*Japanese Banking and Investment
in the United States*

Japanese Banking and Investment in the United States

An Assessment of Their Impact Upon U.S. Markets and Institutions

Peter S. Rose

Q

Quorum Books

New York / Westport, Connecticut / London

Library of Congress Cataloging-in-Publication Data

Rose, Peter S.
  Japanese banking and investment in the United States : an
assessment of their impact upon U.S. markets and institutions /
Peter S. Rose.
    p. cm.
  Contents: Includes bibliographical references and index.
  ISBN 0-89930-622-5 (alk. paper)
  1. Banks and banking, Japanese—United States.
2. Investments, Japanese—United States.   I. Title.
HG2491.R664 1991
332.6'7352073—dc20   91-2275

British Library Cataloguing in Publication Data is available.

Library of Congress Catalog Card Number: 91-2275
ISBN: 0-89930-622-5

First published in 1991

Quorum Books, One Madison Avenue, New York, NY 10010
An imprint of Greenwood Publishing Group, Inc.

Printed in the United States of America

The paper used in this book complies with the
Permanent Paper Standard issued by the National
Information Standards Organization (Z39.48-1984).

10 9 8 7 6 5 4 3 2 1

To My Family

Contents

Illustrations

APPENDIXES

Preface

The rapid expansion of Japanese institutions throughout the world is truly startling and not just from the perspective of what has happened in our own generation. Were man gifted with a life span measured in centuries, today's "Japanization" of foreign markets and institutions would be even more startling than it is to us today. For it was only a century and a half ago—July 8, 1853—that U.S. Navy Commodore Matthew Perry sailed into the Port of Uraga to be received by Japanese officials who were intent on developing foreign trade with the Western world as a possible remedy for a struggling economy. The United States, for its part, saw Japan as a large and untapped market for the products of its farms and manufacturers.

Then, too, there was the growing reality of Japan's key position in the Pacific—a key linkage to trade with China, India, and Southeast Asia. In 1858 Japanese–U.S. negotiations opened a few Japanese ports to trade with the West, reversing a 200-year-old prohibition against foreign intrusion when the Japanese themselves were told to stay at home, and foreign nationals were not allowed to establish residence on Japanese soil. This edict of 1639 was finally swept aside in 1859 when an enclave for foreigners was established in the city of Yokohama.

How incredible the recent worldwide Japanese expansion would seem today to Commodore Perry and his contemporaries were they blessed with superhuman longevity. They would soon discover that it is U.S. consumers, businesses, and governments that are more frequently being targeted as customers by Japanese multinational traders and financiers, rather than the other way around. They would undoubtedly stare in shocked disbelief at large numbers of Japanese ships sailing into U.S. ports from San Diego to Seattle and from New Orleans to Newport. Isolationism has been transformed into internationalism, built upon the solid foundation afforded by Japanese technological innovation and organizational genius.

In this book our focus is far narrower than the wide scope of Japanese global trade or even trade with the United States. In these pages our attention is riveted upon the financial sector—particularly the financial sector of the United States—and the impact Japanese firms and institutions have had and are likely to have on the U.S. financial system and the banks and other financial firms that are integral parts of that system. We must not lose sight of the fact, however, that the impact of the financial system, and Japan's role in it, is far broader and far more important than that in industry alone. The financial markets impact every other market and determine a crucial price in the economic system—interest rates, the price of credit—and, through that price, literally affect every business firm and household. The competitive spur provided by Japanese banks, securities firms, insurance companies, and pension funds operating inside U.S. markets directly or indirectly reaches into every U.S. business and family and every public and private institution. They are a force that cannot and will not be ignored and one that is worthy of our most careful study and deliberation.

The author owes a special debt of gratitude to the Center for International Business at Texas A&M University for its financial support and to the Federation of Bankers Associations of Japan (Zenginkyo), which granted permission to use data it compiled about member banks and foreign banks operating inside Japan and supplied considerable information about recent Japanese deregulation of the financial sector. The book's limitations, however, belong exclusively to the author.

*Japanese Banking and Investment
in the United States*

ONE

The Scope of Japanese Banking and Investment in the United States

INTRODUCTION

This book focuses intently upon a banking and capital investment revolution taking place within the U.S. economy—the rapid expansion of Japanese banks and other foreign investor groups across the U.S. landscape. By year-end 1988 Japanese investments in U.S. real estate and Japanese holdings of U.S. securities had risen 30 times beyond their levels at the beginning of the 1980s. As Federal Reserve Board Chairman Alan Greenspan (May 1990) noted recently, total foreign direct investment in the United States has increased 300 percent since 1980, while foreign purchases and sales of U.S. Treasury securities surpassed $3 trillion in 1988 alone. In the latter year, for the first time since World War II, the total book value of foreign-owned U.S. assets acquired via direct investment, at approximately $390 billion, surpassed the book value of assets held by Americans overseas (which amounted to just over $368 billion). By any measure, the Japanese have represented the most dynamic component of foreign investment in the United States in recent years. Among the most notable recent Japanese acquisitions have been CBS Records, Columbia Pictures Entertainment (a $3.4 billion transaction), Firestone Tire, National Steel Corporation, Rockefeller Center, Union Bank of California, and Washington's Watergate Hotel (see Table 1-1).

The commercial banking industry, perhaps more than any other sector of the global economy, has felt the impact of Japan's business expansion. For example, economist H. Robert Heller, a member of the Federal Reserve Board, reported in a speech before the Bankers' Association for Foreign Trade in 1989 that the 111 Japanese banks represented in the world's 500 largest banking firms held more than 40 percent of that group's aggregate deposits in 1987. In contrast, the 90 U.S. banks represented among the largest 500 in the world held just 11 percent of worldwide deposits. Similarly, the American Bankers Association in the summer of 1989 found Japanese banking firms dominating the list of the world's 100 largest banks. The largest U.S. bank, Citibank of New York, had fallen to twenty-fourth; Dai-Ichi Kangyo Bank, the largest Japanese banking institution, held more than

1

Table 1-1

Leading U.S. Companies in Which Japanese Investors Hold Significant Ownership Interests

Ardent Computer Corp.	National Steel Corporation
Aristech Chemical Co.	Paine Webber
AUX Corp.	Pebble Beach Co.
Best Western Foods, Inc.	Polymer International Corp.
Caddy Corp. of America	Quantum Chemical Corporation
California Portland Cement	Riviera Country Club
CBS Records	Rockefeller Group
CIT Group	Seafreeze Cold Storage
Columbia Pictures Entertainment	7-Eleven Corp.
Cox Creek Refining Company	Shearson-Lehman
CS First Boston Corp.	Silicon Systems, Inc.
Eli Lilly	Stanhope Hotel
Epitaxx Inc. of New Jersey	Texas Copper
Everlasting Value Company	Thermos Co.
Firestone Tire	Tiffany & Co.
General Ceramics	Union Bank of California
Gould Inc.	U.S. Gold Corp.
Healthcare Rehabilitation Inc., Massachusetts	Value Rent-A-Car
	Warrick Controls, Inc.
InterContinental Hotels	Watergate Hotel, Washington, D.C.
Learjet	
Lloyds Bank California	
Lyphomed Inc.	
MCA Corp. (including Universal Studios)	
Merck	
Mohawk Rubber Co.	

double the assets of Citibank.[1] Inside U.S. borders, Japanese banks by the end of the 1980s held close to 60 percent of the assets of all foreign banks present on U.S. shores, far outstripping their nearest competitors, the British, the Canadians, and the Italians (see Tables 1-2 and 1-3).

By the beginning of the 1990s, 15 of the 20 largest foreign banks in the United States were Japanese. Reaching beyond these static measures of industry structure, however, the *dynamics* of international banking emphasize the continuing relative growth of Japanese banks against all the other players in global banking markets. For example, as the author noted in another recent study (1990), while international loans by U.S. banks declined from just over $120 billion in 1983 to less than $100 billion five years later, Japanese banks increased their market share of international lending from just over $25 billion to nearly $130 billion (an increase of 361 percent).

In the securities field, Japan's Big Four securities trading companies—Nomura Securities, Daiwa, Yamaichi, and Nikko Securities—have established themselves as a leading force in international securities underwriting,

Table 1-2
The Growth of Japanese Banking Activities Inside the United States (Dollar Figures in Billions)

Year	Total U.S. Banking Assets Held by Japanese Banks as of Year-End	Total U.S. Banking Assets of All Foreign Banks	Japan's Percentage Share of U.S. Banking Assets Held by All Foreign Banks	U.S. Domestic Bank Assets	Japan's Percentage Share of U.S. Domestic Banking Assets
1982	$113.0	$299.8	37.7%	$1777.8	6.4%
1983	126.0	328.8	38.3	1922.3	6.6
1984	151.3	394.4	38.4	2087.2	7.2
1985	181.3	440.8	41.1	2289.7	7.9
1986	245.4	524.3	46.8	2499.8	9.8
1988	360.9	650.6	55.5	2668.9	13.5
1989	420.7	735.7	57.2	2828.0	14.9

Notes: U.S. domestic bank assets exclude those banks with more than 25 percent foreign bank ownership, though U.S. commercial banks owned by nonbank foreigners are included in the domestic total.

Sources: Federal Reserve Bank of New York, Annual Report, 1989; and Board of Governors of the Federal Reserve System, Structure Data for U.S. Offices of Foreign Banks by Type of Institution, Statistical Release, various annual issues ending with December 31, 1989.

Table 1-3
The Largest Japanese Banking Groups in the United States (Total Assets as of 12/31/89)

Name of Banking Group	Number of Banking Entities in U.S. (Agencies, Banks, Branch Facilities, etc.)	Principal Cities Where Located	Total Assets of Group in Millions of U.S. Dollars
The Bank of Tokyo	10	New York, Coral Gables, Houston, San Francisco, Los Angeles, Honolulu, Portland, Seattle	$ 47,162.2
Mitsubishi Bank	8	New York, San Francisco, Chicago, Houston, Los Angeles	$ 39,463.9
Dai-Ichi Kangyo Bank	7	New York, Atlanta, Chicago, Houston, Los Angeles, San Francisco	$ 37,295.9
Fuji Bank	8	New York, Atlanta, Chicago, Houston, Los Angeles, San Francisco	$ 35,168.8
Sanwa Bank	8	Boston, New York, Atlanta, Chicago, Dallas, San Francisco, Los Angeles	$ 31,806.4
Industrial Bank of Japan	7	New York, Miami, Chicago, Los Angeles	$ 28,770.7

4

Bank	Offices	Locations	Total Assets
Sumitomo Bank	8	New York, Atlanta, Chicago, Houston, Los Angeles, San Francisco	$ 26,719.5
Tokai Bank	6	New York, Atlanta, Chicago, Los Angeles	$ 18,793.7
Mitsui Bank	5	New York, Chicago, Los Angeles	$ 18,712.2
Mitsui Trust and Banking Company	4	New York, Chicago, Los Angeles	$ 13,873.8
Mitsubishi Trust and Banking Corp.	4	New York, Chicago, Los Angeles	$ 13,341.5
Long-Term Credit Bank of Japan	4	New York, Chicago, Los Angeles	$ 12,917.9
Daiwa Bank	4	New York, Chicago, Los Angeles	$ 12,229.7
Sumitomo Trust and Banking Co.	3	New York, Los Angeles	$ 11,372.2
Yasuda Trust and Banking Co.	3	New York, Los Angeles	$ 9,691.2
Taiyo Kobe Bank	5	New York, Chicago, Los Angeles, Seattle	$ 9,664.8

Total Assets for All U.S. Facilities of Japanese Banks $ 420,745.6
Percentage Share of U.S. Domestic Banks' Assets (in 1989)   14.9%

Source: Board of Governors of the Federal Reserve System, Structure Data for U.S. Offices of Foreign Banks by Type of Institution, Statistical Release, December 31, 1989.

offering new securities on behalf of corporate and governmental issuers for resale to investors. In 1978 none of Japan's securities firms ranked in the world's top 20 securities dealers and brokers. By year-end 1988 there were five Japanese firms in this prestigious group—the Big Four plus the Industrial Bank of Japan (Hale 1990). Nomura Securities alone had become the largest financial service firm in the world, with more than $60 billion in capital.

Moreover, Japan's securities dealers now face an even more open door to entry into the United States in the wake of a recent decision by the Securities and Exchange Commission (SEC), known as Rule 144a, permitting unregistered securities to be traded among institutional investors that have more than $100 million in securities under management—a step tailor-made for foreign securities traders eager to establish a beachhead on U.S. shores but who have not yet developed extensive U.S.–client relationships. SEC economists Robert Nachtmann and Fred Philips-Patrick (1990) estimate that by the end of the 1980s foreign securities firms accounted for close to one-quarter of all common stock underwriting inside the United States and underwrote approximately one-fifth of all domestic debt securities offered for open-market sale. Moreover, foreign securities firms appeared to charge lower underwriting fees inside the United States than U.S. securities dealers.

As Professor Faramarz Damanpour (1988) notes, Japanese banks thus far have tended to stress commercial lending, retail banking, and securities trading activity. However, as the 1980s began, these institutions seemed poised to begin an aggressive expansion along several different dimensions, including acquiring property in leading cities in the South as well as capturing larger shares of U.S. manufacturing firms in the industrial Northeast. Most recently, Japanese banking and securities firms have begun to invest heavily in higher education, with substantial endowments flowing to selected U.S. colleges and universities. These investments appear to be motivated by a desire to create greater educational opportunities for Japanese students abroad and to promote a stronger mutuality of interest between the United States and Japan.

THE REASONS BEHIND THE EXPANSION OF JAPANESE BANKING AND INVESTMENT ACTIVITY INSIDE THE UNITED STATES

Japan is now the world's largest creditor nation, holding about $2 trillion in global assets. The rapid rise of Japanese institutions, including banks and securities firms, worldwide as well as inside the United States has not one, but multiple causes. Table 1-4 summarizes the causes most frequently mentioned in business and academic journals in the United States. As we shall see in this section, economic factors and government regulations head the

Table 1-4
Reasons Most Frequently Cited for the Expansion of Japanese Banking and Investment Activity Inside the United States

* Appreciation of the Value of the Yen Against the U.S. Dollar and Other Major National Currencies in Global Foreign Exchange Markets.

* Japan's Large Balance of Trade Surpluses with the United States.

* The More Rapid Growth of the Japanese Economy than in the U.S. and Western Europe.

* The Higher Personal and Corporate Savings Rates in Japan Compared to the United States.

* The Pursuit of Japanese Firms and Individuals Moving to the United States by Japanese Banks.

* The Low Barriers to Entry in Most U.S. Financial Service and Product Markets.

* The Cultural and Economic Similarities Between the U.S. and Japan as a Result of Postwar Occupation and Extensive Trade and Immigration.

* Depressed U.S. Stock Prices.

* The Lower Political Risk of Investing in U.S. Markets Versus Many Overseas Markets Where Governments and Economic Conditions Are More Unstable.

* Constraining Regulations on Japanese Banking and Investment Activities at Home.

* The Longer-Term Investment Horizons of Japanese Investors.

* The Adoption of New Competitive Strategies by Japanese Banks: Targeting of Selected Groups of U.S. Customers.

* The Regulatory Advantage of Japanese Banks over U.S. Banks.

list of driving forces that have ushered Japanese bankers and investors into prominence in the U.S. and global financial systems.

The Rising Value of the Yen in International Currency Markets

One primal cause of Japanese expansion abroad centers on exchange rates and, in particular, the increasing value of the yen relative to the U.S. dollar and other convertible currencies. The Japanese yen nearly tripled in purchasing power in terms of U.S. dollars between 1970 and 1988. As Table 1-5 shows, in 1970 360 yen were required to purchase a dollar of assets inside the United States; by 1988, however, only 135 yen were required to purchase

Table 1-5
Changes in the Value of the Japanese Yen Against the U.S. Dollar
(All Figures Expressed in Yen Per U.S. Dollar)

Year	Average Number of Yen Per U.S. Dollar	Highest Value for the Yen in Terms of U.S. Dollars During the Year	Lowest Value of the Yen in Terms of U.S. Dollars During the Year
1970	¥ 360.00	¥ 357.40	¥ 359.84
1975	296.79	284.90	307.00
1980	226.74	202.95	264.00
1981	220.54	198.70	247.40
1982	249.08	217.70	278.50
1983	237.51	227.20	247.80
1984	237.52	220.00	251.70
1985	238.54	200.40	263.05
1986	168.52	152.90	203.00
1987	144.64	124.05	159.95
1988*	135.50	134.20	137.55

Notes: * Figures are for September 1988.

Source: Federation of Bankers Associations of Japan (Zenginkyo), Japan Financial Statistics 1989, Tokyo, 1989, Table VI-6, p. 55.

the same dollar's worth of U.S. assets, an increase of 165 percent in the yen's dollar purchasing power measured against its 1988 exchange value. Between 1985 and 1988 alone the yen appreciated 106 percent relative to the U.S. dollar. The appreciation of the yen against U.S. dollars sharply increased the buying power of Japanese investors, including banks and securities firms. With the opening of the U.S. domestic market to Japanese goods in the 1970s and 1980s, direct investment in U.S. manufacturing and distribution firms, office buildings, shopping centers, residential structures, and farm and ranch properties was greatly facilitated by the yen's dramatic rise against the dollar.

Higher Savings Rate in Japan Compared to the United States

As Table 1-6 shows, Japan's household savings rate, measured by the ratio of total personal savings to disposable income, has averaged about twice the

Table 1-6
Household Savings Rates for Leading Industrialized Nations
(Savings Rate Is the Percentage of Disposable Income Represented by Total Savings)

Calendar Year	Japan	United States	United Kingdom	Federal Republic of Germany	France
1975	22.8%	10.6%	8.5%	15.1%	15.3%
1976	23.2	9.1	8.1	13.3	12.9
1977	21.8	8.3	6.5	12.2	13.2
1978	20.8	9.0	8.1	12.0	14.2
1979	18.2	8.3	9.1	12.6	18.8
1980	17.9	9.0	10.5	12.8	17.6
1981	18.3	9.4	9.2	13.4	18.0
1982	16.5	8.8	8.5	12.8	17.3
1983	16.3	7.6	6.8	10.9	15.9
1984	16.0	8.6	7.3	11.4	14.5
1985	16.0	7.0	6.3	11.4	13.8
1986	16.6	7.0	4.9	12.1	13.3
1987	----	6.3	----	12.3	12.0

Notes: There is a discontinuity in the series with a new method for calculating the savings rate beginning after 1978.

Sources: Bank of Japan, International Cooperative Statistics, 1988; and Federation of Bankers Associations of Japan (Zenginkyo), Japan Financial Statistics 1989, Tokyo, 1989, Table I-8, p. 12.

U.S. personal savings rate in recent years. Only France and Germany have approached Japan's exceptional rate of household savings during the past decade. The huge volume of savings generated by a 16 percent average savings-to-disposable-income ratio has been invested primarily in Japanese machinery, equipment, and commercial structures, but the balance, still huge by current standards, has flowed principally to the United States to acquire U.S. securities and property.

In the United States, on the other hand, huge federal, state, and local government deficits absorbed more dollars than the total volume of personal savings available for most of the 1980s. In contrast, the government sector in Japan has absorbed less than 20 percent of all personal savings inside that nation over the past decade. U.S. borrowers became increasingly dependent on foreign sources of funds to fully meet their credit needs. Japan has enjoyed almost continuous prosperity for more than two decades, with relatively low unemployment and little inflation—features that have greatly stimulated personal savings and generated large exportable surpluses of loanable funds.[2]

Japan's Large Balance of Trade Surplus with the United States

Closely related to the rising value of Japanese yen, investments in U.S. banks, securities firms, and other assets have been propelled upward by huge surpluses of Japanese exports to the United States relative to Japan's imports from the United States. In 1970 Japanese exports to the United States totaled almost $6 billion while its imports from the United States were about $5.6 billion—an almost perfectly balanced trade position between the two nations. By 1980 Japan's shipments to the United States reached more than $31 billion while imports from the United States totaled only $24.4 billion. But these figures were dwarfed only seven years later in 1987 when Japan's exports to the United States ballooned to nearly $84 billion while its imports from U.S. ports rose to just $31.5 billion, for a net trade surplus with the United States of more than $52 billion, as shown in Table 1-7. Nearly a third of Japan's worldwide exports ($83.6 billion out of a total of $229.2 billion in 1987) flow to the United States, while a little over one-fifth of Japan's imports stem from U.S. sources.

These huge trade surpluses with the United States have been paid for by U.S. firms and the U.S. government by transferring tradable assets to the Japanese—U.S. Treasury securities, bank deposits, corporate stocks and bonds, and deeds to commercial and residential properties. Without question, U.S. trade deficits have played an enormously powerful role in boosting Japan's growing economic advantage and presence in U.S. home markets. As economist Jack Hervey (1990) notes, the last year in which the U.S. merchandise trade balance achieved back-to-back surpluses was in 1970, when the U.S. trade surplus reached almost $3 billion. By the end of 1989, however, U.S. merchandise trade with the rest of the world posted an estimated deficit of $110 billion, which was actually lower than the record deficit of $160 billion reached in 1987.

Historically, U.S. trade with Western Europe, Canada, and nations of Central and South America dominated U.S. trade statistics, and prior to the 1970s Japan's share of U.S. trade ranked well below those of Western Europe, Canada, and the industrialized economies of Central and South America. Even today, Canada leads all other nations in the volume of trade with the United States, though its role in importing goods into the United States has shrunk in recent years. Canada's share of U.S. imports was under 20 percent of all U.S. imports in 1988, although Canadian exports accounted for well over a quarter of U.S. imports for several decades. (Canada continues to lead as a recipient of U.S. exports, however, absorbing just over 20 percent of U.S. shipments abroad as Table 1-8 shows—a remarkably stable proportion that has held up for several years.) Western Europe and the remainder of the Western Hemisphere also have generally lost ground as importers to and exporters from the United States.

It is Japan that has moved to offset previously dominant trading relation-

Table 1-7
Japan's Trade Balance with the United States and Selected Other Nations (All Figures in U.S. Dollars)

Year	Total Trade with the Rest of the World:			Trade Balance with the United States:			Net Trade Balance with the European Economic Community	Net Trade Balance with Middle-East Countries	Net Trade Balance with the Remainder of South-east Asia	Net Trade Balance with China
	Total Exports from Japan	Total Imports into Japan	Japan's Net Trade Balance	Exports to U.S.	Imports from U.S.	Net Trade Balance with U.S.				
1970	$19,318	$18,881	$ 437	$5,940	$5,560	$ 380	$ 186	-$ 1,703	$ 1,889	$ 315
1975	55,753	57,863	-2,110	11,149	11,608	-459	2,304	-10,402	1,957	728
1980	129,807	140,528	-10,721	31,367	24,408	6,959	8,808	-30,142	-841	755
1985	175,638	129,589	46,099	65,278	25,793	39,485	11,126	-17,766	2,999	5,994
1986	209,151	126,408	82,743	80,456	29,054	51,402	16,686	-8,632	12,299	4,204
1987	229,221	149,515	79,706	83,580	31,490	52,090	20,023	-11,020	14,355	849
1988*	65,184	47,331	17,853	21,608	10,451	11,157	5,890	-2,629	4,413	-269

Notes: Data from China are from the People's Republic of China only. *1988 data from second quarter only.

Source: Bank of Japan, International Cooperative Statistics, 1988; and Federation of Bankers Associations of Japan (Zenginkyo), Japan Financial Statistics 1989, Tokyo, 1989, Table VI-2, p. 51.

Table 1-8
Relative Volume of Trade with Leading Trading Partners of the United States (Trade by Country as a Percentage of Total U.S. Trade)

Year	Percentage of U.S. Exports Accounted for by:						Percentage of U.S. Imports Accounted for by:					
	Canada	Japan	Mexico	United Kingdom	Germany	Totals	Canada	Japan	Mexico	United Kingdom	Germany	Totals
1983	19.1%	10.9%	4.5%	5.3%	4.4%	44.2%	19.5%	16.1%	6.3%	4.8%	4.9%	51.6%
1984	21.4	10.8	5.5	5.6	4.2	47.5	19.6	17.7	5.4	4.4	5.2	52.3
1985	22.2	10.6	6.4	5.3	4.2	48.7	19.2	20.0	5.4	4.3	5.9	54.8
1986	20.9	12.4	5.7	5.3	4.9	49.2	17.7	21.8	4.5	4.1	6.8	54.9
1987	23.7	11.2	5.8	5.6	4.6	50.9	16.9	20.8	4.8	4.2	6.6	53.3
1988	21.6	11.8	6.4	5.7	4.5	50.0	17.7	20.3	5.1	4.1	6.0	53.2

Source: Federal Reserve Bank of St. Louis, International Economic Conditions, January 1990, p. 1.

ships between the United States, Canada, and Western Europe to establish the U.S.–Japanese trading connection as the most dynamic international trade relationship. As pointed out in Table 1-8, Japanese imports into the United States reached almost $95 billion in 1989. Shipments of goods and services from Japan to U.S. ports increased more than fifteenfold over the 1970-90 time span, as Table 1-8 suggests. Overall, Japan scored the largest gains in importing into the United States during the 1980s, as its share of total U.S. imports climbed from 16.1 percent to 20.3 percent over the 1983-88 period. U.S. imports from Canada, Mexico, and the United Kingdom were falling in comparable percentage terms.

In contrast, U.S. exports to Japan totaled only 12 percent of total U.S. exports in 1988, placing Japan second to Canada as the target of most U.S. exports. As Alison Butler (1990: 1), economist with the Federal Reserve Bank of St. Louis, observes, "the fact that imports to the United States from Japan are nearly twice the level of exports from the United States to Japan has perpetuated trade frictions between these trading partners." Moreover, these frictions have sharply intensified in the wake of growing Japanese purchases of U.S. property and securities.

While Japanese trade with the United States has grown dramatically in total dollar volume, the *composition* of that trade has also changed significantly in recent years, reflecting predominantly the maturation of the Japanese economy. U.S. exports of farm products to Japan have fallen over the long term as Japan has improved its own agricultural system and found other sources of food and fiber around the Pacific Rim. (U.S. food exports to Japan now appear to be growing again as the Japanese continue to change their dietary habits more in line with Western cuisine.) Exports of heavy machinery from the United States to Japan have fallen slightly as a proportion of all U.S. exports to that country, but U.S. exports of chemicals, computers, and communications equipment to Japan have generally risen. Japan's exports to the United States have changed substantially as well, with automobiles and other transport items increasing rapidly along with computer equipment, office products, and electrical machinery. As the decade of the 1990s began, the Japanese had become the leading importer to the United States of finished goods immediately available for purchase by U.S. businesses and households.

The Rapid Growth of the Japanese Economy

At the same time, Japan's productive base has been growing substantially faster than the United States', principally because of a higher rate of domestic investment. As Table 1-9 indicates, Japan's annual growth in real GNP significantly exceeded this measure of annual production of new goods and services in the United States for most of the 1980s. Moreover, unemployment rates in Japan have averaged less than half of those in the United States

Table 1-9

Key Economic Indicators of the Japanese Economy Compared to the United States and Other Leading Industrialized Nations (Figures for 1987)

Economic Indicator Series	Japan	United States	Canada	United Kingdom	France	Federal Republic of Germany
Annual Growth Rate of Real GNP (in Percent)	4.3	2.9	3.3	3.7	2.1	1.7
Civilian Unemployment Rate (Percent of Labor Force)	2.8	6.2	8.9	10.6	10.4	8.9
Annual Percentage Increase in Consumer Price Index	0.9	3.0	4.2	4.5	3.9	0.7
Population in Millions*	121.5	240.9	---	56.8	55.4	61.0
Per-Capital National Income	$13,859	$15,524	$12,160	$8,401	$6,927	$12,895

Notes: *Population figures as well as the real GNP growth rate for France and Canada are for 1986. National income per capita for France is 1985.

ECONOMIC INDICATORS IN THE
UNITED STATES AND JAPAN

Period	Growth Rates in Real GNP		Growth In Imports		Growth in Exports (FOB)	
	Japan	United States	Japan (CIF)	United States(FOB)	Japan	United States
1984*	5.5%	---	---	---	---	---
1985	4.7	3.6	2.8	5.1	12.3	-4.7
1986	2.1	1.9	-7.8	6.3	9.6	6.1
1987	5.7	5.4	38.7	14.8	15.9	21.6
1988	4.8	3.4	11.8	6.1	13.6	21.9
1989*	3.1	3.1	14.5	4.1	1.5	12.7

	Growth in Production Levels		Rate of Increase in Consumer Prices (Cost of Living)		Money Supply (M1) Growth Rates	
	Japan	United States	Japan	United States	Japan	United States
1984*	---	---	---	---	---	---
1985	0.9	1.7	1.6	3.5	3.2	12.0
1986	-0.6	1.0	-0.3	1.4	12.4	15.6
1987	8.1	5.8	0.8	4.3	4.6	6.4
1988	7.6	5.0	1.1	4.3	9.2	4.3
1989	4.4	2.2	2.9	4.8	1.9	-1.5

Notes: Partial figures for the year.

Sources: Federal Reserve Bank St. Louis, International Economic Conditions, January 1990; U.S. Department of Labor and Department of Commerce; Bank of Japan, Economic Statistics Monthly, and O.E.C.D., Main Economic Indicators Monthly; and International Monetary Fund, International Financial Statistics; and Federation of Bankers Associations of Japan (Zenginkyo), Japan Financial Statistics 1989, Tokyo, 1989, Appendix I, pp. 85-86.

for the past two decades. And this rapid rate of economic growth in Japan has been achieved while maintaining one of the lowest rates of inflation of all industrialized countries in the West. Reflecting the tremendous underlying strength of the Japanese economy, the Nikkei stock index grew at an average annual rate of 31 percent between 1985 and 1989, and at a 13 percent average annual rate between 1980 and 1985.

Japanese business investors appear to be satisfied with lower internal rates of return (by some estimates required investment returns below 10 percent are common inside Japan), suggesting that they are able to raise capital at lower cost. In contrast, U.S. companies generally demand significantly higher internal rates of return on proposed new investment projects (with minimums of at least 12–15 percent according to some estimates). Moreover, in Japan's principal cities real estate prices are generally so high that the rate of return to equity for investors in Japanese commercial property is substantially lower than it is in most markets abroad, particularly the United States, which makes foreign real estate purchases attractive to many Japanese investors. For example, land prices in Tokyo are so elevated that equity returns on real property in Tokyo's financial district average 2–3 percent today. On average, Japanese land prices more than doubled between 1985 and 1990, and the prices of new homes rose to approximately ten times the annual income of the average Japanese employee. In New York, by way of contrast, land prices are well below the price of prime commercial space in Tokyo, promising outside investors average returns of about 8 percent per annum. As we will see later in this book, however, Japanese commercial real estate prices began declining as the 1990s began, due to rising interest rates and new government regulations limiting real estate credit growth, triggering a return flow of some capital previously invested in the United States back into Japan.

Constraining Regulations on Japanese Banking and Investment Activities at Home

In many respects the invasion of U.S. financial markets by Japanese banks is a response to overly restrictive regulations inside Japan. To be sure, Japanese banks have benefited greatly from a number of those restrictions in decades past, particularly the legal interest rate ceilings on deposits imposed by Japan's Ministry of Finance, while other restrictions, especially on investment banking activities, have definitely hurt Japan's banks. Existing financial regulations that limit the returns of Japanese bank depositors have permitted Japanese banks to raise domestic capital at a comparatively low interest cost and to channel those funds abroad to pursue higher investment returns. In contrast, U.S. deposit interest rates were gradually deregulated over the 1981-86 period, resulting in higher average deposit costs for U.S. banks as well as a funding base that is significantly more sensitive to market interest

rate movements, handing the Japanese a key regulatory advantage until their banks' deposit interest rates are fully deregulated.

The Pursuit of Japanese Firms and Individuals Moving to the United States

The first Japanese bank to establish an office in the United States was Mitsubishi Bank, which opened an affiliate in New York City in 1920. The lure that brought Japanese banks and securities firms to U.S. shores in the first place was not American in origin, but Japanese. Japan's bankers and financial service managers saw their largest customers—Japanese and Asian manufacturing firms and international trading companies—setting up shop in the United States to distribute manufactured goods and services. Those customers could easily have been lost to U.S. financial service firms unless bank management acted by setting up their own U.S. branches and agency offices. An added lure to U.S. shores were the thousands of Japanese citizens who immigrated to the United States over the past century to join relatives or to establish and manage businesses. These Japanese expatriates created an opportunity not only to market business-oriented financial services inside the United States, but also to sell household (retail) financial services, particularly consumer loans and deposits.

Japanese bankers have found that many of the services needed by these groups can be provided at lower cost through offices in the United States than from their home offices. While many other banks were closing their branch offices and other facilities abroad due to improvements in transportation and information technology and to problems with the payout of international loans, the Japanese have gone the other way in building more office facilities, especially full service branch offices, agencies, and subsidiary firms inside the United States.

Adoption of New Competitive Strategies by Japanese Banks: Targeting Selected Groups of U.S. Customers

Once inside the United States, Japanese banks as well as other Japanese-owned businesses have generally moved beyond their initial marketing targets—U.S. firms and individuals with Japanese roots—to attract U.S. firms and individuals as customers. What began essentially as a strategic move to follow and facilitate trade between the United States and Japan and to attract the accounts of Japanese expatriates in the United States broadened its beachhead to enter the United States, mainstream markets, reaching out to domestic corporations and small proprietors as well as to individuals and families and state, local, and federal governments. For example, a recent study by Gerald Corrigan (1989), president of the Federal Reserve Bank of New York, finds that foreign bank loans to U.S.–address business customers

represented about one-fifth of all bank-held commercial and industrial loans outstanding in the United States and that Japanese banking affiliates and subsidiaries accounted for close to one-half of these foreign bank–supplied domestic business loans. Corrigan also estimated that the U.S. affiliates of Japanese banks accounted for about one-fourth to one-half of all credit guarantee agreements written annually in U.S. financial service markets. Outside the business sector, Japanese banks have successfully pursued U.S. households with auto and residential loans, credit cards, household deposits, and personal investment plans.

Such a major shift in marketing objectives is by no means unusual among international firms. Inside Japan it is known as *dochakuka,* which (as financial analyst Simon Brady [1988] explains) means the "localization" of an international firm as its management seeks to adapt to the local markets it currently serves and attempts to expand its local market share. A dramatic example of this strategy on the part of Japanese firms (as noted most recently by Rose [1989]) is the recent application to and successful penetration of the exclusive club of U.S. primary securities dealers by the largest Japanese dealer firms. Primary dealers, as we will discuss more fully in chapter 5, are eligible to trade securities directly with the Federal Reserve System as the Fed works to stabilize the U.S. economy and financial markets.

Relatively Low Cultural and Economic Entry Barriers in U.S. Markets

The United States represents a collection of markets less sheltered against foreign entry due to regulation and cultural barriers than in many other foreign countries. Moreover, Japanese banks expanding in the United States have the advantage of entering a country similar to their own in terms of a market-driven economy and in terms of cultural maturity and reliance on advanced banking and financial services technology. While there remain enormous differences between Japan's political and social structure and that of the United States, the market-driven work ethic is shared by both countries and serves to bridge what would otherwise be a forbidding gap between the two nations. (See especially Table 1-10 for a summary of cultural, economic, and other factors that motivate foreign business expansion in U.S. markets.)

There appears as well to be a fundamental difference between the investment horizons of Japanese investors and their counterparts inside the United States. The Japanese, on the whole, appear to be more patient in their investing strategies. They often view more favorably capital transactions that may require many years for full payout than is true of many U.S. investors. Thus, more capital projects will appear to represent profitable investment options, because the Japanese rank longer-term investments higher from the very beginning than do many U.S. investors.

Table 1-10
A Framework for Analyzing the Causes of Foreign Bank and Nonbank Business Expansion Inside the United States

---

Banks and other financial-service businesses abroad are most likely to set up offices and other physical facilities in the United States provided they possess a:

A. Comparative Economic Advantage --

*   When financial services can be provided at lower cost to existing and potential customers abroad by establishing overseas physical facilities than the cost that would be incurred by supplying those same services from the home offices of foreign banks and securities firms.

B. Comparative Financial (Intermediation) Advantage --

*   When the spread between fund-raising costs and earnings on loans and other credit services in a foreign country is greater than the earnings-cost spread at home (after adjustment for differences in relative currency prices).

*   When the establishment of physical facilities in the U.S. provides lower cost or more timely access to dollar trading in order to purchase commodities denominated in dollars in international markets (e.g., oil).

C. Comparative Regulatory Advantage --

*   When foreign banks and other financial-service providers have an advantage in being able to offer more services that are in demand than domestic service firms are allowed to do because of regulation or when foreign financial-service providers face lower regulatory costs than do domestic banks (perhaps because of favorable differences in capital-adequacy requirements, liquidity requirements, etc.).

*   When capital controls are installed abroad, these controls may be successfully avoided by conducting transactions within U.S. borders.

D. Comparative Socio-Cultural Advantage --

*   When cultural attitudes and objectives of the home countries are similar to or at least complementary to those of the host country.

*   When banks and other foreign suppliers have a long history of prior experience with domestic culture and domestic rules of personal and business behavior.

Miscellaneous Factors Influencing Japanese Expansion Inside the United States

In addition to these powerful economic and regulatory factors propelling Japan's investments in the United States, a host of other factors of lesser magnitude are important in shaping recent trends. For example, the depressed prices of U.S. corporate stocks during the early 1980s and as the 1990s began have stimulated increased Japanese purchases of U.S. banks, finance companies, leasing firms, and industrial corporations. This has been particularly true in the U.S. banking sector, where the shares of many of the largest U.S. money-center and regional bank holding companies have recently been trading at close to their book values, giving the Japanese and other foreign investors increased buying power over these U.S. assets.

Still another factor is the comparatively low political risk associated with business operations in the United States. This form of risk arises from changes in laws and regulations that impact the return on private investment. As noted by Samuel Rabino (1981), political risk appears to be much lower in the United States compared to many other areas of the world because political disputes are usually settled peacefully within an agreed-upon framework of laws and elections, which has served to spur greater Japanese interest in U.S. markets. The revolutionary events in Beijing, China in 1989 and Iraq's invasion of Kuwait in the summer of 1990 serve as recent reminders of how relatively low political risk is in the United States. These events further heightened concerns among international investors over political instability and the safety of their investments abroad.

ADDING LONG-TERM PERSPECTIVE TO RECENT DEVELOPMENTS

U.S. policymakers and business analysts must learn to keep Japanese involvement in the United States financial markets in proper perspective. For the U.S. economy as a whole, foreign ownership of U.S. property is still under 10 percent of total domestic capital, whereas in Western Europe the percentage of foreign ownership today is more than double that figure. Of the roughly $1 trillion in funds raised in U.S. credit markets in 1988, foreign investors supplied only 7.5 percent of that total. Foreign holdings of U.S. assets totaled approximately $1.7 trillion, or about 12 percent of all net wealth in the United States at year-end 1988, compared to just 5 percent of aggregate U.S. wealth in 1980. Yet, about one-third of these foreign holdings represent claims against U.S. banks that are roughly matched by U.S. bank claims against foreign assets.

Foreign direct investment still represents only about 3 percent of U.S. fixed capital (about half of the proportion currently prevailing in Western Europe), while foreign ownership of U.S. farmland is estimated at less than 1 percent of the total supply currently available (Johnson 1989:4). Affiliates of foreign businesses account for just under 10 percent of the total assets of U.S. manufacturing companies and less than 3 percent of all U.S. jobs. Moreover, the United States holds far more total direct investment abroad than any other nation and, in most recent years, has been the recipient of substantially larger inflows of payments from overseas than its citizens and institutions send abroad. For example, in the banking sector alone, by the end of the 1980s U.S. bank branches abroad held assets of more than $350 billion booked in more than 900 branches, and the foreign subsidiaries of U.S. banks posted total assets of close to $150 billion. In contrast, foreign bank offices in the United States totaled only about 700, and their assets summed across all the dozens of countries whose banks have come to U.S. shores totaled just over $600 billion.

Of course, the relative importance of Japanese and other foreign investment varies significantly with the type of financial service or product market under consideration. For example, of the $188 billion in new U.S. government securities offered in the open market in 1988, foreign investors purchased $62 billion or close to one-third of the total sold. Clearly the influence of foreign investors on the U.S. government securities market far exceeds their impact on U.S. credit markets as a whole and on most other domestic markets for goods and services. Yet, as Manuel Johnson (1989), former governor of the Federal Reserve Board, noted recently, the percentage of total foreign ownership of the public debt of the United States was less at the end of the 1980s than it was in the late 1970s. As the Japanese share of U.S. government securities rose, other foreign investors generally cut back on their holdings of these securities.

The share of capital assets inside Japan held by U.S. and other foreign investors also has been growing—from an estimated $900 million in 1985 to about $3.2 billion in 1988. Yet, foreign investment still supports only about 1 percent of Japan's industrial base, which means there is probably plenty of room for expansion of foreign businesses in Japan and, as entry barriers fall, the foreign ownership percentage is virtually certain to grow. Moreover, Japan's share of U.S. capital is by no means the largest. At present, Japan is outdistanced by Great Britain's total share of U.S. domestic capital and also ranks below Canada's share of all U.S. capital.

Moreover, we must keep in mind that the United States is not the only target of current and future Japanese acquisitions. Indeed, there is developing evidence of a shift of emphasis among leading Japanese firms toward other areas of the world. One of these areas of high current interest is China and adjacent portions of Southeast Asia. For example, in the fall of 1990 several of Japan's largest city banks announced their preparations for establishing representative offices in Ho Chi Minh City, Vietnam, as a prelude to setting up full service branch offices.

Another key target area for the future is Western and Eastern Europe.

Japanese banks, insurance companies, and leading securities houses operate branch offices, representative offices, or subsidiary businesses in Barcelona, London, Paris, Manchester, Munich, Birmingham, Lisbon, Frankfort, Madrid, and Milan. The Japanese recently have moved to expand their operations in Italy in anticipation that higher European Economic Community (EEC) regulatory barriers may be erected against outsiders after an initial period of openness to outsiders. Japanese financial firms appear to be especially interested in the relatively high propensity to save among Germans and Italians, with the latter currently posting an even higher average savings ratio than currently prevails in Japan.

The EEC has recently issued the Second Co-ordination Directive, permitting foreign banks that are already operating or have been given permission to operate in any EEC member state to offer designated services throughout the European Economic Community. However, reciprocally favorable treatment must also be extended to EEC banks seeking to operate in the foreign country involved. This raises an intriguing question as to whether Japanese domestic banking regulations will be modified sufficiently to make full banking reciprocity with the EEC possible.

PUBLIC AND OFFICIAL CONCERN OVER JAPANESE EXPANSION IN THE UNITED STATES

Despite the fact that Japan's current market stake in the United States is relatively modest, this has apparently done little to dampen the concerns of U.S. bankers, property owners, capital market investors, legislators, and regulatory authorities. A Louis Rukeyser survey of U.S. investors at the close of 1989 reported that 58 percent of those surveyed regarded Japanese investments in the United States as a threat, while only 23 percent saw these ventures as benign. Equally revealing, just 9 percent of the respondents believed foreign investments inside U.S. territory should be encouraged, while 10 percent were unsure of what foreign investment activity might mean for U.S. businesses and consumers. Lee Smith in *Fortune Magazine* (1990) reports that a majority of Americans polled believes that Japanese investment inside the United States should be discouraged and that Japanese imports should be restricted. A *Wall Street Journal*/NBC News Poll found that only 15 percent of Americans surveyed believed that the United States was the undisputed world economic leader; 73 percent of those Americans surveyed identified Japan as having surpassed the United States as an economic power. Only 3 percent viewed the two nations as about equal in economic power. Perhaps most startling, a majority (58 percent) would approve of legislation aimed at restricting foreign ownership of U.S. businesses and property and limiting foreign imports into the United States.

The U.S. Congress has also expressed deep concern over Japanese expansion in the United States. In March 1980, for example, when the Depository

Japanese Investors Show Interest in Property Liquidated from the S & L Crisis

Japanese investors could become a major force in helping U.S. government authorities, such as the Federal Deposit Insurance Corporation and the Resolution Trust Corporation, dispose of the billions of dollars in American real estate taken over for liquidation by the federal government in the wake of the savings and loan crisis. Evidence of the recent interest of Japanese investors in these properties is provided below by a recent FDIC news story of a large resort and ranch facility in Texas put up for bids.

FDIC NEWS RELEASE

Ranch Development Company Recommends Purchaser of Stonebridge Ranch, McKinney, Texas

Mr. Yukio Kitano of Honolulu, Hawaii, and Osaka, Japan, has submitted a bid of $61 million to purchase Stonebridge Ranch, a 6,230-acre master-planned community located in McKinney, Texas, just north of Dallas. Ranch Development Company, whose sole shareholder is the Federal Deposit Insurance Corporation, today filed a recommendation with the U.S. Bankruptcy Court for the Eastern District of Texas to accept the bid.

The recommendation was submitted to the federal bankruptcy court along the lines of the original bankruptcy petition filed on March 14, according to Cody Buck, chairman of the board of Ranch Development Company. Buck said that the original petition indicated that Ranch Development Company expected to receive bids for the property with the purchase price exceeding $45 million.

Marketing of Stonebridge Ranch began in April, with more than 170 investor information packages mailed to prospective purchasers by Ranch Development Company. Three bids were received for the purchase of the property, of which Mr. Kitano's was the high bid.

Each bid was required to be accompanied by $1 million cash deposit to eliminate any but serious and qualified bidders. Mr. Buck indicated that Ranch Development Company was pleased with the interest shown in Stonebridge Ranch and the results of the offering.

The property has more than 270 homes already occupied and approximately 394 homesites sold. An independent research firm based in Dallas has reported that more homes were sold at the community than any other development in the Dallas/Fort Worth area in 1989. Nearly 60 lots were sold for net proceeds of $1.9 million since Ranch Development Company's March bankruptcy filing.

Existing zoning allows for more than 27,500 housing units and 91 million square feet of retail, commercial, office, research and industrial space to be developed. The property contains two championship golf courses, a beach and racquet club with a swim area, a small marina, equestrian facilities and other amenities.

Mr. Kitano is a Japanese businessman and a major shareholder in a Hawaiian bank. The FDIC is manager of the FSLIC Resolution Fund, which Congress created in 1989 to assume the management of assets and liabilities from receiverships of the former Federal Savings and Loan Insurance Corporation (FSLIC). Stonebridge Ranch was acquired by the FSLIC from Gibraltar Savings Association, Houston, which was closed December 28, 1988.

Source: Federal Deposit Insurance Corporation, *News Release*, Washington, D.C., June 20, 1990.

Institutions Deregulation and Monetary Control Act was passed, Title IX of that bill imposed a brief moratorium on foreign bank acquisitions of U.S. domestic banks, spurred on by a declining trend in U.S. banks' share of global markets. Moreover, the actions taken by Congress to deregulate the U.S. banking sector appear to have been motivated, at least in part, by foreign banks' success in penetrating U.S. domestic markets. Further indication of congressional concern over the growth of foreign banks occurred on May 24, 1990, when the U.S. Senate Banking Committee approved a bill that would authorize the federal banking agencies to reject any foreign bank applying for service expansion if officials at the U.S. Treasury Department found that the bank's home nation was discriminating against U.S. banks. The bill, which still faces the formidable hurdles of passing the Senate and House and a threatened veto by President Bush, was labeled the Fair Trade in Financial Services Act.

One reason for these negative attitudes is not so much the size, but more especially the recent rapid growth of Japanese banking and investment in the United States. To many U.S. bankers, capital market investors, and policy-making authorities Japan's *potential* share of U.S. banking and nonbank business activity appears to be so great as to arouse concern about possible future Japanese control over key U.S. assets and decision-making authority. In a sense, the rapid growth of Japanese banking and investment activity inside the United States is a manifestation of U.S. fears of permanently becoming a debtor nation to the rest of the world. Increased foreign investment and ownership seems to convey the threat that, as Federal Reserve Board member Manuel Johnson (1989:2) noted, Americans "will mortgage . . . [their] future since the obligation of interest payments abroad will generate an impossible burden. Also there seems to be a growing fear that increased indebtedness to foreigners will cause Americans to lose control of their destiny."

Then, too, many Americans see foreign investment as a symptom of poor government management and a runaway federal budget deficit. Heavy federal borrowing, this argument runs, has raised U.S. market interest rates and encouraged foreign investors to purchase U.S. securities and real estate. Moreover, capital inflows from abroad, it is contended, have brought about appreciation of the U.S. dollar in international markets, "crowding out" U.S. exports and stimulating imports of goods and services into the United States, contributing to even larger U.S. balance-of-trade deficits.

But there is another side to this argument. Foreign investors seek out those regions of the world whose economies appear sound and whose social and governmental structures appear to be stable. As Manuel Johnson (1989:8-15) recently observed:

Capital will generally flee restrictive, high tax, unsafe economies and migrate to soundly managed economies. Foreign investors, just like domestic investors, will invest where prospects are good. In this sense, foreign investment is consistent with relatively sound economic policy and hence is often a sign of a safe and productive economic environment. [Moreover] . . . if capital inflow is voluntary . . . higher living standards will accrue to both borrower and lender and increased macroeconomic efficiency will result.

Still another factor that makes the Japanese perhaps more visible as foreign business owners centers upon differences in management styles and language. Japanese-owned companies in the United States generally are run by Japanese citizens or Japanese Americans, whereas many other foreign-owned firms typically employ U.S. citizens or English-speaking Europeans in highly visible senior management positions. In addition, few Americans speak Japanese, while many Japanese speak English as a legacy of postwar occupation and due to the attractiveness of U.S. colleges and universities as places for graduate study and continuing education programs.

An added problem arises because of the character of Japan's trading relationships with the United States and other nations. When the Japanese enter U.S. domestic markets, there is often a multiple increase in Japanese exports to the United States, principally because the component parts of electronic equipment, autos, and so forth generally are also made in Japanese plants abroad and must, therefore, be imported as well. This means that Japan depends heavily upon continuing strength of demand in the U.S. economy to provide a sufficient market for its finished products. Indeed, even though Japan's economic and financial system is very different in its key structural features from the economic systems in the United States and Western Europe, the Japanese economy is moving toward more complete integration with the United States and with the remainder of the global economy. Moreover, Japan has an industrial policy that calls for government management and/or oversight of its trade programs, whereas the U.S. government has not been able to reach a sufficient level of agreement within Congress and the administration to successfully launch a cohesive industrial policy.

While there is substantial sentiment within segments of the U.S. banking and investment communities for slowing, and in extreme cases, even rolling back Japanese business and real property acquisitions inside the United States, few Americans appear to have thought through the consequences of such an action. These consequences could include: (1) higher domestic interest rates for all borrowers, foreign and domestic; (2) a slowing in the job creation process and in the availability of employment to U.S. citizens; and (3) a reduction in the availability of long-term capital that sustains the U.S. economy's long-term rate of expansion.

The first of these concerns surfaced in the winter of 1990, when stock and bond prices tumbled on the Tokyo Exchange, resulting in investor paper losses of about 1 trillion yen in the late spring and early summer of 1990. This ignited fears among capital market investors that Japanese investors, particularly multinational banks, securities firms, and insurance companies, would "dump" their holdings of U.S. securities to cover their losses in Japan. Moreover, the interest rate spread between U.S. government bond rates and Japanese government bond rates narrowed sharply from nearly 5 percentage points in favor of U.S.–issued securities early in 1989 to less than 1.5 percentage points in February 1990.

Adding to this developing problem, leading Japanese banks and investment firms have recently suffered severe losses on several large U.S. investments. The most notable of these was the January 1990 bankruptcy filing by Federated Department Stores and Allied Stores Corp. (both subsidiaries of Campeau Corporation), where the total exposure to loss for such leading Japanese lenders as Sanwa and Sumitomo Bank exceeded an estimated $1 billion. Total Japanese investment abroad dropped about 9 percent in 1990 from 1989 and the Japanese invested about 40 percent less overseas in 1990 compared to 1987. These statistics are of considerable concern to U.S. policymakers because roughly half of Japan's investments abroad have been placed in the United States. Moreover, in 1990 total foreign investments in the United States dropped by more than 70 percent from 1989 levels, while U.S. investment overseas rose almost 20 percent. The result was a massive capital outflow from the United States comparable to the hemorrhaging of funds from the United States that followed the October 1987 stock market crash, pushing the exchange value of the dollar down and increasing U.S. interest rates. Simultaneously, Japan's historic trade surpluses with the United States have fallen sharply, dropping about 45 percent between 1987 and 1990.

If a massive transfer of funds back to Japan does occur, the result would likely be soaring U.S. interest rates as billions of dollars in U.S. securities are sold, other factors held equal, choking off growth in an already sluggish U.S. economy. As Manuel Johnson (1989:14–18) then vice chairman of the Federal Reserve Board, noted in his final year in office:

Policies that deliberately prohibit or restrict foreign investments are potentially very dangerous. Attempts to curtail foreign investment could cause the exchange rate to decline sharply and interest rates to increase, thereby crowding out private investment. Such action would also encourage retaliation abroad . . . . The notion of more open markets has become an integral part of the ideas sweeping the globe today. As a principal proponent of [free market] ideas, the U.S. has played an important role in this process. If we are to maintain this leading role, restrictions or prohibitions on foreign investment should play no part in U.S. economic policy.

Plausible arguments have been offered, however, that may lead to a different outcome. For example, there may be a massive shift of global investment emphasis toward such markets as Germany and the remainder of Eastern Europe, where new investment opportunities appear to have surfaced due to the weakening Russian political and military hegemony in Europe. One of the primary missions of this book is to evaluate both the causes of Japanese interest in U.S. property and institutions and the consequences of a significant reduction in Japan's financial involvement in the United States in the years ahead.

NOTES

1. It should be noted, however, that there is considerable dispute about whether or not bank asset size is the relevant measure of the comparative strength of Japanese banks versus U.S. and other banks. As we will discuss in chapter 6, in terms of total stockholders' equity capital, two British banks rank as the world's largest—National Westminster Bank and Barclays Bank. The largest Japanese bank in these terms, Fuji, ranked fourth in total owners' capital, though the Japanese still placed six banks among the world's ten largest in terms of total equity capital.

2. There are reasons to expect some reversal of the large prevailing gap between U.S. and Japanese savings rates. Inside Japan the personal savings rate may begin a long-term decline due to changing life-styles toward greater consumption spending as well as a growing retired population that will draw down accumulated savings. Inside the United States a more slowly growing economy may generate more precautionary savings and an aging work force moving into higher-income jobs could increase the average propensity to save.

TWO

The Japanese Banking and Financial System at Home and Its Links to U.S. and Other Foreign Markets

THE STRUCTURE OF BANKING IN JAPAN

In many ways the banking and financial system of Japan parallels the system of financial markets and institutions in the United States. In part, this is a legacy of the post–World War II influence of the United States' administration of that country for a considerable period after the war. The British influence on Japanese banking is also strong, however, with most private banks modeled along British organizational lines. Today's banking and financial services industry in Japan is, in reality, an amalgamation of the older traditional Japanese system, with its closely intertwined private and government-supported institutions, and a newer and more fractured system, less dominated by a few financial firms and more market driven. Japanese banks today are given more limited government protection and, consequently, have less refuge from the discipline of an increasingly global financial marketplace.

Most of Japan's present-day banks were chartered within the past century, products of the Meiji Restoration launched in 1868 and the passage of the National Bank Act of 1872. The latter sanctioned the formation of *ginko* (national banks) to be modeled after U.S. federally chartered banks. However, passage of the Banking Act of 1890 marked the transition to a British-style banking system, authorizing the chartering of "ordinary banks of deposit," similar to Britain's merchant banks in supplying both commercial accounts and consumer savings plans. At the same time a Savings Bank Act was passed to authorize the creation of consumer-oriented savings institutions to accept small denomination savings accounts from individuals and families. These household-oriented savings institutions eventually were converted into ordinary banks, however, and the Banking Law of 1981 stipulates that ordinary banks are entitled to the combined service powers of commercial banks and savings banks.

Government policies coupled with private market forces have led to gradually increasing consolidation in the domestic banking industry, mainly through merger and acquisition activity. This consolidation trend has been buttressed in recent years by a government policy that limits the number of new branches each bank can build in a year. These branching restrictions virtually guaranteed that mergers and acquisitions would become the primary vehicles for bank growth in the domestic market. Newly chartered banks in Japan usually have come from abroad. Competition in Japanese banking also has been limited by the tendency to charter and nurture specialized banks that possess only selected service powers. Prominent examples include a specialized foreign exchange bank to trade in foreign currency, under rules spelled out by the Foreign Exchange Bank Law of 1954, and credit cooperatives that lend to agriculture. A further impediment to more open competition is the internal policy of allowing some financial institutions to grow into financial conglomerates whose primary clientele are corporations and governmental units, while still maintaining thousands of smaller financial service providers focusing on households and smaller businesses in selected cities and regions of the nation. In many ways this approach mirrors the U.S. bank regulatory system, especially prior to the deregulation movement of the 1980s.

Banking regulations are extensive in Japan. Approval must be sought for all new branches, mergers, and acquisitions, principally from the Ministry of Finance. Holding companies are prohibited under the Antimonopoly Law (1947), which generally outlaws investments of more than a 5 percent share in nonbank business firms. However, Japanese banks may establish and own 100 percent of bank-related firms operating in certain business product lines, such as computer services and the management of bank-owned real estate. There are also restrictions against banks entering the securities industry and engaging in the underwriting of corporate securities. There are capital and liquidity requirements and a loan limit rule on credit extended to a single borrower. (Generally no more than 20 percent of capital and reserves can be loaned to one borrowing customer.) The Ministry of Finance, in cooperation with the Bank of Japan, controls the acquisition of nonbank firms and regulates loan and deposit interest rates. As we shall see, though, there is a significant trend toward interest rate deregulation.

The City or Metropolitan Banks

Japan's banking system is, first of all, split down the middle between the largest money-center banks, which are world-class in size, and smaller urban-based banks that respond primarily to the financial service needs of households and smaller businesses. The largest money-center institutions

Table 2-1
The City Banks of Japan

Bank Names	Location of Head Office	Deposits in Billions of Yen As of:		Number of Branch Offices:			
		June 1989	July 1990	Total Offices		Overseas Offices	
				6/89	7/90	6/89	7/90
Dai-Ichi Kangyo Bank	Tokyo	40,255¥	45,089¥	354	359	14	15
Sumitomo Bank	Osaka	36,140	41,392	326	339	17	19
Fuji Bank	Tokyo	35,723	39,641	273	286	15	16
Mitsubishi Bank	Tokyo	34,600	39,534	257	263	15	16
Sanwa Bank	Osaka	34,080	38,743	260	271	16	17
Tokai Bank	Aichi	21,976	25,156	242	242	10	10
Mitsui Bank*	Tokyo	19,426	42,395	206	534	16	20
Taiyo Kobe Bank*	Hyogo	17,899	42,395	327	534	9	20
Bank of Tokyo**	Tokyo	16,334	20,088	66	66	35	35
Kyowa Bank	Tokyo	10,627	11,734	226	228	6	7
Daiwa Bank	Osaka	10,493	12,778	176	183	7	8
Saitama Bank	Saitama	9,529	10,728	176	180	6	7
Hokkaido Takushoku Bank	Hokkaido	7,616	7,995	183	185	7	7
Totals		294,698¥	335,273¥	3,072	3,136	173	177

Notes: *Mitsui Bank and Taiyo Kobe Bank merged on April 1, 1990 with the deposit figure cumulated for the two banks as of September 1989. The deposit figures include CDs beginning in September 1988. As of the same date the head office is counted in the number of branch offices reported. Deposit figures for selected banks include debentures.
**The Bank of Tokyo is a specialized foreign exchange bank.
Source: Federation of Bankers Associations of Japan (Zenginkyo), List of Member Banks, June 1989, p.1 and List of Member Banks, July 1990, p. 1.

are generally labeled *city banks* or *metropolitan banks*. There were 13 conglomerate banking firms labeled as city banks in 1989, including such well-known global giants as Dai-Ichi Kangyo (Tokyo), Sumitomo (Osaka), Fuji (Tokyo), Mitsubishi (Tokyo), Sanwa (Osaka), Tokai (Aichi), Mitsui (Tokyo), Taiyo Kobe (Hyogo), the Bank of Tokyo, Kyowa (Tokyo), Daiwa (Osaka), Saitama (Saitama), and Hokkaido Takushoku (Hokkaido) (see Table 2-1). However, in April 1990 Mitsui Bank and Taiyo Kobe Bank merged, reducing the number of independently operated city banks to 12. In total, the city banks control about one-fourth of the aggregate loans within the Japanese banking system and about one-fifth of all bank funds raised. Counting both foreign and domestic deposits, the city banks controlled just over 46 percent of all Japanese bank deposits at the end of the 1980s. All of these institutions rank among the top 100 banks in the world in terms of asset size and total capital.

The city banks' principal customers are the largest Japanese manufacturing and service corporations. Nearly half of the city banks' deposits come from corporations, including more than 60 percent of the checking accounts they hold. These metropolitan banking institutions supply a major share of all loanable funds borrowed by Japanese corporations and purchase a significant share of their equity issues as well. Prior to World War II, several of the city banks were members of large financial-nonfinancial corporate groups known as "zaibatsus" and supplied most of the credit needs of these large and complex firms. Today these interfirm arrangements are much looser networks, called "keiretsus," and the city banks play a more prominent role in these interfirm relationships, supplying not only credit, but management consulting and securities underwriting services as well.

The city banks have extensive international office networks and often operate with more freedom abroad than they do at home. In London, for example, a dozen of the largest 25 banks are Japanese owned. While a Japanese bank cannot acquire in excess of half of the equity capital in a foreign firm in most cases, larger ownership percentages may be sanctioned by the Ministry of Finance. Overseas, the city banks underwrite and syndicate loans and securities and trade in foreign exchange, whereas a license is required from the Ministry of Finance to engage in domestic currency trading. City banks also undertake extensive nonbank business activities abroad that usually are prohibited or restricted at home and are striving to become universal banks—full service financial institutions with investment banking, commercial banking, securities trading, asset management and risk management services.

Inside the domestic banking system the city banks raise their funds from selling deposits, from borrowing in the money market, and in the form of loans from the Bank of Japan. While these huge metropolitan banks devote most of their resources to corporate loans, there is evidence that consumer loans, while still relatively small in proportion to total city bank assets, are increasing relative to other forms of domestic credit. Moreover, loans to small and medium-size businesses have more than doubled as a percentage of total city bank loans since 1970. The city banks are the leading holders of all major categories of bank deposits—total deposits, demand accounts, and time deposits, but are especially dominant in the field of corporate deposits, particularly cash-management accounts. Moreover, the city banks have captured a growing share of domestic banking accounts in recent years—both loans and deposits.

Unlike most banks in the United States, Japan's city banks are major players in the capital market as well as in the short-term money market. They are active purchasers of corporate and government bonds and common stocks, and even purchase mortgages. Moreover, while most of the loans these banks make are short-term in character, they also make permanent working capital loans to their business customers.

The Regional Banks

The smaller urban banks inside Japan are generally referred to as *regional banks*. These institutions include such industry leaders as the Bank of Yokohama (Kanagawa), Hokuriku (Toyama), Chiba, Joyo (Ibaraki), Shizuoka, Ashikaga (Tochigi), Hiroshima, Bank of Fukuoka, and Gunma Bank. (Other regional banking institutions are listed in Table 2-2.) In 1990 there were 64 of these institutions, ranging from very small banking firms focused primarily on a single metropolitan area or region to regional banks with extensive domestic branching systems and a few with offices overseas, including facilities in the United States. However, the bulk of the regional banks confine their markets to cities and local political units comparable to states and counties in the United States.

The regional banks offer a wide range of deposits and deposit-like financial instruments to raise funds and, in this respect, closely parallel the city banks in how they raise new working capital. However, the regionals use more deposits relative to money-market borrowings as funding sources than do the city banks. The regionals also draw more heavily upon deposits from individuals and families than do other types of Japanese banks. Popular forms of deposits include maturity-designated time deposits with normal maturity ranges of about one to three years, time deposits with two-year maturities as well as one-year, six-month and three-month time deposits, money-market certificates, and negotiable CDs (which were first permitted in April 1979).

Loans made by regional banks include a full range of business and household credits as well as credit guarantees, factoring arrangements, credit cards, mortgage bonds, equipment leases, and loans to new businesses. These banks make far more loans (relative to the volume of their total assets) to individual consumers and to smaller businesses than do Japan's city banks. While generally successful in their consumer lending programs, the regionals face growing competition in this field from city banks, which are especially concerned about inroads made by foreign banks into domestic trade and are more aggressively pursuing household and smaller business customers today. In reaching out to Japanese households, the city banks have a cultural advantage over foreign banks that have entered Japan, just as many U.S. bankers argue that it is in the household or retail market inside the United States where they possess the clearest advantage over foreign banks. However, as Paul Maidment (1990) observes, the consumer (retail) finance business inside Japan is significantly less well developed than in most industrialized economies of the West. Therefore, Japanese banks must grapple

Table 2-2
The Regional Banks of Japan
(Money Figures in Billions of Yen)

Location of Bank Names	Head Office	Deposits in Yen as of:		Number of Branch Offices:			
		June 1989	July 1990	Overseas Offices		All Branch Offices	
				6/89	7/90	6/89	7/90
Bank of Yokohama	Kanagawa	8,178¥	8,958¥	161	163	3	5
Hokuriku Bank	Toyama	5,130	6,960	172	178	1	2
Chiba Bank	Chiba	5,114	6,694	138	140	1	3
Joyo Bank	Ibaraki	5,011	6,575	136	140	-	1
Shizuoka Bank	Shizuoka	4,999	5,844	179	181	1	2
Ashikaga Bank	Tochigi	4,632	5,451	126	130	-	1
Hiroshima Bank	Hiroshima	4,106	4,803	174	178	1	1
Bank of Fukuoka	Fukuoka	3,845	4,502	171	173	1	2
Hachijuni Bank	Nagano	3,655	4,318	126	128	1	1
Gunma Bank	Gunma	3,339	3,831	115	118	1	1
Chugoku Bank	Okayama	2,766	3,321	153	155	-	2
Yamaguchi Bank	Yamaguchi	2,761	3,180	143	143	1	1
77 Bank	Miyagi	2,652	2,999	120	120	-	1
Nishi-Nippon Bank	Fukuoka	2,600	2,926	176	176	-	-
Bank of Kyoto	Kyoto	2,490	2,754	98	99	-	1
Juroku Bank	Gifu	2,423	2,829	121	125	-	-
Hokkaido Bank	Hokkaido	2,397	2,765	119	101	1	-
Nanto Bank	Nara	2,390	2,625	101	129	-	1
Iyo Bank	Ehime	2,250	2,445	126	104	-	1

Table 2-2 (*Continued*)

Location of Bank Names	Head Office	Deposits in Yen as of: June 1989	Deposits in Yen as of: July 1990	Number of Branch Offices: Overseas Offices 6/89	7/90	All Branch Offices 6/89	7/90
Shiga Bank	Shiga	2,246	2,526	101	91	-	1
Hyakujushi Bank	Kagawa	2,207	2,400	91	91	1	-
Daishi Bank	Niigata	2,167	2,513	124	124	-	1
Suruga Bank	Shizuoka	2,020	2,224	119	120	-	1
Kiyo Bank	Wakayama	1,954	2,180	92	93	-	-
Hyakugo Bank	Mie	1,866	2,118	115	117	-	-
Hokkoku Bank	Ishikama	1,785	2,032	118	119	-	-
Higo Bank	Kumamoto	1,743	1,971	103	104	-	-
Ogaki Kyoritsu	Gifu	1,662	1,841	97	99	-	1
San-in Godo Bank	Shimane	1,557	1,717	122	126	-	-
Fukui Bank	Fukui	1,504	1,656	120	122	-	-
Toho Bank	Fukushima	1,481	1,724	96	97	-	-
Tokyo Tomin Bank	Tokyo	1,466	1,724	69	71	-	-
Shikoku Bank	Kochi	1,432	1,619	103	104	-	-
Kagoshima Bank	Kagoshima	1,413	1,623	111	113	-	-
Musashino Bank	Saitama	1,393	1,583	71	74	-	-
The Bank of Osaka	Osaka	1,362	1,598	69	71	-	-
Hokuetsu Bank	Niigata	1,359	1,431	89	91	-	-
Awa Bank	Tokushima	-	1,351	1,537	87		
87	-						
Oita Bank	Oita	1,310	1,463	101	101	-	-
Yamanashi Chuo	Yamanashi	1,239	1,427	76	79	-	-
Chiba Kogyo Bank	Chiba	1,219	1,426	69	73	. -	-

Table 2-2 (*Continued*)

Location of Bank Names	Head Office	Deposits in Yen as of:		Number of Branch Offices:			
		June 1989	July 1990	Overseas Offices		All Branch Offices	
				6/89	7/90	6/89	7/90
Eighteenth Bank	Nagasaki	1,146	1,298	95	98	-	-
Akita Bank	Akita	1,123	1,274	90	94	-	-
Bank of Iwate	Iwate	1,121	1,441	102	104	-	-
Shinwa Bank	Nagasaki	1,066	1,196	102	106	-	-
Aomori Bank	Aomori	1,054	1,214	95	95	-	-
Senshu Bank	Osaka	1,018	1,144	52	53	-	-
Michinoku Bank	Aomori	955	1,069	98	99	-	-
Yamagata Bank	Yamagata	950	1,038	80	81	-	-
Bank of Ikeda	Osaka	947	1,103	57	58	-	-
Miyazaki Bank	Miyazaki	934	1,053	94	94	-	-
Bank of Saga	Saga	908	1,112	83	85	-	-
Bank of the Ryukyus	Okinawa	861	931	68	69	-	-
Mie Bank	Mie	724	802	65	66	-	-
Bank of Okinawa	Okinawa	688	751	78	77	-	-
Kanto Bank	Ibaraku	658	735	54	55	-	-
Shimizu Bank	Shizuoka	614	740	62	64	-	-
Ugo Bank	Akita	460	525	63	66	-	-
Shonai Bank	Yamagata	414	479	53	55	-	-
Tottori Bank	Tottori	390	475	56	58	-	-
Tajima Bank	Hyogo	389	444	49	50	-	-
Tohoku Bank	Iwate	277	315	47	48	-	-
Chikuho Bank	Fukuoka	251	308	39	41	-	-
Toyama Bank	Toyama	185	210	32	33	-	-
Totals 64 Banks		123,607¥	144,044¥	6,412	6,532	15	25

Notes: Deposit figures include CDs and office figures include the head office.Source: Federation of Bankers Associations of Japan (Zenginkyo), List of Member Banks, 1989, pp. 1-3; and List of Member Banks, 1990, pp. 1-3.

with numerous nonbank financial firms, such as securities houses and insurance companies, for what is inherently a smaller market than in many other industrialized nations.

The regionals also face a strong, more traditional challenge in the household credit market from small loan companies, called *sarakin*, which often lend to individuals and families with little or no collateral, but assess loan interest rates that are usually higher than average bank rates. The *sarakin* cannot take deposits, but borrow from other financial institutions and relend revenues from outstanding loans. A substantial number of the financially stronger *sarakin* have been absorbed by banks that have used them to spearhead their own consumer lending programs. Due to cultural opposition to heavy family borrowing, credit card companies also have presented a strong competitive challenge to both the city and regional banks, giving Japanese individuals access to credit without necessarily inviting the attention of friends and neighbors. One of the nation's credit-card leaders is Credit Saison, a subsidiary of Seibu Saison, whose credit-card loans have grown rapidly in recent years along with its payments services and automated teller machines.

The regional Japanese banks offer investment advisory and management consulting services and are allowed to sell computer software. Like the city banks, the regionals appear to be building up a greater share of domestic financial service markets. For example, the regionals' share of all banking funds raised increased from about 12 percent to over 13 percent as the 1980s drew to a close. Their share of all bank loans booked by Japanese institutions climbed from just under 13 percent to almost 15 percent during the 1988-89 period.

Specialized Bank Lenders

There are a number of specialized banking firms that confine their activities largely to certain customer groups and offer a relatively limited range of services. Mirroring the British banking system, regulations in Japan draw a sharp distinction between short-term and long-term lending institutions. The principal difference between the two is that long-term lenders rely principally upon long-term sources of funding, while short-term lenders look primarily to the money market to derive the funds they require to make loans. For example, a long-term bank can issue notes or debentures bearing maturities of five years, while a short-term banking institution can borrow through deposits and notes generally only up to two-year maturities. Historically the Japanese have distinguished between banks specializing in commercial (and, to a lesser extent, consumer) lending, which are predominantly short-term lenders, and banks specializing in making loans to agriculture and other sectors of the economy that need longer-term credit.

Among the more rapidly growing of Japan's specialized banks are the *trust*

Table 2-3
The Trust Banks of Japan

Bank Names	Location of Head Office	Deposits in Billions of Yen as of: June 1989	July 1990	Number of Branch Offices: Total Offices		Overseas Offices	
				6/89	7/90	6/89	7/90
Mitsubishi Trust and Banking Co.	Tokyo	24,266¥	29,082¥	63	64	6	7
Mitsui Trust and Banking Co.	Tokyo	21,175	22,875	62	64	6	6
Sumitomo Trust and Banking Co.	Osaka	21,026	26,136	59	59	6	6
Yasuda Trust and Banking Co.	Tokyo	16,935	19,502	61	62	5	5
Toyo Trust and Banking Co.	Tokyo	13,866	15,014	63	63	5	5
Chuo Trust and Banking Co.	Tokyo	8,495	9,543	55	55	4	4
Nippon Trust and Banking Co.	Tokyo	2,909	3,126	37	37	-	-
Totals		108,672¥	125,278¥	400	404	32	33

Notes: Deposit figures include money in trust, loan trust, pension trust, and employees' property formation benefit trust.

Source: Federation of Bankers Associations of Japan (Zenginkyo), List of Member Banks, 1989, p. 5; and List of Member Banks, 1990, p. 5.

banks, which develop long-term financial relationships with their customers and are permitted to offer and manage five-year loan trust accounts as a vehicle for supplying long-term capital to businesses. (See Table 2-3 for a list of Japanese trust banks.) Unlike their counterparts in the United States, trust banks do much more than act simply as agents for individuals and corporations; they offer many regular banking services as well as trust services and are active in international markets, including the United States. Trust banks in Japan function as discount securities brokers, keeping a portion of the commissions charged by securities dealers for carrying out the orders of trust banks to buy or sell securities on behalf of their customers. The trusts also manage investment (fund) trusts that contain a corporate customer's accumulated financial assets (cash and securities) that the trust invests on behalf of its customer to protect the customer's property and earn a satisfactory rate of return. Trust companies are one of only two types of financial institutions (the other being insurance companies) that are allowed to control and manage pension and retirement programs inside Japan.

Trust banks have also come to play a prominent role in real estate projects as selling agents and facilitators, and increasingly are participants in domestic business lending and Eurocurrency credit agreements. These banking firms have a history of developing new service innovations. Among the most recent are "property trusts," in which the trust bank takes over the control of commercial property owned by a customer and develops that property to generate a stream of revenue for its customer—an activity that has become highly profitable due to rising land values inside Japan. Their market shares appear to be growing like those of the city and regional banks and, in fact, they have, on occasion, outperformed these institutions. Trust banks' share of all funds raised climbed from about 9 percent to over 10 percent as the 1980s came to an end.

Deregulation, however, is likely to bring the larger city and regional banks into the trust market eventually, creating competitive problems for the trust institutions. In fact, a major battle has developed between Japan's trust and commercial banks and foreign banking firms in global financial markets over so-called *custody services*. As Lori Ioannou (1989) points out, global custodian firms assist international investors by buying promising looking securities employing local currency, collecting any dividends and interest to which investors in these securities are entitled, keeping records for tax and investment planning purposes, and providing investors with periodic reports on their purchases and sales. Among the leading customers seeking custodial services are investment companies (mutual funds), insurance companies, securities dealers, smaller banks, and pension funds. The custody business rakes in substantial fee income for the most aggressive commercial and trust banks and is expected to be an area of continuing revenue growth, due to the expansion of worldwide investments and the growing number of corporations entering the global money and capital markets.

Cooperative banks serve agricultural borrowers as well as the forestry and fishing industries. The cooperatives also provide small businesses and individuals with loans and are regulated predominantly by Japan's regional governments rather than the central government. They are generally restricted from dealing in government securities except as distributing agents and are shut out of most foreign markets. The cooperatives have a coordinating bank, known as the National Federation of Credit Cooperatives, which is designed to provide for liquidity needs and to protect the cooperatives from damaging seasonal swings in loan demand and deposit flows.

Long-term credit banks service capital market borrowers and investors, providing longer-term loans and selling long-term debt securities (up to five years in maturity) in order to fund the growth of credit accounts that represent the bulk of their assets. As Table 2-4 shows, the long-term credit banks

Table 2-4
The Long-Term Credit Banks of Japan

Bank Names	Location of Head Office	Deposits in Billions of Yen As of: June 1989	July 1990	Number of Branch Offices: Total Offices 6/89	7/90	Overseas Offices 6/89	7/90
Industrial Bank of Japan	Tokyo	29,151¥	30,930¥	33	36	8	9
Long-Term Credit Bank of Japan	Tokyo	18,686	20,629	27	31	5	7
Nippon Credit Bank	Tokyo	12,171	13,107	24	24	6	6
Totals		60,008¥	64,666¥	84	91	19	22

Notes: Deposit figures include bank debentures.

Source: Federation of Bankers Associations of Japan (Zenginkyo), List of Member Banks, 1989, p. 5; and List of Member Banks, 1990, p. 6.

are all based in Tokyo and include the Industrial Bank of Japan, the Long-Term Credit Bank of Japan, and Nippon Credit Bank. These banks can collect corporate and government deposits (which are eligible for insurance coverage) but usually are blocked from providing retail banking services to Japanese households. Nevertheless, long-term credit banks are highly leveraged firms that can drive their capital ratios well below the levels maintained by most multinational banks, and their loan limit is generally higher than other banks at roughly 30 percent of capital plus reserves.

The three long-term credit banks have significant ancillary operations in money markets around the world. In their international operations these banks advise corporate and governmental issuers of securities on market conditions and suggested terms for new securities issues and act as agents for both securities offerings and for investors interested in buying securities. Recently these long-term credit institutions have challenged the preeminent position of Japan's city banks in short-term corporate lending and scored slight market share gains from just over 5 percent to almost 6 percent of all bank loans in Japan by year-end 1989. These banking firms also modestly enlarged their share of total funds raised by Japanese banks to about 5 percent by the end of the 1980s.

Banks in Japan must be licensed by the Ministry of Finance to offer foreign exchange trading services (FOREX). This activity is still dominated by a foreign exchange specialist, the Bank of Tokyo, which is normally classified among Japan's city banks and serves Japanese manufacturing corporations and trading firms with foreign currency–denominated loans. The Bank of Tokyo is active abroad in the Eurocurrency market as investment banker and agent. While it is authorized to solicit retail and wholesale deposits inside Japan, its relatively limited branching system at home has caused it to rely more on securities issues and funding from the international Eurocurrency markets. The Bank of Tokyo is now facing strong challenges from both foreign and domestic banks for both international and domestic clients, and no longer plays the exclusive role it once did in serving as one of Japan's few financial service links to the global financial system.

The Sogo and Shinkin Banks

The Sogo and Shinkin banks, along with Japanese cooperatives, are active lenders and service providers to small business firms. *Sogo* banks began early in this century as mutual associations, similar to U.S. mutual savings banks, but shortly after World War II became stockholder-owned corporations. They were and still are active deposit-takers from and lenders to households and smaller business firms as well as active money-market lenders and investors in government bonds.

Ministry of Finance regulations place a ceiling on the size of companies to which Sogo banks can extend credit. Generally they are prohibited from extending loans to businesses with capital resources exceeding $5 to $6 million and with payrolls exceeding 300 workers. This restriction tends to make Sogos direct competitors with Japan's regional banks. The largest Sogos are compelled by Japanese law to keep required reserves with the central bank and receive Ministry of Finance licensing of their operations and approval for any planned branching, mergers, or acquisitions.

A major structural shift occurred among the Sogo banks in 1989. Sixty-six former Sogo banks converted to ordinary banks after February 1989, becoming full-fledged commercial banks. These institutions are now referred to as member banks of the Second Association of Regional Banks, which also includes two Sogos that had not converted to ordinary banks as of the summer of 1990. These institutions include such prominent banking firms as Hyogo Bank, Tokyo Sowa Bank, the Bank of Kinki (Osaka), the Bank of Nagoya (Aichi), Fukuoka City Bank, and Kofuku Bank and Fukutoku Bank (both from Osaka). (Table 2-5 contains a complete listing of these member banks.) By June 1990 there remained only two Sogo banks.

One of the most unique of Japanese financial institutions is the *Shinkin* bank, of which there were over 450 in 1990. Shinkin banks bring smaller nonfinancial business firms together into credit-granting associations. The Shinkins have a strong presence in both rural markets and cities and it is in the latter that they often compete for the same business and household

Table 2-5
The Member Banks of the Second Association of Regional Banks

Bank Names	Location of Head Office	Deposits in Billions of Yen As of:		Total Branch Offices as of:	
		June 1989	July 1990	June 1989	July 1990
Hyogo Bank	Hyogo	3,071¥	3,333¥	129	132
Tokyo Sowa Bank	Tokyo	2,358	2,829	90	93
The Bank of Kinki	Osaka	1,723	2,042	97	98
The Bank of Nagoya	Aichi	1,668	1,910	108	110
Fukuoka City Bank	Fukuoka	1,654	1,984	120	125
Kofuku Bank	Osaka	1,468	1,828	111	112
Fukutoku Bank	Osaka	1,380	1,733	91	95
Aichi Bank	Aichi	1,319	1,508	99	101
Hiroshima-Sogo Bank	Hiroshima	1,305	1,593	90	92
Keiyo Bank	Chiba	1,293	1,594	95	98
Chukyo Bank	Aichi	1,201	1,371	94	96
Towa Bank	Gunma	1,120	1,294	78	78
Daisan Bank	Mie	1,110	1,270	89	90
North Pacific Bank	Hokkaido	1,108	1,239	105	107
Ehime Bank	Ehime	1,103	1,154	77	80
Higashi-Nippon Bank	Tokyo	1,038	1,136	69	69
Tochigi Bank	Tochigi	794	929	55	57
Kyushu Bank	Nagasaki	723	884	63	63
Niigata Chuo Bank	Niigata	710	779	75	75
Hanshin Bank	Hyogo	709	926	62	64
Kita-Nippon Bank	Iwate	707	784	75	75
Biwako Bank	Shija	687	881	62	64
Kagawa Bank	Kagawa	675	754	68	70
The Bank of Kansai	Osaka	658	872	65	66
Taiheiyo Bank	Tokyo	748	748	42	42
Bank of Kochi	Kochi	613	708	73	75
Gifu Bank	Gifu	601	663	57	58
Taiko Bank	Niigata	597	597	52	52
First Bank of Toyama	Toyama	535	590	66	66

Table 2-5 (*Continued*)

Bank Names	Location of Head Office	Deposits in Billions of Yen As of:		Total Branch Offices as of:	
		June 1989	July 1990	June 1989	July 1990
Fukushima Bank	Fukushima	514	566	62	63
Tokushima Bank	Tokushima	508	531	57	59
Setouchi Bank	Hiroshima	504	599	53	55
Kumamoto Bank	Kumamoto	498	558	56	58
Sapporo Bank	Hokkaido	495	588	65	66
Minami Nippon Bank	Kagoshima	491	534	70	72
Ibaraki Bank	Ibaraki	482	555	49	50
Hanwa Bank	Wakayama	467	546	50	50
Kokumin Bank	Tokyo	467	576	35	36
Higo Family Bank	Kennamito	457	555	51	52
Saikyo Bank	Yamaguchi	436	520	53	54
Shokusan Bank	Yamagata	432	499	63	64
Tomato Bank	Okayama	431	510	54	54
Yamagata Shiawase Bank	Yamagata	401	450	66	67
Nagano Bank	Nagano	382	445	44	46
Daito Bank	Fukushima	375	433	59	61
Chubu Bank	Shizuda	367	435	43	43
Ishikawa Bank	Ishikawa	345	436	63	65
Fuso Bank	Tottori	338	409	53	55
Sendai Bank	Miyagi	335	366	57	57
Akita Akebono Bank	Akita	312	356	58	58
Bank of Naniwa	Osaka	279	355	39	41
Wakayama Bank	Wakayama	274	327	45	46
Fukuko Bank	Fukui	272	288	50	50
Kyoto Kyoei Bank	Kyoto	270	325	47	47
Howa Bank	Oita	266	297	47	48
Okinawa Kaiho Bank	Okinawa	264	309	47	47
Miyazaki Taiyo Bank	Miyazaki	262	291	48	49
Shizuoka Chuo Bank	Shizuoka		264		46
Bank of Nagasaki	Nagasaki	221	238	51	51

Table 2-5 (*Continued*)

Bank Names	Location of Head Office	Deposits in Billions of Yen As of: June 1989	July 1990	Total Branch Offices as of: June 1989	July 1990
Fukuoka Chuo Bank	Fukuoka	208	230	41	41
Kanagawa Bank	Kanagawa	207	237	27	27
Tsukuba Bank	Ibaraki	200	234	27	29
Shimane Bank	Shimane				
Taisho Bank	Osaka	151	172	20	20
Saga Kyoei Bank	Saga	142	158	31	32
Nara Bank	Nara	88	105	19	19
Totals		43,472¥	52,438¥	3,963	4,215

Notes: The Second Association of Regional Banks is an association composed of 66 former Sogo (savings-type) banks that converted to ordinary banks under Japanese law after February 1989. By mid-1990 there were only 2 Sogo banks that had not converted to ordinary banks. Deposit figures include CDs as of September 1988 and September 1989 respectively. The head office of each bank is included in total branch offices as of September 1989 and 1990 respectively.
Source: Federation of Bankers Associations of Japan (Zenginkyo), List of Member Banks, 1989, pp. 3-5, and List of Member Banks, 1990, pp. 3-5.

clients as the Sogos and regional banks. Regulations enforced by the Ministry of Finance limit the Shinkins to lending to somewhat smaller businesses than the Sogos normally have dealt with in the past. Generally, the Shinkins must lend to businesses with capital resources of less than about $4 million.

Shinkins also trade government securities and have made some forays into the foreign currency markets. The Japanese government has tried to nurture the Shinkins with more lenient branching restrictions and more liberal deposit terms to enable them to grow and service more borrowers. Money-market activities of the Shinkin banks are generally under the direction of the Zenshinren Bank, which acts as their accommodating bank, investing their excess loanable funds and making loans to those Shinkins facing liquidity pressures.

Two other relatively unusual financial institutions are the *Shoko Chukin Bank*, which is a joint private-government cooperative association, and the *labor credit cooperatives*, which generally serve members of labor unions and consumer associations. Shoko Chukin Bank makes loans to groups of small business firms. Both Shoko and the labor credit cooperatives generally confine sales of their services to members only, though they are more liberal in the groups from which they can solicit deposits and to whom they can sell debentures—the two preeminent sources of funds for these institutions. Shoko Chukin Bank is subject to regulation by the Ministry of Finance whereas the labor credit associations are generally supervised at the regional government level.

Even more specialized financial firms are the Nokyo, Gyoko, and Shinrin cooperatives. These retail and small business lending institutions deal, respectively, with agricultural, fishery, and forestry cooperatives. Farmers, fishermen, and individuals involved in the forest products industry come together in these financial firms for loans, management consulting services, and marketing assistance. Members frequently can access nonbank services, such as life insurance and property and casualty insurance, through some of these cooperatives. The regional governments inside Japan play the principal role in their daily regulation.

Additional support for the agricultural segment of the Japanese economy has been provided for more than 60 years by the *Norinchukin Bank*—a central bank for those cooperative lending institutions serving the forestry, fishery, and agricultural industries. Norinchukin takes deposits from participating cooperative associations, sells debentures, and may also accept some types of corporate deposits. The Norinchukin bank is a major player in national and international securities and foreign exchange markets, buying large quantities of government and corporate bonds as well as supplying money-market loans to other institutions in the domestic and international money markets.

NONBANK FINANCIAL INSTITUTIONS IN JAPAN

The Japanese financial system also includes a significant number of nonbank financial institutions, including at least 300 domestic securities firms, credit card firms and small loan companies, life insurance companies, and property-casualty insurance firms. The most numerous private nonbank financial institutions are securities firms and small loan companies. A government savings institution—the postal savings and insurance system, which is supervised and managed by the Ministry of Posts and Telecommunications—operates out of nearly 24,000 post offices nationwide, selling savings deposits to the public. Until the spring of 1988 the savings placed by the public with the postal system were exempt from taxes and the yields posted on postal savings accounts were generally allowed to be higher than those paid by other depository institutions. Postal savings deposits are guaranteed by federal authorities and continue to be an attractive savings vehicle for thousands of savers of relatively limited means.

Securities Firms Within the Japanese Financial System

Slightly in excess of 200 domestically chartered securities firms represent the core of the Japanese system for the underwriting and distribution of stocks, bonds, and other securities. Out of this total industry population, four giant securities conglomerates far outdistance their competitors in domestic markets and, increasingly, have come to exert a pervasive influence over international securities trading along with the leading U.S. and British investment companies. These well-known firms include Nomura Securities, Daiwa Securities, Nikko Securities, and Yamichi Securities, which account for at least two-thirds of securities sales and underwriting operations inside Japan and the leading actors in underwriting sales of new Japanese government securities. The "Big Four" also are playing a growing role in sales of government securities inside the United States and operate branches and subsidiaries in capital markets all around the world. Daiwa and Nomura have banking licenses in London and primary dealerships in the United States. Leading Japanese securities dealers realize that their success internationally will depend on their ability to offer corporate customers a complete menu of credit, securities, underwriting, portfolio, and cash management services as well as risk-hedging tools with links to all major exchanges and credit markets worldwide. Reflective of this rapid developmental diversity has been the rise of Japan as a leading global center for foreign exchange trading and the creation and trading of currency swaps, not only as an aid to the worldwide expansion of the Euroyen market but to facilitate direct investment inside Japan and abroad.

Much of the rapid expansion of the securities business, especially its growth worldwide, is accounted for by strict regulatory barriers between the securities industry and other financial service firms (particularly commercial banks) in both Japan and the United States. The most notable is the famous Article 65 in Japan's Securities and Exchange Code, which was enacted in 1948. Article 65 parallels the U.S. Glass-Steagall Act in requiring a strict separation between commercial banking and investment banking, but with important differences. Glass-Steagall was aimed primarily at protecting bank depositors, while Japan's rule is in place principally to protect securities firms. Moreover, Japanese banks can invest in corporate stock as an investment security, unlike U.S. banks.

As in the United States, significant holes have been punched in this legally erected wall between commercial and investment banking, particularly in the underwriting of government securities and in offerings of securities in the retail market.[1] However, in Japan as in the United States, securities firms still dominate the underwriting of new issues of corporate stock. In addition to trading on the major exchanges in Tokyo and Osaka and on the smaller exchanges, there is a growing over-the-counter (OTC) market, based principally in Nagoya, Osaka, and Tokyo, designed to serve as a channel for capital flows to smaller business firms. Recent changes in regulation have permitted the development of mutual funds to invest in the equity shares of smaller Japanese firms and the use of smaller companies' stock as loan collateral, both of which should stimulate the further development of Japan's OTC market. However, prevailing opinion inside Japan's financial community suggests that Japanese commercial banks are likely to be kept out of full service investment banking for privately issued securities for some time into the future, stimulating Japanese commercial banks to enter other fields with significant revenue potential. These latter areas include providing investment advice, the placement of private securities, and trading government bonds and futures contracts.

The Ministry of Finance, which is the primary regulator of commercial banking operations inside Japan, also is the principal regulatory agency for the domestic securities industry. Securities companies must be licensed and must meet the capital adequacy standards set by the ministry. Many of the ministry's rules affecting securities firms are spelled out, while others consist of informal "window guidance" that is nevertheless generally quite effective.

The Bank of Japan plays a relatively minor role in securities regulation compared to the Ministry of Finance, but does have some influence on the industry. This is because a few securities firms maintain clearing accounts with the Bank of Japan, and these firms are entitled to request loans from the central bank in emergency situations, though there is little evidence of any significant use of this power in recent years.

The Tokyo Stock Exchange, the regional exchanges, and the Ministry of Finance can set margin requirements on stock purchases. Short sales tend to be more limited than in the West due to the volatility of prices on the Tokyo and Osaka exchanges, but interest in program trading has advanced rapidly due to the wide price swings and the limited number of different corporate shares compared to most major exchanges in Europe and the United States.

Insurance Companies Operating Within the Japanese Financial System

For decades the principle of insurance was little understood and little used in Asian culture, in large part because of institutional arrangements and cultural traditions that protected individuals and families in time of need and provided support for the aged. The rapid industrialization of Japan and the Asian continent has changed that pattern somewhat in recent years, however, and Japan is now one of the leading nations around the world in annual sales of life insurance and in providing life insurance coverage for families. In other forms of insurance, however, particularly in coverage against personal negligence and for the protection of property, insurance sales in Japan (and most of Asia, for that matter) still lag significantly behind insurance sales in the United States.

The regulatory walls that separate depository institutions from one another and divide commercial banking from investment banking have their parallels in the way the Japanese segregate insurance companies from each other. Property and casualty insurers are prohibited from selling ordinary life insurance with few exceptions; concomitantly, property and casualty insurance policies are not generally part of the permitted menu of services that can be sold by life insurance firms. In the United States, property and casualty insurers are important stock market investors, while life insurers hold smaller equity positions except in their management of pension plans, where U.S. life insurance companies can act as agents for pension plan members and their sponsoring employers and purchase large volumes of corporate stock for long-term capital appreciation. Inside Japan life insurance companies also now appear to be outstripping trust banks in the rate of growth of their management of pension plans. Today several Japanese insurers make active use of financial futures trading to hedge their foreign investments. A trade association, the Life Insurance Association of Japan, represents the industry in regulatory matters and keeps extensive industry statistics.

Japanese life insurers have also become leaders in the domestic equity market, helped by favorable regulations that allow Japan's insurance companies to hold a substantial share of the stock issued by Japanese corporations. Life insurance companies also are among the leading buyers of commercial bank notes and stock, helping Japanese banks recently to boost their capital to meet new international bank capital standards set up in the late 1980s. Moreover, Japanese life insurers have become a potent force in international financial markets and highly visible in the United States as purchasers of U.S. property and as underwriters of U.S. Treasury debt securities and the federal government's huge budget deficit.

Further evidence of Japanese plans for expanding involvement in the U.S. insurance market surfaced in 1991 when Dai-Ichi Mutual Life Insurance announced plans to invest just over $300 million in Lincoln National Corporation of Fort Wayne, Indiana, giving Dai-Ichi almost a 10-percent share of this large U.S. insurance and pension management firm. Still, it is not clear that Japanese investments in U.S. insurance firms are motivated principally by the goal of broadening their American market shares of this industry or whether they are seeking to learn management and marketing principles that can be used back home where the insurance market is undergoing gradual government deregulation, posing intense competitive pressure for Dai-Ichi and other Japanese insurers.

Domestic property and casualty insurers have displayed rapid growth in selected insurance lines—notably in automobile-related insurance coverage and in the coverage of shipping hazards. They tend to be heavy investors in shorter-term corporate loans, government securities, and bank CDs, as well as in selected common and preferred stocks. Regulation by the Ministry of Finance includes the establishment of capital adequacy rules and the setting of common insurance fees for each type of policy sold.

BANKING'S IMPORTANCE RELATIVE TO NONBANK FINANCIAL FIRMS IN THE JAPANESE SYSTEM

Overall, Japanese banks play a far greater role in their financial system relative to insurance companies, securities firms, and other nonbank financial institutions than is true in the United States. One reason is the strong

Japanese tradition favoring negotiated markets, where credit is extended after direct negotiation between lender and borrower, rather than through the impersonal sale of securities in an open market where lender and borrower generally do not confront each other directly. Most negotiated loans arise from long-standing bank-customer relationships where, as Thomas Cargill and Shoichi Royana (1990) note, formal risk analysis is limited, not only because of extensive experience with each customer, but also because very often Japanese banks hold the stock of firms to which they lend money and will be actively involved in the management of these customer firms. There is less tendency, too, for "gouging" the loan customer, since many Japanese banks seem to place greater priority on stable earnings and stable growth rather than on high short-term profitability.

Despite the prominent position played by banks in the Japanese financial system, there is evidence of considerable slippage in bank market shares with nonbank financial institutions, foreign lenders, and the government's postal savings system now capturing a portion of the banks' former market share. For example, by 1987 Japanese commercial banks accounted for about 35 percent of all capital market flows inside Japan, while privately owned nonbank financial institutions represented about 45 percent of these flows, with the government sector accounting for most of the remainder of capital market trading. Nonbank financial institutions also captured the biggest share of personal and postal savings at 35 percent in 1988, compared to 33 percent for commecial banks. This growing competitive pressure from nonbank financial institutions and from open-market trading activity explains a significant portion of Japanese banking activity abroad, as these banks seek ways to offset their lagging market shares at home.

THE MINISTRY OF FINANCE AND THE BANK OF JAPAN—THE REGULATORY CENTERPIECES IN THE JAPANESE FINANCIAL SYSTEM

Regulatory responsibility for all financial institutions in the Japanese financial system is in the hands of the Bank of Japan and the Ministry of Finance. Actually, most regulation of financial services is vested in the Ministry of Finance, which sets rules for bank lending, the maintenance of bank liquidity, and required levels of capital adequacy. In contrast, the Bank of Japan, Japan's central bank, oversees the examination of individual banks and other financial intermediaries and is charged with conducting monetary policy for the nation.

The Bank of Japan was chartered in 1882 to control the growth of money and credit and to nurture the development of the Japanese banking and financial system. The central bank is a special quasi-public corporation. The government supplies 55 percent of its capital, and the private sector provides about 45 percent. It is governed by the Bank of Japan Policy Board, established in 1949, and by law is charged with regulating the nation's money supply and financial system to promote a stable value for the yen and a stable pattern of economic growth.

Like the Federal Reserve System in the United States, the Bank of Japan issues bank notes as circulating currency and serves as the fiscal agent for the central government and for private banks. The central bank also sets reserve requirements on deposits and other bank liabilities and the required levels of legal reserves that must be held in an account at the Bank of Japan. As in the United States, legal reserve accounts held in the Bank of Japan are employed to clear checks and to resolve claims between banks and other financial institutions. Mirroring the Federal Reserve System, Japan's central bank purchases and sells government securities and selected commercial instruments (which began in 1962) in order to stabilize money and credit growth and to nudge market interest rates in the desired direction. All policy operations are supervised by the Policy Board, headed by the Bank of Japan's governor, with representatives from the Finance Ministry, government agencies, and private industry.

Loans are made by the central bank, which monitors and frequently changes the standards financial institutions must meet to qualify for these loans as well as the discount rate charged for receiving central bank credit. The Bank of Japan makes heavy use of "moral suasion"—psychological "arm twisting"—in much the same manner as the Federal Reserve System in the United States, through phone calls and private conferences with the managements of banks and other regulated institutions. In this instance Japan's central bank uses a somewhat unique psychological tool known as "window guidance," which consists of suggested guidelines for loan growth given by the Bank of Japan to the financial institutions to which it lends funds.

The Bank of Japan is actually under the supervisory control of the Ministry of Finance, which can appoint the former's management and control the issuance of currency as well as approve major policy changes and the use of monetary policy tools. The ministry has other extensive governmental powers as well, such as drafting the government's budget, issuing government debt, and collecting tax revenues.

The Ministry of Finance is responsible for the operation of the Deposit Insurance Corporation (DIC), which was set up in 1971 and now provides coverage of the public's deposits up to 10 million yen (close to $70,000 in U.S. dollars). However, the Deposit Insurance Corporation does not protect deposits accepted by foreign banks having offices in Japan. The Ministry of Finance also has responsibility for supervision and licensing of the securities markets and uses a form of moral suasion to make sure financial institutions endeavor to follow its policy guidelines. Banks must obtain the ministry's approval for mergers and acquisitions, the establishment of new branches, and other significant organizational changes.

DEREGULATION OF THE JAPANESE FINANCIAL SYSTEM

The Japanese banking system has been closely regulated and supervised from its inception. This regulatory stance has not merely restricted banking services and markets, but has endeavored to protect Japanese banking firms from collapse. Economist Philip Wellons (1985) observes, for example, that the Japanese government has permitted no bank to fail since World War II. Moreover, the Japanese regulatory system may have shaped its supervisory actions to broadly preserve existing relative market shares among the various banks. For example, economist Akio Mikuni in a speech to the 1988 International Banking Conference contends: "It is a cardinal principle of the regulators not to upset the pecking order between the banks. . . . The Bank of Japan's role is to coordinate new loans so as to keep the relative size of each bank intact, judged by loans and assets."[2]

Of course, these unique features of the Japanese banking system are currently under great pressure for change, largely because of a deregulation movement that began in the late 1960s and 1970s, especially after the Arab Oil Embargo and the subsequent escalation of world oil prices. Japan found itself with growing trade deficits and large government budget deficits at home, necessitating great reliance on the financial markets to absorb new government securities. Among the most important results of the deregulation movement have been the increasing importance of open markets in allocating credit and, as a result, the gradually declining role of negotiated credit markets; the rise of nonbank financial institutions inside Japan that have reduced the banks' share of all financial transactions; and an increasing share of financial service sales going to foreign firms, including U.S. banks and securities firms. Moreover, Japanese investors have experienced a substantial broadening in both domestic and foreign financial instruments available to them, and they have received many more options, both at home and abroad, to raise new money.

From the standpoint of Japanese bankers, however, the most consequential trend, unquestionably, is that *both* Japanese banks and foreign banking institutions that compete with them are experiencing a declining share of total funds flows through both the Japanese financial system and the international financial system, as securities markets and nonbank financial service firms become more important. This adverse trend for Japanese bankers has given powerful impetus to them to expand overseas, particularly into the United States, and to seek favorable regulatory concessions at home.

Revamping of the financial system in Japan may be said to have begun with a study conducted in the 1960s by the Financial System Research Council, which serves as an advisory group to the government's Minister of Finance. The council considered possible reforms in the banking system and in financing various sectors of the economy, including international trade. Results of the council's studies were published over the 1967-70 period, and ultimately led to revisions during the 1970s in the laws surrounding mergers among financial institutions and credit flows to smaller Japanese businesses. Other recommendations of this group led to a gradual relaxing of deposit interest rate ceilings beginning early in the 1970s and the launching of a federal deposit insurance system. Over the 1975-84 period numerous restrictions on loan and securities transactions were modified or lifted to respond to a widening government budget deficit and slower economic growth at home. Government bond auctions were expanded, and banks and other investors were freed from various restrictions on trading Japanese government bonds in the secondary market, leading to the growth of a market for repurchase agreements (RPs) using government securities as collateral.

Major changes in the Foreign Exchange and Trade Control Act followed soon after in 1980, which contributed to an expansion of trading in yen-denominated bank deposits overseas. This broadened the international appeal of the yen and raised its value in international currency markets, and enabled Japanese citizens to more easily obtain access to deposits denominated in foreign currencies. Japanese companies began selling their bonds abroad, while domestic institutions thereafter made massive purchases of corporate debt obligations, corporate stock, and government securities from the United States and other foreign countries. The internationalization of the yen, which has occurred largely since 1984, has helped greatly to boost the deregulation of Japan's banking and financial system.

Once international trading in the yen and in yen-denominated instruments became firmly established, Japan's domestic controls on financial services and its internal monetary policies became much less tenable. Because dissatisfied borrowers and investors could flee to other markets abroad, further deregulation of the domestic financial system became inevitable. Repeatedly, in the years since 1984, restrictions on Euroyen trading and yen-denominated securities issuance for both domestic firms and foreign entities have been liberalized, resulting in a massive expansion of the Euroyen market—that is, yen-denominated deposits—around the world. The Euroyen market today is comparable in size to the external market for Swiss francs, but remains smaller than the market for deutsche mark–denominated deposits and, of course, is many times smaller than the Eurodollar market. A major constraint on the future international expansion of the yen is that a relatively small proportion of Japanese exports is actually denominated in yen (roughly one-third of Japan's total exports, according to K. Osugi [1990]).

One of the most important steps in the deregulation of the Japanese domestic banking community occurred in April 1979, when negotiable CDs were first authorized. The first CDs were issued in May of that year. These negotiable time deposits were allowed to carry negotiated interest rates to reflect current market conditions. In April 1983, the government cleared the way for the sale of public bonds to small investors, thus setting in motion the beginnings of a retail bond market. In June 1984 Japanese banks were authorized to deal in public bonds, and in April of that year, investors were allowed to purchase commercial paper and commercial bank CDs abroad. In the same year the United States and Japan concluded an accord calling for the internationalization of the yen, central bank efforts to strengthen the yen, and gradual deregulation of Japan's domestic financial markets.

The year 1985 ushered in new Japanese money-market certificates of deposit and, in June of that year, a yen-denominated bankers' acceptance market appeared. A futures market in government bonds was set up in October 1985, which also saw the liberalization of interest rates on large denomination time deposits. Foreign-owned trust banks were permitted to operate inside Japan beginning in the fall of 1985 and, in December of that year, foreign banks were permitted to establish branch offices in Tokyo as 50 percent subsidiaries to conduct securities trading and record-keeping. In April 1987 Japanese banks were granted permission to issue domestically convertible bonds and, in October 1988, were also approved to securitize their home loans. The process of securitizing a loan simply involves packaging all loans of a uniform type and quality, removing them from the bank's balance sheet, and selling securities against the packaged loans to capital market investors in order to raise more loanable funds. At the same time Japanese banks were empowered to issue commercial paper, both at home and abroad, with fewer constraining regulations.

Even broader powers for Japanese banks were ushered in during 1989, as domestic banks received permission to offer brokerage services in financial futures markets overseas and to offer bond futures brokering services. Moreover, the number of domestic financial markets expanded substantially as a Tokyo financial futures market in Euroyen, Eurodollar, and other currency futures was launched in June 1989, followed by the issuance of three-month government bonds in September 1989 and U.S. Treasury bond futures at the end of that year. In March 1990 Japanese banks were permitted to securitize their corporate loans, and in May 1990 government bond futures began trading on the Tokyo stock exchange.

Major changes in rules applying to foreign investors and foreign loans were made in 1985. Restrictions on medium-term and long-term Euroyen-denominated loans to foreigners were liberalized. In July 1985 Japanese banks received permission to issue foreign currency–denominated convertible bonds in overseas markets. The establishment of Japanese offshore markets in December 1986 served simultaneously to stimulate Japanese banking activity abroad and gave foreign financial firms more open access to Japan's domestic markets. In 1987 the underwriting of foreign commercial paper was approved for the overseas branches of Japanese banks, and these banks plus securities firms and insurance firms were granted access to overseas financial futures markets. Symmetrically, the issuance of commercial paper inside Japan by foreign firms was authorized in January 1988. By July 1989 foreigners could more easily issue bonds in the Tokyo market, and a U.S. Treasury bond futures market was begun in December 1989. A key policy issue that remains is whether and how fast interest rate ceilings and other regulatory restrictions on small denomination savings-type deposits should be lifted to give small Japanese savers access to more generous yields on savings.

One recent deregulation move inside Japan that Western bankers have largely ignored, but could be of considerable significance for their future success in penetrating the Japanese corporate market, was a governmental decision requiring Japan's banks to reduce their equity investments in domestic nonbank corporations. Effective December 1987, Japanese banks were told to retain no more than 5 percent of the stock of all nonbank corporations not specifically exempt (such as financially related companies supplying services, such as data processing or property management services, to their parent banks). There was an almost immediate benefit to Japan's huge city banks from this ruling, as large profits were generated as the now-forbidden stock (which included considerable stock that the city banks held in Japan's long-term credit banks) was sold. However, there was also a cost to the divesting banks: the extensive intercorporate ties between domestic banks and nonbank corporations were significantly weakened. This may open the door wider to foreign banks seeking more corporate business inside Japan. Moreover, as Japanese companies find their stock more widely dispersed and, therefore, become more accountable to new capital market investors, they are likely to deal more "at arm's length" with Japan's banks, seeking financial services from those financial institutions—foreign or domestic—offering the very best terms as opposed to following traditional intercorporate relationships.

PROFITABILITY, TECHNOLOGICAL CHANGE, AND DEREGULATION IN JAPANESE BANKING

It has been argued in the financial press and especially in the banking communities of the United States and Great Britain that deregulation inside Japan will so increase internal competition that Japanese banks will scale back their operations abroad and experience many of the financial problems experienced by banks in the West. Certainly smaller commercial (especially regional) banks and savings banks in Japan will be under great pressure to upgrade their risk management techniques as more interest rates (particularly deposit interest rates) are fully deregulated. However, the largest Japanese banks, particularly the city banks, that have already faced the intense pressures of risk and competition abroad, are likely to gain on their smaller domestic rivals, capturing a growing share of domestic deposits and driving to increase the efficiency of their operations at home and abroad. This should tend to make the largest Japanese banks an even more potent force in both domestic and international markets.

One of the forces that appears to be increasing the efficiency of Japanese bank operations at home and abroad is automation. Japanese banks are highly automated today, which has allowed them to cut staff size and slow the construction of additional full service branches. Computerization has sharply increased employee productivity and allowed many new services such as cash management, smart card systems, where credit cards are equipped with microchips to store and communicate financial information, point–of–sales (POS) terminals, and other customer communications links. This has helped sustain Japanese bank profits reasonably well in an era of deregulation, something U.S. banks have not been able to do as well. Nevertheless, Japanese banks' experience under deregulation began to parallel the U.S. bank experience more closely as the 1980s drew to a close and the 1990s began. The profitability of Japanese banking firms generally declined under the pressure of deregulation of deposit interest rates, losses on securities trading, and the heightened exposure of Japanese banks to international markets due to their growing physical presence abroad and advancing proportion of overseas assets. The most notable decline occurred among the huge city banks and the trust banks, though the regional banks were not far behind.

These recent developments appear to have led to more widespread use of floating-rate loans tied to changes in money-market borrowing costs. Previously many Japanese banks had tied their lending terms to changes in the Bank of Japan's discount rate, but this proved to be too inflexible to faithfully capture frequent changes in international market conditions. Nevertheless, recent pressure to further deregulate the Japanese financial system from the U.S. government and the Ministry of Finance's recently announced plans to lift regulatory ceilings on time deposits have led to widespread predictions of earnings losses, especially among regional, Sogo and Shinkin banks.

Overall, on a return-to-assets basis, Japanese banks have relatively low profits, both in the short run and in the long run. For example, while U.S. and West German bank's average returns on total assets (ROAs) have been close to 1 percent in most recent years, Japanese banks have averaged only 50 to 60 percent of that figure. One explanation for these differences in recent years has been losses on developing country (LDC) loans. Japanese banks account for 10 to 15 percent of the total of these international credits, a substantial portion (at least 80 percent) of which have had to be rescheduled in recent years. However, the Japanese tend to operate with substantially lower ratios of book value capital to total assets (ranging between 3 and 3.5 percent) than U.S. banks (whose book value capital generally averages between 6 and 7 percent of bank assets). Accordingly, Japanese banks' rates of return on equity capital (ROE) are high, especially compared to the United States. Japanese banks averaged a rate of return on owners' equity of 15 to 16 percent during the 1980s, compared to average equity returns of about 13 percent for U.S. banks during the same period.

FOREIGN BANKING FIRMS

Foreign-owned commercial banks have faced a long, uphill battle to gain entry into Japanese home markets. According to the Bank of Japan, their share of total domestic funds raised and of all domestic loans changed hardly at all through the mid-1980s and then appeared to decline later in that decade. However, foreign banks play a much greater role in extending foreign currency–denominated loans to Japanese residents, accounting for about 17 percent of short-term and 7 percent of medium- and long-term foreign currency loans granted to Japanese residents at year-end 1987.

U.S. banks have managed to secure substantial footholds in some key Japanese business centers, these centered principally in Tokyo and Osaka. Leading U.S. banks in Japan today include Bank of America, Chase Manhattan, Citicorp, Chemical Bank, Irving Trust, and Manufacturers Hanover. (See Table 2-6 for a partial list of leading foreign banking companies with Japanese offices.) In the fall of 1985 Morgan Guaranty opened Morgan Trust Bank in Tokyo, while Bankers Trust Company of New York launched Japan Bankers' Trust Company following a 1984 ruling by the Ministry of Finance. While all trust banks must be incorporated within Japan, they can raise capital overseas or form a joint venture between a domestic trust bank and a foreign bank. These friendly arrangements between domestic and foreign trust banks have caused foreign trust companies to rank among the most rapidly growing foreign financial firms inside Japan, though they have faced severe restrictions in their efforts to attract pension accounts. Other leading foreign bank–owned trust funds operating in Japan include Cititrust, Chemical Trust, Union Bank of Switzerland, Credit Suisse, and Barclays Trust.

By February 1989, 83 foreign banks operated nearly 120 branches in Japan, of which 18 had licenses to deal in public bonds and 22 were approved to operate subsidiary firms to carry on securities business in Tokyo. This compares with only 35 foreign bank branches in 1965, 38 in 1970, 73 in 1975, and 82 in 1978. There were also 9 trust banks owned by foreign corporations and 22 foreign firms that held seats on the Tokyo Stock Exchange, including such leading foreign securities firms as Morgan Stanley, Goldman Sachs, Merrill Lynch, Vickers da Costa, Jardine Fleming, and S.G. Warburg. The United States led all other nations with 28 banks operating in Japan early in 1989, followed by Korea with 14.

By April 1991 the number of foreign banks in Japan totaled 86, while their branch offices had grown to 133 total offices inside Japanese home territory. Additionally, the number of foreign banks authorized to operate 50 percent subsidiary companies to trade securities via branch offices in Tokyo had climbed to just under 30 firms. During that same time period there were 9 foreign trust

Table 2-6
Leading Foreign Banks Operating in Japan

Bank of America	Société Générale
Bankers Trust of New York (and its trust banking affiliate, Japan Bankers Trust Co.)	Sparkassen SDS, Copenhagen
	Standard Chartered Bank, London
	State Bank of India
	State Bank of New South Wales, Australia
Banque Indosuez	Swiss Bank Corporation, Basel
Barclays Trust and Banking Co.	Swiss Volksbank, Bern
Chase Manhattan Bank	Texas Commerce Bank, National Association
Chemical Bank (and its trust banking affiliate, Chemical Trust)	The Korea Development Bank
	The National Commercial Bank, Saudi Arabia
Citicorp of New York (and its trust banking affiliate, Cititrust)	The Royal Bank of Canada
	The Toronoto-Dominion Bank, Ontario
Credit Suisse	Union Bank of Finland
Deutsche Bank	Union Bank of Switzerland
Irving Trust Company of New York	United Overseas Bank, Ltd., Singapore
Manufacturers Hanover Bank (and its trust banking affiliate, Manufacturers)	West LB International SA, Luxembourg
Merchants Bankers Ltd.	Westpac Banking Corporation, Sydney
Morgan Guaranty (and its trust banking affiliate, Morgan Trust)	Philadelphia National Bank
	Philippine National Bank, Manilla
National Bank of New Zeland Limited	Royal Trust Bank (Switzerland)
National Westminster Bank PLC, London	Scotiabank, Canada
NCNB Texas National Bank	Seattle - First National Bank
Overseas Union Bank Ltd., Singapore	Security Pacific Corporation
	Singapore International
	Skandinaviska Enskilda Banken, Stockholm, Sweden

banks set up inside Japan, about 70 licensed foreign dealers engaged in the public trading of bonds, and nearly 40 foreign investment management services operating in Tokyo and in other financial centers inside Japan.

Current rules allow foreign banks to set up branch offices and create subsidiary corporations inside Japanese territory, though currently the majority of these facilities have been in the guise of branch offices. In theory at least, foreign banks have the same service powers as domestic commercial banks (including both Japanese city and regional banks) and can offer a full range of credit, deposit, and ancillary services as dictated by the Ministry of Finance. They must also keep required reserves with the Bank of Japan, but cannot qualify for government-subsidized deposit insurance coverage. Until recently foreign banks were not allowed to offer a full range of trust services or participate in the underwriting of securities issued by Japanese governmental units, but these service powers have recently been extended to all foreign banks that formally qualify.

Many foreign banks, including some U.S. banking institutions, have been bitterly disappointed by their lack of progress in carving out greater market shares inside Japan. They have found, for example, that some Japanese financial regulations hurt them more than those same rules limit domestic banks. Most notable here are branching restrictions that have limited foreign financial firms in their attempts to establish national branch office networks and tend to favor those domestic banks that already have extensive networks of satellite banking offices. This constraint appears to have forced many foreign banks to draw on their headquarters back home for funds, which has tended to raise their operating costs above those of Japanese competitors and to limit their ability to make more credit available inside Japan.

Moreover, the government-supported postal savings system has proven to be a formidable competitor with foreign banks for small-denomination deposits. Then, too, traditional and informal bank-customer relationships in Japan frequently have been resistant to penetration by outside competitors. This has been especially true of credit and other services for Japanese corporate customers, where long-standing ties can be broken only with great difficulty by outsiders. The result is to confine the activities of foreign banks largely to servicing foreign corporations that have established facilities or have building projects underway inside Japan.

Another service area more easily penetrated by foreign institutions, as we saw above, is trading in Japanese government bonds or bond futures, as well as granting loans in U.S. and Canadian dollars, francs, pounds, and marks to Japanese firms and governmental agencies that need to make purchases or pay debt obligations overseas. Foreign exchange trading has recently accounted for a major share of foreign bank profits inside Japan, especially following the revocation of the "real demand" proviso in 1984, which required foreign exchange trading to be connected to commerce overseas. Thereafter, foreign banks could conduct arbitrage and hedging transactions in convertible currencies—an area where they possessed a distinct advantage over Japan's domestic banking firms.

The biggest gains scored by foreign financial institutions have been in the open markets for securities and loans—the kind of financial markets U.S. and other Western financial institutions are more familiar with. Foreign securities firms were first allowed entry into Japan in 1971, which Merrill Lynch took advantage of the following year. Late in the 1970s Bache Securities, Smith Barney, Jardine Fleming, and Vickers da Costa also entered. Following deliberations by the Japan–U.S. Yen-Dollar *Ad hoc* Committee, foreign financial firms were granted permission to trade Japanese government bonds beginning in October 1984. This spur to entry by foreign financial institutions was further strengthened by a government decision announced in October 1985 to allow foreign companies to set up trust banks. A number of foreign heavy weight securities dealers established respectable market positions, including Salomon Brothers Asia, Jardine Fleming Securities, Merrill Lynch Japan, Bache Securities of Japan, Morgan Stanley International, W.I. Con, First Boston of Asia, Goldman Sachs of Japan, S.G. Warburg, Kidder Peabody, and Smith Barney. It soon became evident to leading banks and securities firms on all continents that real competitiveness in global markets required a physical presence in Japan and a full menu of services available through offices in Tokyo as well as in New York and London.

In December 1985 foreign banks were permitted to establish Tokyo branch offices through the creation of 50 percent–owned subsidiaries to conduct securities trading operations. Chase Manhattan Bank entered early with its L.M. Securities and Citicorp came in with Vickers da Costa. Deutsche Bank and Security Pacific National Bank were allowed to open offices in Japan representing their subsidiary securities firms under the stipulation that the parent bank could own no more than 50 percent of the securities affiliate. (A parallel privilege was simultaneously granted Japan's securities companies that were allowed to set up banking subsidiaries abroad.) As the number of new financial markets expands inside Japan, this step will, almost assuredly, provide additional avenues for growth by foreign banks and other foreign financial service firms.

NEW INTERNATIONAL CAPITAL REQUIREMENTS: THEIR LIKELY IMPACT ON JAPANESE BANKING FIRMS

In 1987 the central banks of the United States, Great Britain, France, Japan, and eight other industrialized countries agreed, in principle, on a set of common capital standards for all the banks under their jurisdiction. For many countries the new standards seem to spell trouble, since many multinational banks appeared to have lower capital ratios than the new capital guidelines require. It was assumed by many observers that Japan's banks could be caught with capital ratios well below the new international standards and would be forced to slow their future growth drastically.

It has also been alleged that privately owned Japanese banks benefit from great implicit or explicit support from the Japanese government, which allows them to hold lower capital-to-asset ratios due to their governments' superior guarantees and to raise new capital at lower cost. As economist Herbert Baer (1990) of the Federal Reserve Bank of Chicago observes, such an argument suggests that the banking organizations that have captured the most significant shares of U.S. banking markets in recent years have benefitted significantly from a low, government-supported cost of capital. However, Baer finds that Japanese banks frequently have the highest ratios of market value capital to total assets of all international banks, followed by Swiss and German banks. In fact, Japanese banks' market value of capital relative to their total assets ranged from approximately 16 percent to more than 20 percent. In contrast, the U.S. multinational bank with the highest ratio of market value capital to total assets reported a ratio value of 5 percent, and three leading U.S. banking institutions reported capital-to-asset ratios of less than 3 percent. Swiss and West German banks ranked below Japanese banks, but were still significantly ahead of the largest U.S. banks in their market value capital ratios.

THE JAPANESE FINANCIAL SYSTEM IN RETROSPECT

At first glance, the Japanese financial system seems markedly different from the system that prevails in the United States and in most other nations of the Western world. Concentration ratios are somewhat higher in the most important financial industries, especially in banking, insurance, and securities transactions. Foreign banks, insurers, and securities firms have appeared inside Japan in growing numbers in recent years, but most still hold relatively small market shares.

Regulation is also concentrated in the hands of a dominant government agency—the Ministry of Finance—with the Bank of Japan playing a supporting role, whereas in the United States there has been a proliferation of government agencies regulating the financial system with a dispersal of power and, thus far, only limited success in regulatory cooperation. Japanese financial regulation has helped to maintain significant separation between the services and markets served by different financial institutions, with the result that there is still less interindustry financial services competition in Japan than in the United States. And the Japanese government remains more actively involved in the allocation of credit and in encouraging savings from the public than currently is countenanced within the United States.

Still, it is easy to lose sight of the important parallels and similarities between the U.S. and Japanese financial systems. For example, both are deregulating the financial sector of their economies, though at different speeds, and both are experiencing the increasing globalization of their markets along with growing internal financial services competition. Both are having to deal with significant market risks and the need to make their institutions more flexible and more responsive to shifting public demands for services if they are to survive in an increasingly high-pressure and unforgiving marketplace.

NOTES

1. Ordinary banks are permitted to underwrite and trade in central government and local government bonds as well as government-guaranteed bonds, as in the United States. Unlike the United States, however, ordinary banks are allowed to purchase corporate stock. In the underwriting field, Japan's regional banks are the

principal securities underwriters for local government borrowings through privately placed securities.

2. See, in particular, A. Mikuni, "Evaluating Japanese Banks," presented to the International Banking Conference, Washington, D.C., February 17, 1988.

THREE

Japanese Ventures into U.S. Banking Markets: Organizational Forms, Strategies, and the Household Financial Services Market

The shock wave created by Japanese and other foreign banks invading U.S. markets has captured the public's attention primarily because this development is so different from most of the United States' past. Except for the colonial period and the early nineteenth century, when British banks supplied much of the credit required by U.S. merchants, U.S. banking was relatively isolated from strong foreign competition until the post–World War II era. Moreover, the majority of U.S. banking markets were and still are *local* in nature—confined to cities and counties where households and smaller businesses rely primarily upon local institutions for their financial service needs—and most local banks are of very modest size. Only the largest businesses in the United States access financial services across broader regional, national, and international markets and have come to expect contacts from foreign banks—especially British, Canadian, and Japanese banking units—seeking their corporate accounts.

One of the key reasons most U.S. banks have not been exposed to the full impact of foreign bank competition until recently is the plethora of state and federal laws that have blocked domestic banks from crossing state lines or even, in some cases, from branching outside their own home community or county. For example, the McFadden-Pepper Act passed by Congress in 1927 prohibited domestic banks from full-service branching across state lines unless the states involved expressly granted permission to do so. The states were permitted to further restrict or even prohibit branching activity within their own borders and, until the 1970s and 1980s, a majority of states did just that—either outlawing full service branching or confining it to selected cities, counties, or special districts. When the Bank Holding Company Act was passed by Congress in 1956, the Douglas Amendment to that law prohibited holding companies from acquiring 5 percent or more of the equity shares of banks located outside the acquiring bank's home state unless the states involved gave its express approval.

These federal and local laws helped to insure that, for decades, U.S. banking would be characterized by predominantly modest-size, locally oriented banks, subject mainly to competition from other locally based financial institutions. And there was often as much cooperation as there was competition among banks headquartered in different cities, due to a vast and uniquely American correspondent banking network in which banks cleared checks for each other and jointly participated in loans to their largest corporate customers. In this kind of industry environment foreign banks were more of a nuisance than a potent competitive force. Foreign-owned banks held a *de minimus* share of U.S. financial service markets as recently as the mid-1960s, when their share of all U.S. bank loans to business firms was less than 2 percent; in the local markets for household financial services—consumer cash and installment loans, credit cards, savings deposits, and checking account services—the foreign impact was scarcely measurable during this period.

In fact, a recent study by Rang Roe Cho, Suresh Krishnan, and Douglas Nigh (1987) concludes that nearly three-quarters (74 percent) of foreign banks currently operating inside U.S. territory established their U.S. offices after 1970. By the end of the 1980s, however, the foreign bank share of U.S. business loan markets had expanded fourteenfold. Moreover, the foreign banking sector was racking up a growing share of household financial service markets, particularly along the West Coast and in the New York area.

As Federal Reserve economist Herbert Baer (1990) notes, the fractured structure of U.S. banking, populated heavily with small community banks, coupled with tight regulation, has placed U.S. banks at a real competitive disadvantage in an increasingly internationalized banking system, particularly in dealing with multinational corporations and governments. Moreover, restrictions against U.S. banks undertaking full service expansion across state lines have so confined most U.S. banks to narrow geographic areas that they have fallen victim to one credit binge after another—leveraged buyouts, real estate development credit, energy loans, and agricultural commodity credit, to name just a few, while their best and largest customers— major corporations—have left the banks to raise their own funds directly from the open market. Deregulation similar to that proposed by the U.S. Treasury Department in February 1991 is a necessary step for the future.

ORGANIZATIONAL VEHICLES USED BY JAPANESE BANKS TO ENTER U.S. MARKETS

Japanese banks first entered the United States in 1952, when a total of ten branch offices and three representative offices were established almost simultaneously in New York City. (That same year the Japanese also established banking offices in London.) However, until the 1970s and 1980s, growth was modest, focusing predominantly on trading foreign currencies and providing trade financing for Japanese firms. That growth became explosive in the latter 1970s, however, as the Japanese sharply expanded their direct investments in plant and equipment and real estate and made large securities investments abroad. Moreover, the international capital markets were opening wide to admit major borrowers from all over the world, so that Japanese bankers and the businesses they served no longer had to rely exclusively on the Japanese homeland for funding. Japanese banks moved rapidly to take advantage of these new sources of capital and established a position of global leadership in the 1980s.

Japanese banks have chosen a wide variety of organizational vehicles to penetrate their target markets inside the United States, as outlined in Table 3-1. Where possible, full service *branch offices* have been established (especially in New York, Illinois, and California) to capture rapidly growing business deposits. By 1989 the Japanese had bank branch offices in Los Angeles, San Francisco, Chicago, New York, Seattle, and Portland. Branches are considered to be an integral component of the parent bank back home with the power to offer the complete menu of home-bank services, including taking deposits and granting loans to businesses and households. Initially, most branches began by servicing the U.S. operations of companies rooted in Japan, but increasingly these branches have become active competitors for the accounts of U.S. corporations and, more recently, U.S. households. However, many Japanese and other foreign-owned bank branches do not aggressively seek out households as customers because they would then be forced to apply for Federal Deposit Insurance Corporation (FDIC) insurance on their deposits. In the wake of the savings and loan crisis the FDIC has sharply increased deposit insurance fees and has petitioned Congress for authority to set even higher fees in the future.

A related organizational form, the *subsidiary bank,* is usually established to offer deposits that could qualify for federal deposit insurance and, therefore, be in a position to compete for the savings accounts of U.S. consumers as well as smaller, locally oriented businesses. Subsidiaries possess the same service powers as domestic U.S. banks and are regulated in much the same way as U.S. banks are. Japanese firms have secured an interest in U.S. subsidiaries either by acquiring an established U.S. bank or by building a new bank. The largest subsidiary operations of Japanese banks are located in California, where these institutions have generally made their strongest efforts to enter the U.S. household financial services market.

Outside the state of California, Japanese banking subsidiaries typically are found in relatively large metropolitan areas surrounded by heavily populated states, such as Illinois and New York. U.S. interstate banking laws have been a significant barrier to Japanese efforts to offer a full range of banking services across the nation. Beginning in the mid-1980s, however, several states permitted the Japanese and other out-of-state acquirers to move into their

Table 3-1

The Kinds of Banking Organizations Japanese Banks Operate Inside the United States

* Branch Offices are similar to any full service office operated by a U.S.-chartered bank and usually offer a complete range of banking services to U.S. customers and provide their foreign customers with financing and technical support to carry on commercial trading activity inside the United States; branch offices are empowered to raise funds by selling deposits, borrowing in the money market, or by receiving loans from the foreign bank that owns them or from any other company that is part of their conglomerate organization.

* Agency Offices are designed to provide funds to support exports and imports (mainly from Japanese-owned companies with U.S. customers) and to carry out borrowing and lending activities and securities trading for the controlling foreign bank and its customers; under U.S. rules, agencies may sell only a restricted set of financial services which usually do not include taking deposits, but the agency office can be drawn upon by the foreign firm that controls it or any of its other affiliated businesses for a loan of funds.

* Representative Offices act to identify new customers and provide a convenient point of contact for existing customers, but cannot accept deposits or grant loans, though they often serve as conduits for channeling payments, loan applications, and other customer requests back to the home office; these offices usually are the first step in establishing an overseas presence.

* Edge Act Subsidiaries are bank-affiliated companies that both U.S. and foreign banks can operate inside U.S. territory (even crossing state lines) once they are

sufficiently capitalized and approved by the Federal Reserve Board and provided that the major portion of their activities arise from business transactions with overseas customers.

* Subsidiary Firms operate as banking corporations headquartered inside the United States, receiving their charters from state or federal banking agencies, but are wholly or partly owned (directly or indirectly) by a foreign banking firm that possesses the same service powers as any U.S.-chartered bank and are subject to identical laws and regulations as those faced by U.S. domestic banking firms. Subsidiaries can support themselves by selling deposits, tapping money-market borrowings, and through loans obtained from the controlling firm.

* Commercial Banking Corporations operate under charters of incorporation issued either by state banking authorities or by the Comptroller of the Currency. They may offer the same services and must comply with the same banking laws and regulations as any U.S.-chartered bank.

* International Banking Facilities (IBFs) are computerized sets of records maintained by a U.S. or foreign bank or by foreign-owned banking agencies or branch offices, and are located inside the United States; IBFs possess both lending and deposit-taking powers without having to comply with certain U.S. banking regulations (e.g., IBFs do not have to post reserve requirements behind their deposits).

* Agreement Corporations are similar in service powers and responsibilities to Edge Act subsidiaries, except that they are chartered by individual states.

territory. (Recent examples include Georgia, Florida, Massachusetts, and Texas.) By the middle of 1989, however, Japanese bank subsidiaries existed predominantly in Los Angeles, San Francisco, and New York.

More limited organizational forms have also been rapidly pressed into service. For example, *investment companies* were created to carry out securities transactions for Japanese customers and other clientele attracted by the quality and price of the services they offer. These companies, too, soon began to reach out to smaller U.S. firms and to wealthier individuals and families as clients. Currently they are confined to the state of New York, however.

Banking *agencies* are created to supply a more complete line of banking services than investment companies, but, like the latter, are not permitted to offer checking accounts or take savings deposits (though customers can hold credit balances arising from the unused portion of currently active credit lines or stemming from cash receipts stemming from overseas trade). Agencies, typically, are centered around large international commercial trading centers. For example, Japanese agency offices at the end of the 1980s included 19 offices in Los Angeles, 4 in San Francisco, 1 in Coral Gables, 4 in Atlanta, 1 in Honolulu, 1 each in New York and Dallas, and 3 in Houston. Agencies can grant business loans, but usually are restricted from offering household loans and, therefore, have been important in reaching U.S. businesses, but have not become major players in the domestic market for household financial services. Agencies continue to be heavily oriented toward financing and record-keeping for international trade, including the issuance of letters of credit and acceptance financing.[1]

For a number of Japanese banking firms and other foreign banks, the Federal Reserve System has approved the creation of *international banking facilities* (IBFs), which permit foreign customers to trade and purchase investments inside the United States. Thus, IBFs gave Japanese firms access to dollar deposits and dollar credits to purchase goods and services inside the Untied States and to access international commodities (most notably, oil) that are valued in U.S. dollars.

To avoid the most burdensome of U.S. banking regulations, some Japanese banks sought and received approval from the Board of Governors of the Federal Reserve System to charter *Edge Act* companies—corporate entities whose principal banking functions are centered around facilitating international transactions. In fact, Edge Act companies must devote the majority of their business activities to funding or facilitating international commerce, not domestic business. Both foreign and domestic banking organizations can apply to the Federal Reserve Board to launch Edge Act companies, provided they pledge adequate capital. Once established, Edge Act companies are not bound by U.S. antibranching laws and may expand across state lines.

Representative offices are established to identify potential U.S. customers for Japanese banks back home and to help their affiliated companies operating inside the United States gain access to banking services. Representative offices also supply vital marketing information regarding opportunities in the United States to Japanese export/import firms and investors, but cannot take deposits nor make loans. Instead they often forward customer loan applications and payments to headquarters back home.

Japan's representative offices are situated in such diverse locations as Washington, D.C., and Lexington, Kentucky, where representative offices of Japanese banks serve the Georgetown auto assembly plant of Toyota Motor Corporation. The Lexington office is particularly interesting because it illustrates another important role fulfilled by representative offices—protecting and monitoring the interests of the bank in the investments it has made abroad. Modern banking theory suggests that commercial banks are relatively unique business firms because of the thoroughness and professionalism with which they monitor the behavior of borrowers. Presumably, depositors are willing to pay service fees or accept lower rates of return on their deposited funds in return for receiving the bank's professional monitoring services to insure the safety of their funds. Bank monitoring activity is particularly valuable to depositors when overseas loans are involved, because few depositors have the knowledge or capital necessary to effectively monitor how their funds are being used in distant countries. In the Lexington case, the Japanese banks represented there are among the principal stockholders in Toyota Corporation.

Recent Changes in Organizational Structure

Initially, Japanese banking ventures in the United States were confined almost exclusively to leading financial centers, particularly New York, Chicago, San Francisco, and Los Angeles. In fact, a recent study by L.G. Goldberg and A. Sanders (1990) finds that three heavily urbanized states— New York, California, and Illinois—accounted for close to 95 percent of all foreign bank assets in the United States. Growing familiarity with U.S. markets and U.S. financial service needs, however, soon led to a widening of the beachheads previously established. The cities of Atlanta, Boston, Dallas, Houston, Seattle, and the Miami area attracted increasing attention from the Japanese, not only because of rapidly developing investment opportunities in those regions but also because the emphasis within Japanese banking firms has been swinging toward accommodating smaller U.S. businesses and serving the vast household (retail) banking market in the United States—the single largest concentration of affluent consumers in the world.

As Table 3-2 indicates, by year-end 1988 Japanese banking organizations operated more than 100 banking units inside the United States, or nearly one-fifth of all foreign-owned banking units located in the United States. These Japanese banking affiliates held more than $360 billion in assets compared to a total of about $650 billion in assets held by all foreign-owned bank

Table 3-2

Types of U.S. Banks and U.S. Banking Offices Controlled by Japanese Banking Organizations (As of Year-End 1988)

Type of Organization Operating in the U.S.	Number of Each Type of Organization Affiliated with Japanese Banking Organizations	Total of All Foreign-Owned U.S. Banking Units in this Organizational Category	Percentage of Total Number of Foreign-Owned U.S. Units Affiliated with Japanese Banking Organizations in Each Organizational Category	Total Assets in Millions of Dollars Held by U.S. Affiliates of Japanese Banking Organizations in Each Organizational Category (in Millions of Dollars)	Total Assets of All Foreign Owned U.S. Banking Units in Each Organizational Category (in Millions of Dollars)	Percentage of Total Assets of All Foreign-Owned U.S. Banking Units Held by Japanese Affiliates in the U.S. Under Each Organizational Type
U.S. Agency Offices	32	206	15.5%	$47,590.4	$83,600.2	56.9%
U.S. Branch Offices	59	346	17.1	259,074.2	430,154.0	60.2
U.S. Commercial Banks More Than 25 percent Foreign Owned (Subsidiaries)	24	84	28.6	53,923.5*	132,348.2	40.7
New York State Investment Companies Majority-Owned by Foreign Banks	1	10	10.0	16.3	4,213.0	0.4
U.S. Offices of Banking Edge Act or Agreement Corporations Majority Owned by Foreign Banks	1	28	3.6	249.3	2,928.3	8.5
Total or Percentage of Total	117	674	17.4%	$360,853.7	$653,243.5	55.2%

* Data for three banks more than 25 percent owned by Japanese banking organizations was not available.
<u>Source</u>: Board of Governors of the Federal Reserve System, Structure Data for U.S. Offices of Foreign Banks by Type of Institution, Statistical Release, December 31, 1988.

affiliates (55 percent of the foreign bank total). The Japanese accounted for 12 percent of total U.S. bank assets and 16 percent of U.S. bank business loans by 1989—both of these percentages were more than all other foreign banks combined. Within the Japanese banking sector, as Table 3-2 shows, most Japanese banking assets and offices were in full service branch offices, with year-end 1988 assets of nearly $260 billion. Banking subsidiaries ranked third, with U.S. subsidiary banks controlled by the Japanese holding almost $54 billion in total assets at the end of 1988, followed closely by Japanese agency offices with close to $48 billion in assets. New York investment companies were the least important type of organizational firm employed by the Japanese in the United States.

The New York offices of Japanese banks represent well over half of all their assets held in U.S. offices ($283 billion out of a total of $421 billion at year-end 1989). California accounts for roughly another quarter of all Japanese banking assets in the United States ($99 billion at year-end 1989). Counting just agency offices, most bank agency assets are kept in the state of California (California agencies held $50 billion out of a total of $55 billion in Japanese agency assets at year-end 1989). In contrast, the bulk of Japanese branch office assets have been captured by their branch offices in New York ($259 billion out of $306 billion at the end of 1989), followed distantly by Illinois branches ($31 billion). Among the leading U.S. subsidiary banks controlled by the Japanese by year-end 1989 (as Table 3-3 indicates) were Union Bank in California, with assets of more than $15 billion, and the Bank of California, holding aggregate assets of more than $7 billion. By the end of the 1980s the city of New York led all other U.S. cities with nearly 80 Japanese banking offices (including 38 branches, 17 subsidiary banking firms, 20 representative offices, and an agency facility), followed by Los Angeles with nearly 30 offices (including 5 branch offices, 4 banking subsidiaries, and almost 20 agencies). Chicago ranked third with 22 offices, made up of 14 branches and 8 representative offices, followed by Houston with 16 offices, San Francisco with 15 offices, and Atlanta with 13. Other cities with a significant Japanese presence included Boston (1), Cleveland (1), Columbus (1), Coral Gables (1), Dallas (3), Honolulu (1), Lexington (3), Miami (2), Portland (2), Seattle (1), and Washington, D.C. (2).

The Bank of Tokyo exceeded all other Japanese banking firms in the volume of assets held by its U.S. offices, with $47 billion as of year-end 1989; most of this total was almost evenly split between California agency offices and New York branch offices. Mitsubishi Bank and Dai-Ichi Kangyo Bank were not far behind, as Table 3-4 shows. Seven Japanese banking organizations accounted for almost $250 billion out of a total of $421 billion (or 60 percent) of total Japanese bank assets inside the United States.

As Table 3-5 indicates, the United States leads in every category of banking office as a site for Japanese overseas expansion. More branches, subsidiary banking firms, and representative offices have been opened in the

United States by the Japanese than in any other nation. The Japanese operate more than twice as many representative offices in the United States as are operated by the nearest two competitor nations, Australia and the United Kingdom. The United States also holds an edge in numbers of banks and banking subsidiaries over both Hong Kong and the United Kingdom, the next most important countries as far as Japanese banking units are concerned. Moreover, U.S. branch offices controlled by the Japanese exceeded their branches in Great Britain and Hong Kong by more than threefold.

Factors That Influence Japanese Organizational Choices

Recent research on the factors that influence the choice among different organizational forms by multinational banks and other international firms suggests that such choices depend upon firm size, market conditions, product differentiation possibilities, and the bank's experience with the same or similar markets (see especially Ball and Tschoegl [1982]). Presumably the experience factor reflects the costs of expansion into foreign markets. Where experience is lacking, the tendency is to employ a "step-wise" strategy of gradual expansion into new markets. This is one reason most international banks begin with such limited service facilities as representative offices and agencies and pursue their existing customers abroad first—they already possess substantial information concerning these customers, which makes for speed of decision making and relatively lower costs.

Product differentiation arises as a factor when an international bank develops a service line or clientele that domestic banks in the nation it plans to enter cannot easily replicate. This is why Japanese banks, by and large, saw their initial marketing targets inside the United States as firms and individuals of Japanese origin (see, for example, Grubel [1977]). Bank size also plays a role in the overseas expansion decision, because multinational banks are generally large enough to take advantage of any arbitrage opportunities that arise due to differences in currency prices, interest rates, and regulations—opportunities that purely domestic banks cannot access as easily.

Economists Clifford A. Ball and Adrian E. Tschoegl (1982) recently constructed a binary choice model in an attempt to explain the establishment of foreign branch banking offices in Japan and the acquisition by the Japanese of subsidiary banks in California. Their model attempts to explain foreign branch entry according to each bank's knowledge of the host nation, the distance between the parent bank's home office and the host country to be entered, the level of experience by each international bank in overseas operations, and the relative advantages possessed by banks in the home country. Ball and Tschoegl find that prior experience and time—representing the depth of knowledge of the country entered—dominate the choice between establishing foreign branches or acquiring subsidiary companies abroad.

Table 3-3
Principal Corporate Subsidiaries of Japanese Banks Operating in the U.S. (As of Year-End 1989)

Japanese Banking Organizations	Name of Subsidiary Company in the United States	Total Assets of Subsidiary Corporations in Millions of Dollars
Bank of Tokyo	Union Bank, California	$15,220.8
Mitsubishi Bank	Bank of California	7,234.2
Bank of Tokyo	Bank of Tokyo Trust Company	6,537.4
Sanwa Bank	Sanwa Bank California	6,128.7
Industrial Bank of Japan	Industrial Bank of Japan Trust Co., New York	5,575.0
Sumitomo Bank	Sumitomo Bank of California	4,400.7
Fuji Bank	Fuji Bank and Trust Co., New York	3,679.0
Industrial Bank of Japan	IBJ Schroder Bank and Trust Co., New York	2,646.9
Daiwa Bank	Daiwa Bank Trust Co.	2,318.1
Mitsui Bank	Mitsui Manufacturers Bank, California	1,346.6
Tokai Bank	Tokai Bank of California	1,127.2
Long-Term Credit Bank of Japan	LTCB Trust Company of New York	992.4
Sumitomo Trust and Banking Co.	Sumitomo Trust and Banking Company, U.S.A.	586.8

Dai-Ichi Kangyo Bank	Dai-Ichi Kangyo Bank of California	531.0
Mitsubishi Trust and Banking Corp.	Mitsubishi Trust and Banking Corp. (USA)	441.4
Mitsui Trust and Banking Corp.	Mitsui Trust Bank, USA	252.9
Yasuda Trust and Banking Co.	Yasuda Bank and Trust Co., USA	228.3
Kyowa Bank	Kyowa Bank of California	108.2
Toyo Trust and Banking Co.	Toyo Trust Company of New York	58.2
Taiyo Kobe Bank	Taiyo Kobe Bank and Trust Company	51.5
Dai-Ichi Kangyo Bank	Dai-Ichi Kangyo Trust Company of New York	----
Mitsubishi Bank	Mitsubishi Bank and Trust Company, New York	----
Mitsui Bank	Mitsui Finance Trust Company	----
Sumitomo Bank	Sumitomo Bank New York Trust Company	----
Tokai Bank	Tokai Trust Company of New York	----
Total Assets of the U.S. Subsidiaries of Japanese Banking Organizations		$ 59,465.1

Source: Board of Governors of the Federal Reserve System, Structure Data for U.S. Offices of Foreign Banks by Type of Institution, Statistical Release, December 31, 1989.

Table 3-4

Ranking of Japanese Banking Organizations in the United States as of Year-End 1989

Organizations	Total Assets Held (in Billions of Dollars)	Agency Offices	Branch Offices	Other Subsidiary Firms	Affiliated Firms
Bank of Tokyo	$ 47.2	$3,076.8	22,320.7	$21,758.2	$ 6.5
Mitsubishi Bank	39.5	507.8	31,567.9	7,234.2	154.1
Dai-Ichi Kangyo Bank	37.3	5,309.0	31,456.0	531.0	---
Fuji Bank	35.2	5,395.2	26,084.3	3,679.0	10.2
Sanwa Bank	31.8	1,381.7	24,296.0	6,128.7	---
Industrial Bank of Japan	28.8	6,308.8	14,158.5	8,221.9	81.4
Sumitomo Bank	26.7	1,262.8	21,056.0	4,400.7	---
Tokai Bank	18.8	5,035.8	12,630.7	1,127.2	---
Mitsui Bank	18.7	2,020.9	15,344.7	1,346.6	---
Mitsui Trust and Banking Corp.	13.9	3,795.2	9,825.7	252.9	---
Mitsubishi Trust and Banking Corp.	13.3	2,841.2	10,058.9	441.4	---
Long-Term Credit Bank of Japan	12.9	2,879.6	9,045.9	992.4	---
Daiwa Bank	12.2	1,844.9	8,066.8	2,318.1	---
Sumitomo Trust and Banking Co.	11.4	1,851.2	8,934.2	586.8	---
Yasuda Trust and Banking Co.	9.7	3,605.9	5,857.0	228.3	---
Taiyo Kobe Bank	9.7	1,193.3	8,419.9	51.5	---
Nippon Credit Bank	7.4	1,999.2	5,357.8	---	---

Kyowa Bank	5.2	1,355.2	3,776.5	108.2	---
Toyo Trust and Banking Co.	5.1	1,263.8	3,750.8	58.2	---
Saitama Bank	4.9	---	4,948.3	---	---
Hokkaido Takushoku Bank	4.1	697.5	3,407.4	---	---
Norinchukin Bank	3.9	---	3,944.2	---	---
Chiba Bank	3.3	---	3,301.9	---	---
Joyo Bank	2.7	---	2,735.4	---	---
Chuo Trust and Banking Co.	2.7	474.7	2,218.7	---	---
Bank of Yokohoma	$ 2.1	241.9	1,900.5	---	---
Shizuoka Bank	1.6	448.4	1,157.7	---	---
Hokuriku Bank	1.5	---	1,481.1	---	---
Hiroshima Bank	1.4	---	1,436.7	---	---
Shoko Chukin Bank	1.3	---	1,349.1	---	---
Zenshimen Bank	1.2	---	1,225.9	---	---
Hyakyishi Bank	1.1	---	1,077.5	---	---
Hachijuni Bank	0.9	---	886.5	---	---
Bank of Fukuoka	0.7	---	671.8	---	---
Bank of Kyoto	0.6	---	601.0	---	---
Hokkaido Bank	0.6	---	552.0	---	---
Gunma Bank	0.5	---	539.5	---	---
Ashikaga Bank	0.4	---	418.3	---	---
Suruga Bank	0.2	---	223.1	---	---
Iyo Bank	0.1	---	137.4	---	---
Tokyo Tomin Bank	0.0*		0.0		
	$ 420.7	$54,790.8	$306,237.3	$59,465.1	$ 752.4

* Less than $50 million.

Source: Data provided by the Board of Governors of the Federal Reserve System, Structure Data for U.S. Offices of Foreign Banks by Type of Institution, Statistical Release, December 31, 1989.

Table 3-5
Japanese Banking Offices in the United States and Selected Other Countries
(Figures as of June 30, 1989)

Country of Location	In Each Nation the Total Numbers of Each Office Type Are:			
	Banks	Branch Offices	Subsidiaries	Representative Offices
United States	33	89	34	70
Australia	--	--	22	33
Canada	--	--	11	18
United Kingdom	23	23	26	22
Federal Republic of Germany	11	13	5	16
France	5	5	1	9
Hong Kong	26	26	26	18
Singapore	22	22	21	1

Source: Federation of Bankers Associations of Japan (Zenginkyo), Japan Financial Statistics 1989, Tokyo, 1989, Table II-12, p. 27.

Regulatory Rules on Bank Organizational Choices

As we have seen, Japanese and other foreign banks can reach U.S. customers through more than one organizational channel, but these avenues for expansion face different regulatory rules dictated by the 50 states and the federal government. If Japanese banks choose to establish additional branch offices of subsidiary banking firms on U.S. soil, these full service facilities are bound by the same federal and state regulations as U.S.–chartered banks.

Moreover, if a foreign banking corporation owns at least 25 percent of the stock of a U.S. bank or otherwise exercises a controlling influence over that bank, it will be labeled a *holding company* by the Federal Reserve Board. It will thus be required to file periodic financial reports and to receive board approval for any banks or nonbank businesses it plans to acquire. Foreign bank holding companies do have an advantage over domestic banks inside the United States, however. While U.S.–based bank holding companies cannot own a nonbank business that is not "closely related to banking," foreign holding companies can own nonbank firms abroad if their own countries' regulators approve, and still be permitted to own or control a bank inside the United States. This situation arises because the United States follows the doctrine of *national treatment*, which allows other nations to regulate their banks as they see fit without the United States contradicting those foreign rules, provided U.S. banks receive reciprocal, equal treatment abroad. The essence of national treatment is to allow foreign and domestic banks operating in the same country to have parallel privileges.

Moreover, if a foreign bank operates a branch office inside U.S. territory, that branch is *not* considered a separate corporation for purposes of U.S. regulation. Thus, the foreign-owned branch office is not subject to the same restrictive rules as a domestically chartered U.S. bank (though the state where the branch office is situated has the right to examine the branch's books for purposes of determining its eligibility for a license to operate). Of course, foreign banks can serve U.S. businesses and households from off-shore without operating offices inside U.S. territory. In this instance U.S. banking regulations do not apply, and the bank in question can provide its U.S. customers with any services its home country allows it to offer.

The International Banking Act of 1978

A key limiting factor on the expansion of Japanese and other foreign banks into both business and household banking services inside the United States was passage of the International Banking Act (IBA) in 1978. The key provisions of the IBA are summarized in Table 3-6. This federal law was spawned by growing fear of the impact that foreign banks were having on the U.S. banking industry as far back as the 1960s and early 1970s.

The IBA requires each foreign-owned banking organization to designate a "home state." The foreign institution must then confine its branching activity and acquisitions of local banks to that particular state unless other states give express permission to enter their territory. Foreign banks that had already crossed state lines were allowed to continue with those activities under grandfather provisions of the IBA, however.

The International Banking Act's geographic restrictions have tended to fall hardest on retail banking activities because most individuals and families prefer to deal with a local bank, particularly for checking accounts and small loans. Instead of being able to branch nationwide, the Japanese must acquire different banks in a variety of states, something they are hesitant to do without more confidence in the economies of distant states and local areas and without favorable regulations to fall back on. The notable exceptions are several Japanese-owned banking units that made interstate acquisitions prior to passage of the IBA, especially in Illinois and Texas, that they continue to operate. Fundamentally, the IBA helps to explain why the Japanese have tended to concentrate most of their banking activities in two states—California and New York—that permit statewide branching and have the largest concentration of population and financial transactions.

RESEARCH EVIDENCE ON THE CAUSES OF JAPANESE BANK EXPANSION IN THE UNITED STATES

We are not sure of all the reasons for Japanese banks and banking operations having expanded so rapidly in recent years. Several recent research

Table 3-6
Provisions of the International Banking Act (IBA) of 1978

* <u>Purpose of the IBA</u>: To establish the principle that foreign banks operating in the United States should operate under comparable sets of rules to those faced by domestically chartered U.S. banks. Moreover, foreign bank operations must not be allowed to interfere significantly with the monetary policy activities of the Federal Reserve System.

* <u>Regulatory Power Reserved by the States</u>: All offices and facilities owned by foreign banks are subject to U.S. banking regulations at the federal level and the states are free to impose their own regulatory restrictions on the activities of foreign banks.

* <u>Access to Deposit Insurance</u>: U.S. retail banking customers who deal with foreign banks are entitled to protection. Foreign banking offices in the United States selling deposits with denominations of less than $100,000 will be required to apply for and receive insurance coverage from the Federal Deposit Insurance Corporation. Moreover, the Federal Reserve Board is empowered to impose reserve requirements on U.S. retail deposits and on other reservable liabilities of foreign banks booked through their U.S. agency and branch offices.

* <u>Grandfather Provisions of the IBA</u>: Foreign banks already operating in the United States before July 26, 1978 may continue with those activities they had begun before the International Banking Act was passed.

* <u>Expansion Across State Lines</u>: Foreign banks must designate a "home state" within the U.S. and then are subject to the same interstate banking restrictions as U.S. banks (except for any grandfathered interstate facilities).

* <u>Licensing Rules</u>: Federal licensing of branch offices and agencies of foreign banks is generally required.

* <u>Edge Act Powers</u>: U.S. Edge Act corporations are granted broader powers to compete on more equal terms with foreign-owned U.S. banks, but foreign banking companies can also acquire or start Edge Acts inside the United States.

* <u>Restrictions on Owning Nonbank Businesses</u>: Foreign banks with U.S. agencies and branch offices must abide by the restrictions on nonbank business activities contained in the Bank Holding Company Act and Federal Reserve Board regulations.

studies offer a variety of explanations, and there seems to be some significant measure of truth to most of the alternative explanations offered by earlier researchers.

One of the most extensive of earlier research studies by economists Charles Brecher and Vladimir Pucik (1980) identifies *market access* as a key factor driving Japanese expansion inside the United States, particularly the ability to secure strategic positioning in the markets for short-term loans and long-term capital in which New York, Los Angeles, and San Francisco represented key locations for fund-raising, the execution of securities transactions, and for identifying good loan customers. A related factor cited by Brecher and Pucik was the close relationship between Japanese manufacturers engaged in exporting to U.S. and Japanese commercial banks. As Japanese commercial trading ventures in the United States expanded, Japanese banks fell in step with this expansion to provide the credit, deposit, and agency services that Japan's export firms required.

Once here, these researchers suggest, some Japanese banks seized on unfolding opportunities to sell their services to U.S. business customers and households. At the same time, Brecher and Pucik found evidence of a "division of labor" that appeared to characterize Japanese banking operations in the United States, with most of the retail (household) service sales directed toward West Coast markets, particularly Los Angeles, San Francisco, San Diego, Seattle, and Portland, and most of the securities and trade-related service activity conducted through New York and, to a lesser extent, San Francisco.

Certainly other reasons have been found for Japan's success in U.S. banking markets. For example, prior to passage of the International Banking Act of 1978, there appeared to be key regulatory advantages from aggressive foreign bank expansion inside the United States. U.S. banks could not underwrite corporate securities and were limited in the type of securities transactions in which they could legally participate. This situation created a "vacuum" that Japanese banks (along with banking firms headquartered in Canada and Western Europe) were only too happy to step in and fill.

As the 1980s began L.G. Goldberg and Anthony Saunders (March 1981) analyzed the determinants of foreign banks' share of all U.S. commercial bank assets over the 1972-79 period. These researchers found that interest rate differences between U.S. and overseas loans and deposits were key factors, along with changes in U.S. bank price-earnings ratios, the volume of foreign direct investment inside the United States, and the global depreciation of the dollar. Confirmation of the findings of Goldberg and Saunders was offered later by Charles W. Hultman and Randolph McGee (1989), who found that the growth of foreign bank branch and agency offices was most closely related to the international value of the U.S. dollar, passage of the International Banking Act of 1978, and the volume of foreign direct investment in the United States.

Looking specifically at Japanese banks, Hultman and McGee found Japan's share of total U.S. banking assets to be inversely related to the yen-dollar exchange rate and positively related to the volume of direct foreign investment in the United States as well as passage of the Japanese Banking Act of 1982, which allowed foreign banks greater latitude inside Japan. Additional evidence was offered by Robert Grosse and Lawrence G. Goldberg (1990), who found that banks from more volatile national economies tended to have an above-average involvement inside the United States, as did banks from nations displaying greater geographic distances and cultural differences from and with the United States.

One of the broadest, most complete, and carefully reasoned studies of the causes of foreign bank expansion was conducted by Robert S. Dohner and Henry S. Terrell (1988) at the Federal Reserve Board. These economists built and tested a model to explain the growth in total assets of a cross-section of the world's largest banks, including seven Japanese banking firms (Dai-Ichi Kangyo, Fuji, Sumitomo, Mitsubishi, Sanwa, Tokai, and Mitsui) as well as leading banking institutions in the United States, Canada, France, Switzerland, Germany, and the United Kingdom over the 1972-86 period. During this period U.S. banks grew the slowest and Japanese banks the fastest of any major industrialized nation in the world.

In the short run, Dohner and Terrell found that changes in real exchange rates had a significant impact on the growth of international banking assets through their effects on the dollar value of each bank's home-currency assets. In the long run, however, economic growth in each bank's home country, the overall growth of foreign trade and investment capital, and the capacity of banks to preserve their shares of their own domestic banking markets proved to be more important than movements in exchange rates in explaining each bank's asset growth. Moreover, the authors found that all foreign banks, including the Japanese, tended to behave in similar fashion in responding to the foregoing factors.

Interestingly enough, Dohner and Terrell observed, the growth of Japanese banks seemed to pass through two different phases. During the 1970s, Japan's multinational banks' assets grew more slowly than the Japanese economy (measured by nominal GNP), indicating that these banks were relatively less competitive abroad than they were at home. However, during the 1980s, the assets held by leading Japanese banks outraced the growth of their home economy. In fact, the banks' asset growth relative to the home economy's growth was faster than for banks from any other industrialized economy, including the United States, where U.S. bank growth actually lagged behind the growth of the U.S. economy. In this sense the Japanese operated the most competitive and successful banking institutions abroad after 1980.

Dohner and Terrell found that, for the 1972-86 period at least, the growth of assets denominated in yen, not U.S. dollars, were the most important reason that Japanese banks outdistanced their U.S. counterparts. In contrast, leading banks from Canada, France, and Great Britain grew faster than U.S. banks due to the growth of their overseas assets. Moreover, these researchers found that in the most recent period of their study (1984-86) the majority of the growth differential between Japanese and U.S. multinational banks could be traced to differences in the growth of yen-denominated versus dollar-denominated assets. Change in real exchange rates accounted for about two-fifths of the growth differential between Japanese banks and U.S. banks over the period of their study.

Finally, Dohner and Terrell found that the largest Japanese banks have substantially higher ratios of domestic assets to Japan's GNP than is the case in the United States, indicating a higher ratio of domestic intermediation inside Japan than in the United States. These researchers argue that Japanese banks play a larger role in their domestic financial system than U.S. banks play in U.S. financial markets because:

1. The decline in U.S. banks' share of domestic financial markets has occurred due to deregulation, the growth of nonbank intermediaries, the intrusion of foreign banks, and the growing role of securitization and direct borrowing by U.S. corporations and has been greater inside the United States than in Japan

2. Superregional banks have arisen inside the United States to challenge the biggest U.S.–based multinational banks, whereas Japan's huge city banks have not faced as stiff a challenge at home from Japanese regional banks

3. Loan quality problems have been more severe among U.S. banks, particularly in the form of loans to lesser developed countries (LDCs) and domestic real estate, farm, and energy loans, than has been the case in Japan

4. U.S. banks have faced more stringent regulatory capital constraints

5. New bank management strategies have emerged in the United States that emphasize fee income growth and service diversification rather than bank asset expansion, which receives greater emphasis among Japanese-owned institutions

A somewhat older study by Samuel Rabino (1981) looked at differences between the way Japanese and other Asian banks manage their operations versus foreign banks from other countries. Rabino surveyed foreign banks operating in New York and found that Asian banks, including the Japanese, placed greater emphasis on serving companies from their home countries and on appealing to households and smaller U.S. businesses than was true of other foreign banks. Only Canadian banks appeared to place as much emphasis on these aspects of their U.S. operations as did Asian institutions. Moreover, Asian bank operations tended to be more centralized with more of their activity directed by the home office, while European banks tended to conduct their U.S. operations with greater independence from their home offices.

Most recently, Herbert Baer (1990) of the Federal Reserve Bank of Chicago has analyzed the causes of rapid foreign bank expansion, particularly through branch offices inside the United States, during the decade of the 1980s. Among the factors he identifies as linked to foreign bank growth on U.S. shores are:

1. The continuing integration of the nonfinancial sectors of the U.S. economy with global markets through trade and direct investment
2. Growing sales of domestic commercial and industrial loans by U.S. banks to foreign banks (which, Baer estimates, accounted for about two-fifths of the growth in market share of the U.S. branches of foreign banks during the 1980s) as U.S. banks have reached for stronger capital-to-asset ratios and greater diversity in their loan portfolios
3. The relatively large market value capitalization ratios of Japanese, Swiss, and German banks due to the higher market value of their stock which, in turn, has enhanced their ability to borrow low-cost funds and use high proportions of financial leverage

Baer believes that Japanese and other foreign banks will continue to grow relative to U.S. banks until the market price of Japanese bank stock falls significantly or the market value of U.S. bank shares increases significantly. He points to a direct relationship between market value capitalization as a percentage of total bank assets and the growth in any bank's holdings of foreign assets. Of course, a bank with a rising stock price could choose to pay out any gains in market value in the form of special dividends to its stockholders. However, those dividends would be taxable (in Japan, at an approximate marginal tax rate of 52 percent). On the other hand, retaining the additional market capital puts the bank's portfolio in disequilibrium because of higher-than-optimal funding costs. The preferred alternative has been to issue additional securities and purchase more assets abroad as well as to expand domestic assets. This is the dominant global strategy the Japanese have employed for over two decades.

JAPANESE BANKS AND U.S. HOUSEHOLDS

Beginning in the 1970s and continuing to the present day, many U.S. banks, besieged by foreign bank competition, have chosen to turn *inward*, focusing on a market where they seem to possess an unassailable advantage—the U.S. consumer's huge demand for credit, for savings plans, and for financial advice. For example, leading consumer-oriented banks, like BancOne of Ohio, Citicorp and Chemical Bank of New York, and NCNB of Charlotte, North Carolina, have taken advantage of the falling barriers to interstate banking in recent years to reach into distant states and find new pockets of demand for household financial services. U.S. families are, by now, used to buying Japanese automobiles, televisions, and stereos, but *not* to dealing with Japanese banks. Presumably, the unique American culture would be a major, if not unconquerable, barrier to Japanese bankers in selling a product—credit and deposit service—that is perhaps the most personal and sensitive of all the products Americans buy. The market for personal financial services, it was reasoned by many U.S. bankers, is a market in which U.S. banks hold the high ground. As we will soon see, however, that high ground is eroding away.

Of course, Japanese expansion into retail (household) financial services has not always been achieved by acquiring or starting new banks; in a number of cases the Japanese have entered the U.S. consumer banking markets via the "back door"–acquiring a *nonbank* financial services firm. One prominent example occurred in September 1989 when Dai-Ichi Kangyo Bank of Tokyo announced that it was buying a 60 percent controlling interest in CIT Group, a $10 billion finance company operating 50 loan offices across the United States. CIT was then owned by Manufacturers Hanover Corporation of New York, and Dai-Ichi agreed, as part of the same transaction, to purchase 4.9 percent of Manufacturers' outstanding stock, providing the latter with badly needed capital to deal with problem loans, particularly those arising from credits to Third World nations.[2] Another prominent example of a U.S. nonbank financial service acquisition by the Japanese is the Heller International Corporation, now owned by Fuji Bank, which is a U.S. finance company supplying asset-based business loans.

One key factor inhibiting the further expansion of household financial services offered in the United States by Japanese banks is their limited use of deposits from local areas, especially deposits from small businesses and families. At year-end 1988, for example, U.S. agency and branch offices controlled by Japanese banks had borrowed $22.8 billion in deposits from U.S. residents (not including U.S. banks). In contrast, they raised nearly twice as much, $44.3 billion, from foreign institutions and individuals and even more, $45.9 billion, directly from U.S. banks. When Federal Reserve economists Henry S. Terrell, Robert S. Dohner, and Barbara R. Lowrey (1990) traced the various sources of funds for the U.S. branch and agency operations of the Japanese, close to two-thirds of all funds raised by these banking units were ultimately traceable to Japanese banking customers.

This heavy reliance on foreign and domestic institutional funding—so different from what U.S. banks do—has severely limited the contacts between Japanese bankers and U.S. households. Most individuals and families will borrow primarily from those banks that also hold their checking and savings accounts. To the extent that Japanese banks have chosen to rely principally on commercial (wholesale) sources of funding, as opposed to retail sources, this strategic choice has also served to severely restrict the growth of their revenues and assets arising from the sale of household banking services.

Indeed, there does appear to have been some erosion in the Japanese share of such key retail banking markets as personal loans and small de-

Table 3-7

Proportion of All U.S. Bank Loans Going to Individuals and Families (Personal or Consumer Loans) Accounted for by the U.S. Offices of Foreign Banks

	Year-End Data as a Percentage of All Consumer Loans Extended by U.S. Chartered Banks and Foreign Banks with U.S. Offices:								
Name of Country	1980	1981	1982	1983	1984	1985	1986	1987	1988
Japan	0.853	0.847	0.797	0.140	0.693	0.734	0.912	0.783	0.716
South Korea	0.019	0.021	0.021	0.019	0.028	0.023	0.021	0.018	0.016
Australia	0.016	0.020	0.019	0.019	0.014	0.011	0.011	0.009	0.008
Canada	0.796	0.911	0.876	0.820	0.652	0.617	0.607	0.548	0.537
Hong Kong	1.019	1.057	1.205	1.339	1.472	1.468	1.760	1.659	1.814
United Kingdom	2.074	1.939	1.812	1.676	1.723	1.695	2.752	2.411	2.015
France	0.098	0.100	0.098	0.106	0.095	0.100	0.118	0.108	0.115
Italy	0.141	0.156	0.147	0.106	0.089	0.087	0.092	0.025	0.023
The Netherlands	0.211	0.198	0.231	0.202	0.230	0.156	0.272	0.258	0.248
Spain	0.394	0.383	0.400	0.449	0.440	0.546	0.559	0.608	0.549
Ireland	0.184	0.214	0.210	0.235	0.241	0.259	0.336	0.316	0.309

Source: IBA Reports from the Report of Condition Tapes Supplied by the Board of Governors of the Federal Reserve System through the National Technical Information Service.

nomination deposits. As Table 3-7 relates, the Japanese percentage of all personal (or consumer) loans extended by the banks with U.S. offices fluctuated significantly during the 1980s, but had declined slightly in 1988 relative to its 1980 level. In contrast, British banks as well as those from Hong Kong, France, the Netherlands, Spain, and Ireland generally increased their share of U.S. bank personal loan total over the same period. Table 3-8 reveals that this modest decline for Japanese banks over the 1980-88 period was broadly based, including all three major consumer loan categories—residential mortgages, credit card borrowings, and nonmortgage household cash and installment loans. Moreover, as the data in Table 3-8 also suggest, the declines were particularly evident when the Japanese share of the retail credit market was measured against other foreign banks' holdings of U.S. consumer loans.

Table 3-8

Percentages of U.S. Retail-Type Loans Held by Japanese Banks Relative to All U.S. Retail-Type Loans Held by All Foreign Banks with U.S. Offices

Type of Loan	Percentage of Each Retail Loan Type Held by Japanese Banking Offices in the United States Relative to All U.S. Offices of Foreign Banks:								
	1980	1981	1982	1983	1984	1985	1986	1987	1988
Residential Real Estate Loans	17.3	19.10	18.4	17.8	16.4	15.8	10.8	13.6	16.5
Credit Card Loans	8.3	8.6	7.2	7.2	2.7	2.1	1.9	4.7	6.5
Total Nonmortgage Cash and Installment Loans to Individuals and Families	14.1	13.9	13.2	11.0	11.7	12.8	12.4	11.8	11.3

Source: IBA Reports of Condition Tapes Supplied by the Board of Governors of the Federal Reserve System through the National Technical Information Service.

On the deposit side the picture was mixed. Japanese banks gained ground in checkable (demand) deposits between 1980 and 1988, as Table 3-9 reveals. However, they lost ground relative to other foreign banks in their holdings of time and savings deposits, as reflected in Table 3-10. Much of this loss appeared to be captured by British, Spanish, and Hong Kong banks.

There are good reasons to expect a gradual change in the Japanese funding mix, with heavier direct reliance by Japan's banks on U.S. households and businesses for loanable funds in the future. One significant reason is that the Japanese have been losing market share to other financial service providers inside Japan itself. On a percentage basis, the share of total assets held by *all* private financial institutions that is accounted for by Japan's depository institutions fell from over 80 percent in 1981 to little more than 75 percent in 1988. Domestic regulations have hurt the competitiveness of Japanese banks inside their own financial system, principally because regulated deposit rates could not keep up with the higher interest rates offered to Japanese investors by nonbank financial institutions (though their banks' rate of loss in domestic market share may decline as financial deregulation proceeds inside Japan). Foreign markets, including the United States, have come to look relatively more attractive to Japanese bankers in recent years and tended to make them gradually more dependent on their banking units overseas.

Table 3-9

Percentages of U.S. Retail-Type Deposits Accounted for by Japanese Banks Relative to the Retail Deposits Held by All Foreign Banks with U.S. Offices

Type of Deposit	Proportion of All Foreign Bank Holdings of U.S. Deposits Booked Through Their U.S. Offices Accounted for by the U.S. Offices of Japanese Banks At Year-End:								
	1980	1981	1982	1983	1984	1985	1986	1987	1988
Checkable (Demand) Deposits of Individuals, Partnerships, and Corporations	16.2	15.9	15.3	14.0	12.7	11.3	16.3	13.3	17.3
Total Time and Savings Deposits	27.5	27.4	32.0	33.9	40.0	18.9	17.6	16.0	18.4

Source: IBA Report of Condition Tapes Supplied by the Board of Governors of the Federal Reserve System through the National Technical Information Service.

Japanese Banks in the U.S. Credit Card Market

Recently, the largest credit card issuer in Japan—JCB (Japan Credit Card) Company—announced plans to sell its cards in U.S. markets by offering them through U.S. banks, beginning in the fall of 1990. Roughly comparable to American Express, JCB serves primarily an upper-income credit market. The first phase of the JCB marketing plan will focus on an estimated 190,000 Japanese living in the United States. However, phase two will be aimed at the more than half-a-million U.S. citizens who journey to Asia annually. Ultimately JCB's U.S. unit, JCB International Credit Card of Los Angeles, hopes to reach a million credit card customers by 1995.

JCB is a joint venture, launched in 1961 by several Japanese financial service firms, led by Sanwa Bank and Daiwa Bank. The firm accounts for close to 40 percent of credit card volume in Japan (about 17 million domestic customers), and has customers in about 100 countries worldwide. In an effort to attract U.S. banks to sign on as agents for JCB's venture, the Americans are being offered half of any fees collected from U.S. merchants who agree to accept JCB cards. To give JCB an edge, the card membership fee has been set, at least initially, below the fees charged by several leading U.S. contenders, such as American Express.

It is not at all clear that the Japanese will be successful on a significant scale in the North American market. Established domestic competitors are

Table 3-10
Proportion of Total Time and Savings Deposits Held by U.S. Chartered Banks and Foreign Banks in the U.S. Accounted for by the U.S. Offices of Foreign Banks

Name of Country	Year-End Data Expressed as a Percentage of Total Time and Savings Deposits of U.S. and Foreign Banks with U.S. Offices For:								
	1980	1981	1982	1983	1984	1985	1986	1987	1988
Japan	2.954	3.146	4.648	5.121	7.619	1.221	1.371	1.227	1.412
Canada	1.115	1.389	1.241	1.451	1.759	0.651	0.628	0.582	0.554
Hong Kong	0.656	0.628	0.806	0.747	0.770	0.667	0.700	0.786	0.791
United Kingdom	2.390	2.443	2.751	2.566	2.594	1.866	2.851	2.827	2.610
France	0.584	0.471	0.518	0.572	0.787	0.070	0.066	0.066	0.072
The Netherlands	0.800	0.739	0.855	0.703	0.649	0.475	0.570	0.590	0.534
Spain	0.378	0.417	0.474	0.484	0.350	0.477	0.501	0.546	0.509
Switzerland	0.690	0.557	0.709	0.771	0.845	0.025	0.027	0.027	0.028

Source: IBA Reports of Condition Supplied by the Board of Governors of the Federal Reserve System through the National Technical Information Service.

growing and some potent newcomers have appeared. One of these, of course, is the huge Citicorp credit card program, which had issued 36 million cards by the summer of 1990. Citicorp's credit card receivables at the end of the 1980s generated an estimated annual net income of about $600 million. Substantial net earnings such as these have attracted other competitors into the markets JCB hopes to enter. In March 1990 American Telephone & Telegraph Company announced its own Universal Card, and Prudential Insurance Company revealed, three months later, that it would soon offer its own versions of the familiar Visa and MasterCard programs. American Express is already well entrenched, holding close to $80 billion in card receivables in 1989, followed by Citicorp, Sears Roebuck, Bank of America, First Chicago, and Chase Manhattan Corporation. Moreover, these firms are aggressive advertisers and promoters, with rapid response telephone service, mass solicitation programs, and significant discounts that generally bring in thousands of new members each year.

California: The Apex of Japanese Retail Bank Operations in the United States

The centerpiece of Japanese banking's retail operations in the United States has been, and probably will remain, the state of California, an area already well known to many Japanese because of decades of immigration to the Pacific Coast of the United States. Moreover, there are several thousand Japanese-owned businesses there, representing a natural target for Japanese banking firms. And, despite California's statewide branch banking system and its movement toward nationwide interstate banking in 1991, California is home to numerous small and medium-size banks that Japanese bankers may see as potential future acquisition targets.

As senior economist Gary Zimmerman of the Federal Reserve Bank of San Francisco (1989) notes, the assets of Japanese-owned banking firms in California rose almost threefold over the 1982-88 period. By year-end 1988 these banks accounted for about one-fourth of California's total banking assets and for more than 30 percent of all commercial loans granted by banks in that state. While much of this growth could be traced to Japanese buyouts of existing California banks, it has also been true that Japanese-owned California banks have, on average, grown faster than domestically owned California banks.

However, what is particularly remarkable about Japan's forays into California banking is that most of that gain in market share generally has come at the expense of other foreign banks, not home-owned California institutions. Indeed, as Zimmerman (1989) notes, the foreign banking sector as a whole has gained relatively little at the expense of California's domestically owned institutions. From 1982 to 1988, foreign banks' share of all California banking assets rose from 30.8 percent to just 31.7 percent. In particular, Japanese banks have largely supplanted the British as the dominant foreign banking group within the state of California. The purchase of Lloyds Bank-California by Sanwa Bank and the sale of British-owned Crocker Bank to Wells Fargo Bank in 1986 were the two most noteworthy examples of British banking's retreat from the California market during the 1980s.

As of mid-1989, 8 of 25 Japanese-owned U.S. subsidiary banks—the prime vehicle for offering most households banking services in the United States— were in California (4 subsidiaries each in Los Angeles and San Francisco). Moreover, 23 of Japan's 34 U.S. agency offices are situated in Los Angeles (which has 19) and San Francisco (with 4). While Japanese agency offices in New York emphasize the sale of trust services, California agency offices sell household savings, credit card, and payment accounts. The Japanese have successfully invaded the top 10 California banks, holding 4 of the top 10 banks represented by such institutions as the Bank of California (BanCal Tri-State Corp.), acquired in 1984 by Mitsubishi Bank Ltd. (which also has grandfathered banking offices in Oregon and Washington), and the Union Bank, acquired by California First which became a subsidiary of the Bank of

Tokyo in October 1988. Other key Japanese subsidiary banks in California include Sanwa Bank–California (which acquired Lloyds Bank–California in 1986), Sumitomo Bank of California, Mitsui Manufacturers Bank, Tokai Bank of California, Dai-Ichi Kangyo Bank of California, and Kyowa Bank of California.[3]

California is the key to the future of Japanese retail banking operations in the United States because of the development of interstate banking. Beginning in 1991, California voted to allow banks and bank holding companies from any other state to enter that state, provided reciprocal entry privileges are granted to California's banks. Thus, any Japanese-owned bank in California will have the capacity to set up facilities that can offer household banking services in any state that permits California-based banks to enter its home territory. In effect, California may have opened up virtually unlimited opportunity for the expansion of retail banking by the Japanese in the United States. How fast this expansion will take place no one knows, but it does appear inevitable, especially if the U.S. Congress approves the banking reform proposals put forward by the U.S. Treasury in February 1991 which call for eventual nationwide branching.

Do Japanese banks seem to have a specific long-term strategy in their U.S. operations, particularly in California? Financial analyst Dennis Holden (1983), after studying several leading Japanese banking firms, concludes that there is no one agreed-upon, long-range plan, except perhaps "strategic accommodation," in which Japanese bankers try to remain flexible in the face of changing events to take maximum advantage of any opportunities that suddenly become available. One reason for the apparent lack of a long-range plan is the ongoing changes in U.S. banking resulting from federal and state deregulation and the rise of interstate banking. As stated earlier, the International Banking Act of 1978 limits Japanese and other foreign bankers to a single home state unless other states expressly allow entry from the outside. Moreover, the Japanese are especially concerned about the adverse reaction of the U.S. public (and especially the U.S. Congress) to further Japanese acquisitions. As Holden notes, this has led the Japanese banks to a strategy of "study and wait," and to the acquisition of moderate-size U.S. banks whose shareholders frequently have been offered substantial purchase premiums over the book value of their stock.

Reasons Behind the Expansion of Japanese Banking in California

The rapid growth of Japanese banking units inside California undoubtedly has multiple causes. Certainly at the top of the list is the growing trade volume between the United States and Japan. California is strategically situated for trade with Japan, Australia, Southeast Asia, and the remainder of the Pacific Rim. As Pacific-area trade volume has grown, so has the need for those banking services that support international trading activity, especially export/import financing, execution of payments, funds transfers, currency exchanges, and exchange-risk hedging facilities. Federal Reserve economists Gary Zimmerman (1989) and Henry Terrell (1979) argue that Japanese banks possess certain comparative advantages in serving this region of the world, particularly their knowledge of Japanese and Asian culture as well as Pacific-area trade practices, laws, and market conditions. Their greatest comparative advantage, however, probably lies in serving multinational corporations from Europe and North America that desire to enter Asian markets and service corporations from Japan that wish to trade in the United States.

A second key reason for the rapid growth of Japanese banking activity in California relates to capital investment from overseas. Japan has generated large balance-of-trade surpluses with the United States and, thereby, acquired huge dollar deposits—a significant portion of these reinvested in U.S. companies and real estate. Though a much larger proportion of Japanese investments in California have been outside of California's financial sector, the huge volume of Japan's trade surpluses and accumulated dollar deposits has ensured that Japanese investments in California banking have a significant impact upon that state's banking industry. Indeed, Japanese banking operations in California have been at the confluence of massive funds flows associated with (1) financing the production and shipment of goods to California from Japan; (2) supporting the growth of Japanese businesses establishing production and distribution facilities inside the United States; and (3) direct U.S. investments by Japanese banks that plan to serve U.S. retail and wholesale customers as well as expatriated Japanese citizens.

Still another factor propelling the Japanese expansion in California, as noted above, has been the prospect of using California as a strategic base for interstate banking. California was *not* one of the first states to pass enabling legislation to support interstate banking. States east of the Mississippi River, in the troubled Southwest, and from the upper Midwest led the interstate banking revolution. In contrast, California during the late 1980s passed its first bill allowing outside entry only from the Western region, encompassing the Pacific Coast and Rocky Mountain states. However, debate over a nationwide banking bill began in the California legislature soon after the regional interstate bill was enacted. The nationwide reciprocity law that finally received approval in Sacramento established 1991 as the year in which entry into California by full-service banks was permitted.

Most recently, evidence has been accumulating that the Japanese also view California as a base for gathering pertinent data and skills to offer selected new services worldwide. The most dramatic example is the rapid entry by leading Japanese-controlled banks in California—the Bank of California, Union Bank, and Sanwa Bank—into the personal and business trust field, offering trust services to U.S. customers having high net worth and middle-market corporate pension and agency accounts. Moreover, the Japanese are using this California-based trust service network to offer international securities trading services to other banks, and they have plans to offer trust services inside Japan once that market is deregulated back home. This is another example of how Japanese banking regulations have stimulated Japanese banks to offer "forbidden" services abroad. Thus far, as Alice Arvan (1990) notes, most of the Japanese trust customers are American, including employee benefit plans and financial planning for small and medium-sized U.S.- and Japanese-owned businesses, as well as for wealthy investors.

We must also recognize that California is the largest retail financial services market and the largest wholesale trade market in the United States. The state has a population of over 20 million and its thousnads of small- and medium-sized business firms represent a marketing target with sufficiently large volume to justify a full range of banking services. Moreover, California has generally grown faster than the United States as a whole, closer to the growth rate of Japan itself. This permits Japanese banks to more fully diversify their sources of funding and their loan portfolios. At the same time, California is the gateway to entry into the U.S. money market and the huge interbank market in federal funds (overnight loans of reserves) upon which Japanese banking affiliates in the United States have come to depend heavily.

Evidence in support of a number of these observations was provided by Federal Reserve economist Gary Zimmerman (1989) in a comparative study of Japanese-owned banks operating in California versus domestically owned California banks. Pursuing the notion that the growth of trade with Japan prompted much of the rapid expansion of Japanese banks in California, Zimmerman found that Japanese banking's share of all commercial and industrial loans, commercial credit letters, and credit standbys rose significantly during the 1980s. He discovered that Japanese-owned California banks devoted almost 30 percent of their total assets to commercial and industrial loans, compared to just under 20 percent of all the assets of domestically owned banks in the state. Moreover, the Japanese-owned institutions held substantially higher proportions of their total assets in commercial real estate loans that was true of other California banks.

On the funding side, Japanese-controlled banks appeared to rely less on deposits to fund their assets and, within the deposit category, more heavily on large denomination ($100,000+) CDs purchased mainly by corporations than did their domestically owned counterparts inside California. Borrowings from the interbank market and from securities dealers through repurchase agreements ranked higher among the Japanese banks than among other California banks. However, there was little supporting evidence that substantial funding of Japanese-owned U.S. banks was provided by their parent firms back home in Japan. Moreover, Zimmerman could find no evidence that Japanese banking affiliates in the United States held any funding cost advantage over their U.S.–owned counterparts in raising borrowed funds, suggesting again that their parent banks do *not* supply large amounts of cheap funds that make a significant difference in their operating costs.

Equally important, however, the Japanese banks in California revealed evidence of their growing role in retail banking markets for consumer loans and deposits. For example, Zimmerman found no statistically significant difference in the proportion of Japanese bank assets committed to consumer installment loans and single-family home mortgage loans than was true for domestically owned California banks, indicating that Japanese banks have become significant players not only in commercial credit, but also in household lending. Moreover, there was evidence of significant growth in the proportion of household-type deposits held by Japan's California banks. For example, Zimmerman found that small denomination time and savings deposits held by Japanese banks actually grew faster than similar deposits held by U.S.–owned banks over the 1980-88 period.

THE FUTURE OF THE JAPANESE IN THE U.S. RETAIL FINANCIAL SERVICES MARKET

Whether the Japanese can continue expanding their share of California's banking markets at the pace set during the 1980s is an intriguing and difficult question. Much depends upon the course of U.S.–Japanese trade and the strength of the U.S. economy, which must be able to absorb a continually increasing flow of Japanese goods. Japanese bank operations in the United States clearly have been supported and propelled by the trade relationships between the two countries. However, for the sake of long-run stability in cash flows and earnings, Japanese bankers would be well advised to consider alternative product lines to solidify their position.

One way to achieve long-run earnings stability is to pursue U.S. household customers and retail banking services. By seeking a larger role in serving U.S. individuals and families, Japanese banks are displaying behavior similar to that of many international banks in the past, broadening their involvement in those domestic markets they entered earlier in order to support commerce with the home country.

There is, however, no guarantee of success for the Japanese in expanding into retail financial service markets. They appear to have no significant operating cost advantage over domestically owned U.S. banks in funding themselves and in delivering retail banking services. Moreover, they face a significant cultural barrier which will matter to some U.S. consumers. And, potentially at least, they face possible retribution from the U.S. Congress concerning Japan's trade barriers.

There is also the important issue of *infrastructure*—the Japanese, for the most part, do not have the extensive automated teller networks and branch office systems needed to reach convenience-oriented U.S. household customers, except in California. Moreover, U.S. banks are gaining broader authority to expand beyond state lines such that, by 1990, more than 47

states had granted authority for out-of-state banks to enter, usually by acquisition.

In short, it is not at all clear that the Japanese can succeed in retail banking
as they have in wholesale banking in the United States. On the other hand,
the flexibility of Japanese banking in facing new market environments has
been demonstrated repeatedly. Because they have accumulated an enormous amount of experience in providing multiple financial services to their
domestic customers, Japanese banks appear to be especially well positioned
to offer and manage diverse sets of services abroad.

Regulations at home, particularly interest rate ceilings on deposits, have
granted Japan's banks access to ample supplies of loanable funds at relatively
low cost to fuel foreign expansion. In addition, until recently Japanese banks
have experienced historically unprecedented gains in the market value of
their capital, which has allowed them to expand their loans in order to
restore a more normal (market-driven) relationship between risk-exposed
assets and capital. Thus, as long as the ratio of market value capital to assets
for Japanese banks remains substantially above comparable capital-asset
ratios for other international banks, Japanese financial firms will have a
strong economic incentive to widen their financial services beachhead in the
United States and around the world.

NOTES

1. Initially and through the 1970s, agencies were the principal vehicle for expansion by foreign banks inside U.S. borders. Because they are an integral component of
foreign-owned companies, agencies were exempt from U.S. banking regulations until
the International Banking Act was passed by Congress in 1978.

2. See especially "Japanese Bank Buys Stake In Manufacturers Hanover," *Bank
Notes*, Federal Reserve Bank of Boston, 17, 39 (September 22, 1989), p. 1.

3. As of year-end 1989 the Union Bank held $15.2 billion in total assets and the
Bank of California held $7.2 billion. These institutions are the two largest Japanese
subsidiary banks in the United States. Sanwa Bank-California held $6.1 billion in
assets, while Sumitomo Bank of California held assets of $4.4 billion, ranking fourth
and sixth among all Japanese subsidiary banks operating in the United States.

FOUR

Serving U.S. Commercial Customers: Japanese Banking Strategy in Domestic Business Financing

While Japanese bank expansion into U.S. retail (household) financial service markets has been limited to date, the intrusion of these banking firms into the market for financial services sold to business firms, particularly corporations, has reached truly huge proportions. For example, close to 30 percent of commercial and industrial loans inside the United States at the end of the 1980s were on the books of foreign banks, compared to less than 2 percent during the 1960s. And at least one-third of the U.S. business credit total supplied by foreign banks was accounted for by the Japanese.

There is evidence that much, if not most, of this rapid expansion of Japanese commercial lending from U.S. shores is closely related to trade financing, particularly to support Japanese exports to the United States.[1] Moreover, Japanese trade surpluses from goods and services sold in the United States have generated huge dollar deposits in Japanese banks and stimulated these banks to set up operations in the United States to lend those dollar deposits. By the end of the 1980s more than 700 Japanese companies had launched manufacturing operations inside the United States, funded heavily by Japanese banks with U.S. offices. At the same time, Japan acted to liberalize its rules regarding the export of domestic funds when the Foreign Exchange and Foreign Trade Control Law was amended in 1980, allowing significantly increased direct investment by Japanese firms and investors in the United States as well as in Southeast Asia and Western Europe. Not only have the Japanese become major players in the U.S. corporate loan market, but also in related financial services, including the clearing of checks and drafts, funds transfers, the discounting of commercial notes, and the issuance of standby credit letters guaranteeing corporate borrowing. In this chapter we look at the dimensions of Japanese banking activity in financing U.S. companies.

ADVANTAGES OF JAPANESE BANKS IN ATTRACTING U.S. COMMERCIAL CUSTOMERS

The rapid expansion of Japanese banks in funding U.S. business activity reflects a number of significant advantages possessed by these banks over competing institutions inside the United States. One of these advantages is the direct links the U.S. offices of Japanese banks have to Japan and Southeast Asia and their vast markets, something that is attractive to scores of U.S. businesses seeking entry into Asia and other markets around the Pacific Rim. Like other foreign banks with a U.S. presence, Japanese banks have followed Japanese companies moving their operations to the United States to set up manufacturing plants, establish wholesale trading operations, and pursue real estate investments. These mobile corporations usually prefer to deal with the same banks they patronize back home rather than undergo the substantial costs involved in establishing new banking relationships. At the same time, Japan's multinational banks have capitalized on the thousands of Japanese expatriates who, for generations reaching back into the nineteenth century, have come to the United States to live and establish businesses. These individuals often feel more comfortable from both a cultural and practical standpoint in transacting business with a Japanese bank.

While dealing with businesses and individuals of Japanese origin still appears to represent the majority of accounts attracted by U.S. affiliates of Japanese banks, it was almost inevitable that, once established inside U.S. borders, these banking units would seek out U.S. businesses, households, and even federal and local governments as customers. However, business firms—both Japanese and American—have been and remain the principal target of Japanese banking firms operating within the continental United States. Several studies (most recently Zimmerman [1989]) have found that Japanese banks' U.S. affiliates report significantly higher ratios of commercial and industrial loans, commercial real estate and construction loans, commercial credit letters, and standby business credit agreements relative to their total resources than do U.S. banks, affirming the former's well-known bias in orientation toward the business sector of the economy.

There is also considerable evidence that, on average, Japanese banks depend far more heavily than their U.S. counterparts on attracting business deposits to support their lending and other activities. These banks draw especially heavily on sales of large denomination ($100,000+) CDs, which are purchased principally by corporations, on interbank loans from both U.S.–owned banks and foreign banks operating in the United States, and securities sales under repurchase agreements in the U.S. money market to meet their funding requirements. Thus, even more than most U.S. banks, Japanese banks having a U.S. presence actively borrow from corporations at home and abroad to fund other corporations and governments. It is in this business-oriented financial services market that Japanese banks appear to possess the greatest comparative advantage vis-à-vis the U.S. banks and affiliates of foreign banks that compete head-to-head with them in domestic markets. Moreover, they possess a significant product differentiating advantage in their depth of knowledge and experience in dealing with Asian customers and markets and in their professional contacts around the Pacific Rim.

It is a well-established fact in history that trade-related foreign banking activity soon leads to direct foreign investment in U.S. production and marketing facilities. Initially, in the case of the Japanese, such investment was tightly related to the flow of Japanese goods and services to U.S. shores, much of it motivated by a desire to expedite and efficiently manage sales to U.S. customers. Soon after, however, Japanese banks became key players in direct investment projects within the United States' borders in order to escape existing or anticipated trade barriers. For example, the establishment of an automobile assembly plant by Toyota in Georgetown, Kentucky undoubtedly sprang from concern over possible new trade restrictions imposed by the U.S. government. Moreover, investments such as these tend to attract still more banks from the home country into U.S. localities to take full advantage of the spin-off economic benefits from those direct investments. For example, after the new Toyota plant was launched in Lexington, Kentucky, new representative offices from Sanwa Bank and Tokai Bank were established in that community to pursue collateral business.

Japanese banks—like scores of foreign banks that have preceded them to U.S. shores—have encouraged and stimulated investment in the United States by overseas companies that otherwise might not have occurred. For example, Dai-Ichi Kangyo Bank, Japan's largest bank, strongly encouraged Kobe Steel to locate a new plant in the state of California—a plant that was subsequently built. Still another dimension of Japanese banking involvement in the United States centers on the financing of U.S. exports to Japan and Southeast Asia. Frequently this has been carried out by joint lending programs with U.S. financial institutions, as was the case when Morgan Guaranty Bank and Mitsubishi Bank teamed up in the 1980s to support a joint project of Chrysler Corporation and Mitsubishi Motors to assemble and sell cars. It is a relatively easy step from there to the granting of direct loans to U.S. firms not closely connected to trade with Japan.

Interestingly enough, economists Terrell, Dohner, and Lowrey (1990) of the Federal Reserve Board recently found that, among the U.S. branches and agency offices of Japanese banks, loans extended to business borrowers with U.S. addresses were the largest and most rapidly growing single component of their loan portfolios. As of the end of 1988, commercial and industrial loans extended to U.S.–address borrowers by these Japanese banking firms totaled more than $60 billion, which was about one-fifth of the total of $300 billion in business loans held at that time by all U.S. money-center banks. By comparison, business loans extended to foreign-address borrowers by these same Japanese agency and branch offices moved very little between 1980 and 1988, climbing from $9.5 billion to only $13.4 billion. Of course, many of the businesses with U.S. addresses receiving Japanese bank credit were, in fact, Japanese manufacturing companies operating inside the United States or Japanese trading firms selling goods in the United States. Terrell, Dohner, and Lowrey (1990) find, after further investigation, that direct claims against Japanese individuals and firms held by U.S. agency and branch offices of Japanese banks totaled $106 billion in 1988, compared to a total for all such claims of just over $300 billion. Moreover, when these bank claims were grouped under the borrowers ultimately responsible for them, loans to Japanese-controlled business accounted for nearly two-thirds of the total loan risk exposure of Japanese bank agency and branch offices in the United States. Moreover, loans made through these same U.S. banking offices generally grew much faster than the same loans granted from inside Japan by leading Japanese multinational banks.

The essence of international banking is the ability of multinational banks to borrow funds in one set of markets and lend funds in other markets, perhaps thousands of miles distant. (This is known as the *international arbitraging of funds.*) Japanese banks carry out heavy borrowings of Eurodollar deposits in London and around the Pacific Rim and tap relatively inexpensive funds inside Japan, a major portion of which is used to supply credit to support trade with Canada and the United States. Deposit interest rates are artificially low inside Japan due to the slower pace of deregulation there compared to the United Kingdom and the United States. These artificially low deposit rates have resulted in excess demand for loanable funds on the part of Japanese banks from their homeland. A substantial percentage of these incoming funds are then invested in loans to U.S.–address firms.

The United States is an advantageous target for Japanese lending because it is politically stable and largely unregulated, with strong trade links to Japan itself. In this sense Japanese multinational banks are able to reap the best of both situations—borrowing a substantial portion of their total funding requirements in relatively regulated markets and devoting a growing portion of their loan portfolio to credit extended in relatively unregulated markets.[2]

Regulation at home has also encouraged Japanese banks to shift a substantial volume of their business loans to the United States, with much of this loan volume circuitously passing through the U.S. affiliates of Japanese companies, but ultimately reinvested inside Japan itself. As economists Terrell, Dohner, and Lowrey (1990) note, this fact suggests that the public, especially in the United States, may be misled by statistics that purport to show the prominence of Japanese banking activity in U.S. domestic markets by counting all Japanese-held U.S. assets. To the extent that many of these funds are initially borrowed from Japanese depositors and then routed through U.S. banking offices back into Japan, loan and deposit totals booked inside the United States can be highly misleading concerning both the sources and uses of funds of Japanese banking firms.

More important, as financial deregulation continues to make progress in Japan, there is likely to be less need to circuitously route Japanese borrowings and loans through U.S. offices. This should be particularly true if the remaining Japanese restrictions on short-term money-market borrowings and retail bank deposits are eventually lifted. Japanese banks and other financial firms will be able to book more loans and securities acquisitions at home. Moreover, continuing deregulation inside Japan may also cool the ardor of Japanese investors for U.S. government securities and the stocks and bonds of U.S. corporations. If other factors are held constant, this action will tend to reduce the prices of U.S. securities and drive their interest rates higher, putting a greater restraint on future growth inside the U.S. economy.

THE U.S. CORPORATE LOAN MARKET AS A KEY TARGET AREA FOR JAPANESE BANKS

The principal target of Japanese banking and securities activity in the United States has been and remains *corporations*, both domestic and foreign-owned, with most of them, as we have seen, having trading ties with Japan. However, the Japanese are also becoming major players in financing U.S. mergers, acquisitions, and leveraged buyouts, and in underwriting new U.S. stock and bond issues. We examine their involvement in each of these service areas in the sections that follow, but first take an overview of the relative importance of the Japanese banks in U.S. commercial banking activities.

Trends in Japanese Commercial Lending Inside the United States

The Japanese have made their most dramatic gains in U.S. markets, not primarily against U.S. banks, but against other foreign banks that also operate inside the United States. Moreover, those market share gains relative to other foreign banks have occurred across a broad spectrum of loan categories, as revealed by the financial reports submitted annually to the Federal Reserve Board by foreign leading institutions. As Table 4-1 suggests, Japanese banking offices in the United States began the 1980s with foreign banks accounting for about 17 percent of all U.S. bank real estate loans. By 1988, however, the Japanese accounted for more than one-third of all such loans made by foreign banks operating in the United States. Particularly significant market share gains in U.S. real estate lending were made in construction and property development lending, where the Japanese nearly doubled their market share relative to other foreign-owned banks. Commercial real estate mortgages, extended mainly to fund shopping centers, office buildings, and manufacturing and transportation facilities, also rose significantly, from less than 22 percent to almost 28 percent of all such loans extended by foreign banks through their U.S. offices.

Table 4-1

Proportion of U.S. Bank Loans and Credit-Related Instruments Held by Japanese Banks with U.S. Offices Relative to All Foreign Banks with U.S. Facilities

Year-End Data Expressed as a Percentage of All Foreign Bank Held U.S. Loans Accounted for by Japanese Banks:

Credit Portfolio Items	1980	1981	1982	1983	1984	1985	1986	1987	1988
Total Real Estate Loans Outstanding	17.29	17.65	16.59	15.96	14.69	14.86	15.86	23.29	34.58
Construction and Land Development Loans	13.46	14.77	15.58	15.84	15.89	14.47	18.47	16.48	25.71
Commercial Real Estate Loans	21.76	22.26	20.94	19.34	23.42	24.16	21.13	21.80	27.59
Standby Letters of Credit Outstanding	14.12	11.76	19.13	9.13	32.83	4.85	8.46	48.54	52.79
Acceptances Outstanding	28.11	38.08	43.45	46.12	65.24	16.55	15.43	72.53	72.92
Loans to Commercial Banks in the U.S.	50.94	44.17	46.63	45.63	49.37	48.41	53.56	51.35	57.56
Loans to Overseas Banks	16.27	19.05	21.66	21.65	30.87	10.76	9.27	8.05	18.92
Loans to Other Financial Institutions	13.48	14.23	11.68	13.42	30.54	30.43	47.27	57.08	50.52
Loans for Purchasing or Carrying Securities	17.11	20.13	15.66	25.38	21.37	27.09	44.74	45.91	64.33
Commercial and Industrial Loans	30.67	30.57	30.32	31.80	35.69	21.21	22.85	23.63	30.77
Agricultural Loans	8.13	11.88	12.74	9.34	10.87	12.51	23.19	26.91	34.48
Total Loans	29.56	29.11	28.85	29.66	33.22	26.27	30.55	34.32	42.20
Total Assets	26.13	27.50	30.03	31.07	38.08	30.01	32.73	35.56	42.00
Book Value of U.S. Treasury Securities Held	15.58	17.66	16.56	14.82	16.03	13.72	14.90	17.12	18.80

Source: IBA Reports of Condition Tapes Supplied by the Board of Governors of the Federal Reserve System through the National Technical Information Service.

Even more remarkable was the rise in standby credit guarantees granted by Japanese banks. These contractural arrangements that pledge the issuing bank's credit rating and borrowing capacity to back up the borrowings of its corporate or governmental customers, should the latter be unable to pay, are particularly advantageous for Japan's multinational banks because of their huge size and excellent credit ratings and because standby credit guarantees generate fee income, but normally do not use up scarce bank funds. Japanese banks held only 14 percent of all standby credit guarantees issued by foreign banks in 1980, but the Japanese share of this service market had soared to more than half the foreign bank total in 1988.

Equally dramatic was the rise in Japanese bank loans to nonbank financial institutions, which advanced from about 13 percent to more than 50 percent of all foreign bank credit to nonbank financial firms booked inside the United States. Similarly, loans to purchase securities booked by Japanese banks tripled their share of the foreign banking sector in the United States, climbing from just over 17 percent to more than 64 percent of the foreign bank total. The Japanese share of loans to finance farms and ranch operations rose from about 8 percent to just over one-third of total agricultural loans booked by foreign banks' U.S. offices. Growth in acceptance credit, which arises mainly from financing international trade, also advanced strongly, as the U.S. offices of Japanese banks recorded a 28 percent share of all foreign bank acceptances outstanding in 1980 and almost 73 percent of this total by year-end 1988.

Of course, as Table 4-1 also suggests, not all categories of loans registered a gain for the Japanese relative to other foreign banks operating in the United States. For example, the Japanese share of U.S.–booked total commercial and industrial loans fluctuated and, on balance, changed hardly at all during the 1980s. Moreover, Japan's share of all loans granted by foreign banks to U.S. commercial banks changed modestly from about 51 percent of all such loans in 1980 to just under 58 percent of the total. Loans to overseas banks rose only slightly, climbing from 16 percent to almost 19 percent of all these overseas loans extended by the U.S. offices of foreign banks. However, on balance, Japanese banks ended the period holding about 42 percent of all loans booked by foreign banks inside the United States, compared to approximately a 30 percent share in 1980. Moreover, their share of total foreign bank assets in the United States rose from about 26 percent in 1980 to 42 percent in 1988.

Despite these impressive gains, the Japanese share of total business lending by all banks in the United States, both domestic and foreign-owned, still remains relatively small, as Table 4-2 indicates. The Japanese share of total commercial loans booked by all banks operating within the United States fluctuated considerably during the 1980s and ended the period down slightly at 4 percent in 1988, compared to 5.9 percent in 1980. The biggest gains in direct loans scored by the Japanese against all U.S.–chartered banks and foreign banks with U.S. offices centered on real estate loans, which climbed 3 percentage points between 1980 and 1988, according to the figures presented in Table 4-3. Most of this gain was accounted for by construction and land development loans, where the share held by the U.S. offices of Japanese banks climbed from about 1 percent in 1980 to more than 3 percent of the U.S. bank office total in 1988. Japanese banks also made headway against all U.S.–chartered commercial banks in securities lending as their share jumped from under 2 percent to nearly 19 percent of the U.S.–office total. Moreover, their share of agricultural loans rose from inconsequential levels to over 1 percent of all U.S.–bank agricultural credit in 1988. However, the Japanese actually lost ground over the 1980-88 period to U.S. banks in lending to both U.S. and overseas banking firms.

Outside of direct lending, Japanese banks have clearly registered their most significant gains vis-à-vis U.S. banking firms in contingent credit mar-

Table 4-2

Proportion of All U.S. Bank Commercial and Industrial Loans Accounted for by the U.S. Offices of Selected Foreign Banks

| Name of Country | Year-End Data Expressed as a Percentage of All Commercial and Industrial Loans Extended by U.S. Chartered Banks and Foreign Banks with U.S. Offices: | | | | | | | | |
	1980	1981	1982	1983	1984	1985	1986	1987	1988
Japan	5.928	5.967	5.870	6.240	9.231	2.106	2.677	2.947	4.127
South Korea	0.144	0.105	0.184	0.199	0.407	0.029	0.029	0.031	0.036
Saudi Arabia	1.959	2.033	1.784	1.930	1.867	1.705	1.890	2.040	1.792
Canada	1.637	2.265	2.175	2.149	3.140	0.991	0.961	0.988	1.046
Hong Kong	1.196	1.221	1.326	1.367	1.279	1.243	1.306	1.317	1.236
Mexico	0.008	0.033	0.029	0.017	0.373	0.023	0.025	0.032	0.037
Denmark	0.003	0.005	0.006	0.016	0.040	0.009	0.013	0.018	0.021
United Kingdom	3.851	3.705	3.902	3.778	4.013	3.176	4.393	4.637	4.341
France	1.311	1.262	1.106	0.921	1.031	0.081	0.079	0.064	0.080
Italy	0.820	0.924	0.792	0.839	1.495	0.190	0.164	0.059	0.074
Spain	0.351	0.356	0.352	0.339	0.359	0.423	0.428	0.495	0.535

Source: IBA Reports of Condition Tapes Supplied by the Board of Governors of the Federal Reserve System through the National Technical Information Service.

kets. For example, in issuing and accepting letters of credit to backstop international and commodity loans, Japanese banking offices inside the United States held just under 10 percent of the amount of these acceptances held by all U.S. banks in 1980. However, their bookings of these acceptances climbed above the entire U.S.–bank total by 1988, reaching 116 percent of all U.S.–bank-issued acceptances outstanding in that year. The jump in standby credits was equally pronounced, rising from just 2 percent of the U.S.–bank total to almost 62 percent in 1988. Thus, the lesson seems reasonably clear: in direct lending, Japanese banks operating in the United States have achieved their most significant successes against other foreign banks, while in contingent credit obligations (including letters of credit and acceptance financing) the Japanese have made major market share gains relative to both U.S. and foreign banks.

Still, despite recent gains, Japanese banks do not lead in all categories of foreign bank activity in the United States. For example, as Table 4-2 reports, the Japanese share of all U.S.–booked commercial and industrial loans hovered at around 3 to 4 percent of the total for all U.S. and foreign bank loans, which was actually slightly smaller than the British share of just over 4

Table 4-3

Proportion of All Real Estate Loans Held by U.S. Banks Accounted for by the U.S. Offices of Selected Foreign Banks

Name of Country	Percentage of All Foreign Bank Held U.S. Real Estate Loans Accounted For By Japanese Banks:								
	1980	1981	1982	1983	1984	1985	1986	1987	1988
Japan	1.168	1.310	1.277	1.166	1.140	1.155	1.635	2.601	4.240
South Korea	0.006	0.005	0.006	0.013	0.018	0.023	0.036	0.043	0.048
Australia	0.012	0.015	0.014	0.010	0.015	0.021	0.048	0.048	0.055
Denmark	0.000	0.001	0.001	0.003	0.009	0.008	0.008	0.018	0.017
France	0.055	0.062	0.070	0.063	0.086	0.106	0.120	0.131	0.146
West Germany	0.002	0.003	0.003	0.002	0.003	0.003	0.005	0.021	0.046
Greece	0.012	0.016	0.018	0.020	0.033	0.047	0.048	0.046	0.071
Ireland	0.190	0.216	0.208	0.225	0.234	0.248	0.281	0.316	0.348
Italy	0.079	0.082	0.076	0.070	0.069	0.087	0.111	0.056	0.061
The Netherlands	0.378	0.412	0.387	0.323	0.320	0.350	0.440	0.381	0.230
United Kingdom	3.050	3.154	3.107	2.945	2.713	2.576	4.048	4.163	3.652
Switzerland	0.026	0.027	0.033	0.027	0.031	0.046	0.052	0.056	1.683
Spain	0.206	0.265	0.261	0.252	0.220	0.267	0.300	0.337	0.351
Canada	0.764	1.100	1.417	1.261	1.802	1.698	1.542	1.347	1.071
Hong Kong	0.519	0.520	0.486	0.489	0.517	0.595	0.883	0.923	0.900

Source: IBA Reports of Condition Tapes Supplied by the Board of Governors of the Federal Reserve System through the National Technical Information Service.

percent of these loans. Not only British banks, but also banks from Hong Kong, Denmark, Mexico, and Spain appeared to gain market share at the expense of the Japanese in U.S.–booked commercial and industrial loans. Much the same pattern characterized U.S. real estate lending (as reflected in Table 4-3), where the Japanese share approached 2 percent of all U.S.–booked real estate loans, but trailed British banks, which held between 3 and 4 percent of all real estate loans listed in bank accounts inside the United States. To be sure, the Japanese share of U.S. real estate credit rose, but so did the shares of Australian, Danish, French, West German, Greek, Irish, British, Swiss, and Hong Kong banks, according to reports filed with the Federal Reserve Board.

Overall, Japanese-owned U.S. banks held more U.S.–booked loans of all types than any other institutional group in the foreign banking sector. They began the decade of the 1980s with a 1 percent lead over the British, as Table

Table 4-4
Proportion of Total Loans Extended by All U.S. Banks Accounted for by Foreign Banks from Selected Countries

| Name of Country | Year-End Data Expressed as a Percentage of Total Loans Extended by U.S. Chartered Banks and Foreign Banks with U.S. Offices: | | | | | | | | |
	1980	1981	1982	1983	1984	1985	1986	1987	1988
Japan	4.535	4.789	4.980	4.958	6.448	4.215	5.414	6.369	8.516
Canada	1.157	1.595	1.640	1.553	2.028	2.109	1.987	1.837	1.654
Hong Kong	0.910	0.996	1.107	1.101	1.038	1.043	1.280	1.313	1.316
United Kingdom	3.439	3.615	3.761	3.579	3.129	2.942	4.239	4.248	3.757
France	0.828	0.914	0.898	0.768	0.814	0.590	0.488	0.474	0.449
West Germany	0.688	0.602	0.587	0.424	0.394	0.264	0.307	0.265	0.282
Italy	0.878	0.961	1.071	1.066	1.654	0.736	0.797	0.715	0.750
Spain	0.358	0.359	0.401	0.396	0.425	0.493	0.486	0.522	0.563
Switzerland	0.902	0.883	0.883	0.801	0.830	0.620	0.649	0.660	0.574

Source: IBA Reports of Condition Tapes Supplied by the Board of Governors of the Federal Reserve System through the National Technical Information Service.

4-4 suggests. The Japanese widened that lead, holding more than 8 percent of total U.S.–recorded bank loans in 1988, compared to about 4 percent for banks from the United Kingdom. Canadian banks were a distant third at about 1.7 percent of total U.S. loans recorded inside the United States by foreign and domestic banks. To fund all these loans, the Japanese banks turned primarily to borrowings in the U.S. money market and overseas. As Table 4-5 indicates, the Japanese banks' share of U.S. deposits of various kinds relative to other foreign banks either declined or held fairly steady over the 1980-88 period, with the exception of interbank time deposits from U.S. banks, where the Japanese held 26 percent of these deposits posted by all foreign banks in 1980 but jumped their share to 36 percent near the end of the decade. However, the biggest change on the fund-raising side came in nondeposit borrowings (predominantly in the form of purchases of federal funds and security repurchase agreements) where the Japanese share of all such short-term U.S. borrowings by foreign banks soared from less than 15 percent to more than 36 percent over the 1980–88 period. Thus, the Japanese in the United States increasingly are playing the money-market inter-

Table 4-5
Proportion of U.S. Bank Deposits Held by Japanese Banks Having U.S. Offices Relative to All Foreign Banks with U.S. Offices

Portfolio Item	Percentage of All Foreign Bank Held U.S. Deposits Accounted for by Japanese Banks with U.S. Offices:							
	1980	1981	1982	1983	1984	1985	1986	1987
Large-Denomination ($100,000+) Time Deposits in Domestic Offices	32.35	28.30	27.89	28.02	27.27	24.59	31.78	30.58
Total Demand Deposits	13.69	10.92	10.69	10.04	10.35	10.11	11.89	13.17
Demand Deposits of Commercial Banks in U.S.	8.72	6.00	5.90	6.62	4.76	2.41	4.31	4.73
Total Time and Savings Deposits	23.17	22.98	27.68	29.50	35.87	14.24	14.03	12.74
Time Deposits of U.S. Commercial Banks	26.01	31.22	58.45	61.54	70.39	21.32	28.63	36.00
Time Deposits Greater Than $100,000	30.67	27.58	32.53	35.31	43.83	24.45	31.90	31.16
Federal Funds Purchased and Securities Sold Under Repurchase Agreements	14.47	13.78	14.84	18.84	24.06	27.62	31.76	36.57

Source: IBA Reports of Condition Tapes Supplied by the Board of Governors of the Federal Reserve System through the National Technical Information Service.

mediary role—making short-term money-market loans to corporations and governmental units seeking credit inside the United States and borrowing heavily on a short-term basis from many of those same institutions that have U.S. operations.[3]

Japanese Bank Entry into the U.S. Merger and Acquisitions Market

U.S. securities firms, particularly investment banking companies like Morgan Stanley, First Boston Corporation, Salomon Brothers, and Goldman Sachs, enjoyed unparalleled growth and prosperity for much of the 1970s and 1980s before their merger and securities underwriting business began declining precipitously as the 1990s began. The cause of the rapid growth in earlier periods was a massive wave of mergers and acquisitions as U.S. companies searched both home and foreign markets for new firms to acquire and control. U.S. investment bankers encouraged these profitable deals by helping the acquirers arrange financing, leading to a booming market in corporate stock and especially in corporate bonds (led by a dramatic rise in lower-quality "junk" bonds that are rated as speculative investments by credit rating agencies such as Standard & Poor's and Moody's Investors Service).

Seeing the potential for profit and noting that their corporate customers were frequently bypassing banks as funds sources and tapping global securities markets for funds instead, Japanese banks began to penetrate the investment banking market seriously in the 1980s. Sumitomo Bank, for example, established a department for international mergers and acquisitions in the mid-1980s. But Japanese financiers were in for a shock early in the game as the accumulated experience and market contacts of U.S. and European investment banks initially all but drove the Japanese from the acquisitions market. By the late 1980s, however, the foundations of a successful Japanese invasion of the global mergers and acquisitions field were being laid down. First, the rapid expansion of Japanese bank lending and borrowing activities in North America and Western Europe had given them deeper knowledge of cultural differences, greater familiarity with Western investment banking practices, and essential market contacts with potential merger clients. Moreover, the financial resources of Japanese manufacturing and trading firms at home had increased so rapidly that, in growing numbers, these firms began to look abroad for acquisition and merger targets. For these nonfinancial companies, Japanese bank acquisitions services appeared to possess a significant comparative advantage over foreign investment banking programs.

There were also strong signals coming from Japan's Ministry of Finance to domestic financial firms to spread their operations abroad and establish beachheads in distant countries. Moreover, financial pressures on Japanese banks, as a result of the Basle Agreement on International Bank Capital Standards, were forcing Japanese bankers to open up new sources of earnings and capital, and the developing mergers and acquisitions business seemed to fill the bill as a potential source of ample bank earnings. Moreover, the rapid appreciation of the yen in international markets was allowing many smaller Japanese companies to become large enough and strong enough to consider foreign acquisitions that previously were reserved only for the largest multinational corporations. Examples included Paloma Co., a Nagoya appliance firm, which purchased a subsidiary of Pace Industries, and Aoki Corporation of Osaka that acquired Westin Hotels and Resorts.[4]

Japanese banks soon found that they possessed a significant advantage in aiding middle-size Japanese firms with launching their acquisitions programs, because these firms are still heavily dependent on their banks for both funds and financial advice. Recognition of this advantage was not slow in coming. Soon other Japanese banks—for example, Sanwa Bank, Long-Term Credit Bank of Japan, the Industrial Bank of Japan, and Mitsubishi Trust and Banking Corp.—moved to establish their own business acquisition departments, competing on the streets of Tokyo's financial district with such formidable U.S. investment bankers as Morgan Guaranty Trust Co. and First Boston Corporation. While Japanese banks still frequently have to take a back seat to the largest U.S. and European investment banking firms in dealing with multinational clients, the tables are often turned in favor of Japan's banks when it comes to helping midsize Japanese corporations bent on making foreign acquisitions.

As Henry Sender (1988) has noted, the competitive struggle between Japanese investment bankers and those from the West has essentially become a contest between "expertise" and "relationships." Western merger specialists offer experience in analyzing and consummating merger agreements, but, for merger-bound companies inside Japan, Japanese banks offer established lending and consulting relationships that have generally withstood the test of time. To be sure, U.S. and European investment banking firms have developed extensive merger programs with comprehensive support packages to aid their clients. Indeed, the evolution of investment banking has been toward a broader and broader view of what *full service* implies to a corporate client—from securities marketing to strategic planning, options management, and risk hedging. Japanese M&A advising programs usually have a narrower focus, however, helping to identify merger targets for customers and to go through the mechanics of securities offerings needed to finance a merger, but usually do not become more broadly involved in the planning and consulting side of the business.

Certainly, evolution toward a fuller service menu is likely to occur (and, indeed, is already happening) among Japanese investment banking firms. Moreover, some Japanese banks have formed working relationships with U.S. and European investment bankers in an effort to gain additional knowledge about how merger consultants can more fully serve their customers as well as to build stronger contacts with potential clients. A case in point is the Long-Term Credit Bank of Tokyo, which recently established a merger and acquisition joint venture with Peers & Company of Chicago, with the latter supplying information on promising merger targets to the Japanese. Other Japanese merger and acquisition firms have signed on U.S. investment bankers as technical consultants to assist in completing their more complicated acquisition deals.

The Role of Japanese Banking Firms in Leveraged Buyouts (LBOs)

Related to the growing interest of Japanese companies in U.S. and European mergers and acquisitions, Japanese bankers moved in the 1980s to enter the U.S. market for leveraged buyouts. In these typically huge transactions to acquire operating companies, 80 percent or more of the purchase price of a merger-targeted firm may be covered by a combination of bond issues (frequently "junk" bonds)[5] and bank loans. The acquiring firms in these LBO transactions (which often include members of senior management in the business being acquired) count on their ability to better manage the firms they purchase. Presumably, with improved management, these newly acquired businesses will generate cash flows sufficiently large to cover the heavy debt-service costs of the leveraged buyout and still turn a profit for the acquirers. So rapid has been the growth of LBOs that their volume in the United States advanced a hundredfold between 1980 and 1988 to more than $100 billion.

Clearly, there is substantial risk inherent in LBO transactions, not only because the acquirers may suffer from hubris—the tendency to overestimate their managerial skill and their ability to make a company more profitable— but also because fluctuations in the economy, which are beyond management's control, can swamp the most optimistic forecasts and drive the acquiring company into bankruptcy as revenues fall short of the LBO's high borrowing costs. Consequently, bank regulatory authorities in the United States, as the decade of the 1990s approached, moved quickly to limit bank lending for this purpose. For example, the Federal Reserve Board announced that it would empower bank examiners to adversely classify highly leveraged corporate loans and demand more capital if the banks involved appeared to be excessively exposed to loss from too many LBO loans. In November 1989 all three federal bank regulatory agencies in the United States—the Federal Reserve System, Federal Deposit Insurance Corporation, and Comptroller of the Currency—agreed upon a definition of socalled "highly leveraged transactions" (HLTs), including acquisitions, buyouts, and recapitalizations of existing businesses. An HLT was held to exist if the transaction at least doubled a business customer's liabilities, or resulted in a leverage ratio of aggregate liabilities to total assets of more than 50 percent, or if a loan syndication agent declared the transaction to be an HLT.[6] In these instances the bank or banks involved in these transactions would have their loans entered on a special classification list and federal examiners could ask that the bank strengthen its long-term capital to protect against possible loan losses in the future.

These new U.S. regulations coupled with evidence that some previous LBO loans were in trouble caused several U.S. money-center banks to retreat from the LBO and corporate acquisitions market. To no one's surprise the Japanese and other foreign banks and securities firms moved to fill in the partial vacuum left by the U.S. banks. For example, LBOs involving Federated Department Stores, Beatrice Companies, Safeway Stores, Southern Pacific, and others attracted well over $10 billion dollars in Japanese bank funds late in the 1980s, with the expectation of more to follow. Recent estimates made at the beginning of the 1990s suggested that the Japanese have provided roughly one-quarter of all LBO-related U.S. corporate loans in recent years, while U.S. banks themselves accounted for just over 50 percent of this market, but with a definite trend toward fewer LBO transactions still remaining on the books of federally regulated U.S. banking firms.

There is evidence that Japanese banks and securities firms view LBOs as a channel of opportunity for them to become not only major players in the short run, but also regular players on a long-term basis in the U.S. LBO market and the broader U.S. merger and acquisitions market that surrounds it. Entrée to U.S. merger and acquisitions financing is viewed by the Japanese as a door to building permanent banking relationships with U.S. corporations. Japanese banks and securities firms want to be included in the set of firms that U.S. companies look to whenever they have significant financial service needs, whether those needs involve LBOs or more conventional credit, deposit, and agency services. They wish to compete on equal terms across the full spectrum of banking services and to take a leadership position in their share of major corporate loans, including LBOs and other corporate merger transactions.

Advantages Conferred on Japanese and Other Foreign Banks by the U.S. Glass-Steagall Act (1933)

As Japanese and other foreign banks have sought to broaden their U.S. beachhead in financing and managing mergers and acquisitions, they have been aided by a regulatory roadblock thrown into the path of U.S. banks by the U.S. Congress more than 50 years ago. One of the most serious regulatory barriers faced by the largest U.S. banks in meeting the challenge of foreign bank competition inside the United States is the Glass-Steagall Act. Since 1933, U.S. commercial banks have been prevented by federal law from purchasing and holding corporate stock for their own accounts, allegedly to prevent these banks from taking on excessive risk and in an effort to separate the public's savings from speculative activity. The contrast with Japan is particularly striking: current estimates suggest that Japan's banks hold at least 20 percent of all corporate equity shares issued and outstanding in that country. The legal capacity of Japanese banks to purchase both debt and equity securities from their corporate customers confers on them a distinct advantage in the international competition for major corporate accounts.

Equally important, however, Glass-Steagall's prohibitions aimed at lessening bank risk may actually subject U.S. commercial banks to more, not less, risk exposure. This is the implication of a recent study by Federal Reserve economist Stephen Prowse (1990), who finds evidence of stronger "principal-agent" conflicts involving U.S. banks and their corporate customers than appears to be true inside Japan. The basic argument here centers around business customers that have both substantial debt obligations (including bank loans) and equity securities outstanding. Inside these firms, stockholders may have an incentive to seize some portion of corporate wealth that might otherwise accrue to the company's debtholders, such as by substituting higher-risk investment projects not previously revealed to the creditors of the corporation or by turning down investment projects expected to be profitable if most of the projected gain would accrue to the creditors rather than to the stockholders. If debtholders (including banks) perceive these conflicts, they will demand higher interest yields from any loans they make to such firms. As a result, borrowing companies will also tend to use less debt financing, reducing their preferred (optimal) ratio of debt-to-equity financing. If debtholders (including banks) are not cognizant of these conflicts, however, and the shareholders can successfully remove some portion of a corporation's wealth from its creditors, the creditors will tend to receive lower average returns, and the corporations in which they have invested money will have taken on significantly greater risk exposure.

Prowse (1990) finds that such creditor-stockholder conflicts are substantially less frequent in Japan, arguably because Japanese banks can be both creditors and owners (stockholders) of the companies they service. By serving as part owners of corporations, Japanese bankers presumably are able to influence the companies' internal financing and investment decisions. Indeed, Japanese commercial banks routinely hold positions on the boards of directors of Japanese corporations and have representatives among the managements of many domestic firms. With Japanese banks represented significantly as both debtholders and stockholders, the economic inducement of borrowing companies to benefit their shareholders at the expense of their creditors is reduced or eliminated, and overall corporate risk exposure may be reduced.[7]

In contrast, a recent study of the Fortune 500 companies by P. Clyde (1989) carried out at the University of California in Los Angeles suggests that not only do U.S. banks not hold significant equity investments in U.S. corporations, but also those U.S. financial institutions that do hold substantial amounts of corporate stock (principally pension funds, mutual funds, and insurance companies) usually do not hold substantial amounts of debt securities in the same firms. By way of comparison, Prowse (1990) finds that Japanese financial firms display a significant positive correlation between their debt security and equity security holdings—that is, for those corporations in which they have substantial debt holdings, they also tend to hold substantial stockholder positions as well.

U.S. banks face imposing institutional restrictions that severely restrict their ability to monitor their corporate customers' behavior and performance. In addition to the Glass-Steagall Act's prohibition on outright stock investments in nonbank corporations, U.S. banks also cannot underwrite corporate bonds and equities unless they are specifically authorized to do so by the Federal Reserve Board. Moreover, U.S. bankruptcy law threatens banks with loss of their creditor status (and, therefore, the ability to enforce their preferential claim on a defaulted borrower's assets) if they become actively involved in the management of a borrowing firm.

The comparative advantage Japanese and other foreign banks currently possess over U.S. banks in being able to underwrite both equity and debt securities for their corporate customers appears to be eroding, however, albeit slowly. In January 1989 the Federal Reserve Board granted bank holding companies permission to sell newly issued corporate bonds in the open market. However, in an effort to prevent U.S. banks from using the public's deposits, backed by federal insurance, to finance securities transactions, the Federal Reserve Board stipulated, first of all, that it would approve underwriting of corporate securities only on a case-by-case basis—that is, each banking company interested in acquiring underwriting powers for privately issued securities would have to file its own application for approval. Secondly, the underwriting of corporate securities would have to be carried on through a separate subsidiary firm, independent of the banks belonging to the same holding company. Moreover, the underwriting subsidiary would not be permitted to borrow from any banks that belong to the same holding company.

Despite these stringent regulations, several leading U.S. banking organizations moved aggressively to take advantage of whatever security powers the Federal Reserve Board was willing to grant. For example, J.P. Morgan and Company applied for Board approval to underwrite corporate debt the same month that the Fed announced its new policy and, within days of receiving approval, participated in the underwriting of $10 million in notes issued by Xerox Corporation along with other securities dealers. In October 1989 Bankers Trust New York Corporation established itself as the first U.S. bank holding company in the 50 years since the Glass-Steagall Act was passed to assume the role of sole underwriter of a corporate bond. Another unique feature of this particular transaction was the fact that "junk" bonds were involved—securities with such a low credit rating that the bank itself would not be permitted under federal regulations to buy any of them. The Bankers Trust underwriting subsidiary had to place $150 million of these risky securities with other corporate and individual investors.

Then, in the fall of 1990, J.P. Morgan and Company became the first U.S. banking organization to win Federal Reserve Board approval to underwrite corporate stock, subject to restrictions similar to those applying to the underwriting of corporate debt securities. Financial analysts generally anticipated approval from the Fed for J.P. Morgan's application because the bank is well capitalized and experienced in the investment banking field. The stock underwriting must be conducted through a subsidiary firm, J.P. Morgan Securities, Inc., which can receive no more than 10 percent of its total revenue from underwriting corporate stock and other so-called "ineligible" securities (including municipal bonds, mortgage– and consumer credit–backed securities, and commercial paper). Applications for stock underwriting powers were also pending from Citicorp, Chase Manhattan, Bankers Trust, Canadian Imperial Bank, and the Royal Bank of Canada at the time J.P. Morgan's application was approved. Finally in 1991 the U.S. Treasury Department posed sweeping reform proposals that would break down the barriers to U.S. bank involvement in corporate security underwriting as well as in insurance and mutual fund sales.

If more U.S. banks had the ability to offer both commercial banking and investment banking services, they would presumably be less affected by shifting trends in how corporations choose to finance their operations. Thus, the recent trend away from bank loans toward open-market corporate borrowing through the issuance of securities would have been of much less significance for the preservation and growth of bank profits and capital if U.S. commercial banks already possessed broad investment banking powers. Then, too, the ability of U.S. banks to provide both debt financing and equity financing for their clients helps to gauge and control the amount of risk exposure any bank faces from a given firm, industry, or region. Moreover, with the growing use of securitization in banking, in which banks package together groups of loans and issue securities against them, the traditional distinctions between investment banking and commercial banking seem to be rapidly eroding away.

Japanese Banks' Entry into Underwriting U.S. Corporate Securities

Not to be left behind, Japanese banks operating in the United States moved quickly to win Federal Reserve Board approval to deal in corporate securities and other business-oriented financial instruments issued inside the United States. On May 9, 1990 Mitsui Toyo Kobe Bank's application to acquire up to 10 percent of the outstanding common shares of Security Pacific Financial Services System of San Diego was approved by the Federal Reserve Board, giving Mitsui access to a securities trading unit. On May 21, 1990 the Bank of Tokyo was allowed to acquire, through its wholly owned subsidiary, BOT Financial Corporation of New York as well as certain assets from the Bank of New England Corporation of Boston and to engage in making, acquiring, and servicing loans, providing investment and financial advice, leasing personal and real property, and supplying data processing services. On May 29, 1990 the Long-Term Credit Bank of Japan (LTCB) gained Federal Reserve approval to engage, through its Greenwich Capital Markets affiliate, in underwriting and dealing in residential mortgage-related securities, municipal revenue bonds, commercial paper, and consumer receivables–related securities, as well as to act as a futures commission merchant and to buy and sell gold and silver. LTCB had previously been admitted to the "exclusive club" of primary dealers in U.S. government securities and was already a broker-dealer registered with the U.S. Securities and Exchange Commission.

Late in March of 1991 the Mitsubishi Bank Limited of Tokyo applied for permission for its New York subsidiary, Mitsubishi Capital Market Services, Inc., to market interest-rate swaps and currency swaps. The Federal Reserve Board granted permission for Mitsubishi to act as an originator and principal as well as a broker, agent, and advisor in risk-reducing swap agreements, interest-rate caps, floors, and collars, and for sales of options on these same financial products. At the time of its application the Board estimated that Mitsubishi ranked fourth among all banks worldwide and controlled a bank subsidiary in San Francisco, an agency office in Houston, and branch offices in Chicago, Los Angeles, and New York City. Mitsubishi's U.S. offices at the time of this latest application were engaged in lending and property leasing as well as investment advising and trust management, and were acting as a futures commission merchant in Chicago.

Shortly before the Federal Reserve Board announced the approval of Mitsubishi's swap-market activities, that company in collaboration with Hambro International Equity Partners announced the formation of a $150-million venture capital fund. The new fund is designed to invest in American start-up companies interested in selling on the continent of Asia. Mitsubishi would appear to have a distinct advantage in advising American firms trying to market their goods abroad due to its depth of knowledge of Pacific Rim markets and its superior capital strength.

These Federal Reserve Board approvals of Japanese securities activities have not always been unanimous, however. For example, Governor Wayne Angell dissented from the Bank of Tokyo decision discussed above, arguing that the transaction was so complex as to obscure its possible effects on the public interest, making it impossible to determine if the public benefits of the proposal outweighed any potentially adverse effects.[8] Perhaps the strongest statement of dissent was registered by Governor Martha Seger who, responding to the Mitsui Toyo Kobe Bank application approved in May of 1990, expressed concern about the essential unfairness to U.S. banks of allowing foreign institutions to enter U.S. markets with lower capital positions than permitted domestic banks. Governor Seger also pointed to the barriers to entry into Japan still faced by U.S. banks. Governor Seger stated:

I dissent from the Federal Reserve Board's action in this case. I believe that foreign banking organizations whose primary capital, based on U.S. accounting principles, is below the Board's minimum capital guidelines for U.S. banking organizations have an unfair competitive advantage in the United States over domestic banking organizations. In my view, such foreign organizations should be judged against the same financial and managerial standards, including the Board's capital adequacy guidelines, as are applied to domestic banking organizations. The majority [of members on the Federal Reserve Board] concludes that applicant's primary capital meets United States' standards. . . . To do so, however, the majority makes adjustments that are not available for U.S. banks under guidelines that have not yet become effective for U.S. or foreign banking organizations.

In addition, I am concerned that while some progress is being made in opening

Japanese markets to U.S. banking organizations, U.S. banking organizations and other financial institutions, in my opinion, are still far from being afforded the full opportunity to compete in Japan.

The Current Transition Toward Services for Smaller U.S. Businesses

There is little question now that medium-size U.S. business firms have become a key target market for foreign banking units active inside the United States, especially by Japanese and Canadian banks. As economist Suzanna Andrews (1984) observes, U.S. firms with annual sales of $5 to $125 million are particularly important targets. These midsize businesses have been especially appealing to foreign bankers due to:

1. Falling spreads on loans and other services sold to large U.S. corporations (particularly high-volume syndicate loans), reflecting increasingly greater competition in the corporate loan market, while spreads on loans to middle-market firms appear to be much larger
2. Declining demand for bank credit by the largest U.S. companies, which increasingly have turned to the open market for funds by issuing their own securities rather than borrowing from banks
3. Greater growth potential among medium-size firms than appears to be true of many other customer groups with whom banks deal
4. Problems with many overseas loans, which have encouraged bankers to pursue smaller business clients in more protected domestic markets

Among the leading Japanese banks active in this so-called "middle market" are Fuji, Mitsubishi, and the Bank of Tokyo. For example, in January 1984 Fuji Bank announced a $425 million purchase of two finance company operations from Walter E. Heller International Company—an acquisition aimed at expanding Fuji's beachhead in the U.S. middle-business sector. A similar motivation appeared to be behind Mitsubishi's offer in 1984 to take control of BanCal Tri-State Corporation in California for $282 million, the 1988 acquisition of Union Bank of California by the Bank of Tokyo's subsidiary, California First Bank, and the 1986 acquisition by Industrial Bank of Japan of J. Henry Schroder Bank. Similarly, the 1981 purchase of California's Manufacturers Bank by Taiyo Kobe Bank also appeared to represent the strategic objective of lending to small and medium-size U.S. business firms.

More recently, in 1989 Daiwa Bank acquired more than a dozen U.S. offices (including full service branches and representative offices) from Lloyds Bank. In the same year Dai-Ichi Kangyo Bank purchased a controlling (60 percent) interest in CIT Group, a finance company making loans and leases to midsize firms that was controlled originally by Manufacturers

Hanover. Later, in September 1990, Dai-Ichi and Manufacturers Hanover Corporation of New York applied to the Federal Reserve Board for authority to offer through the CIT Group the leasing of personal property and services as agent, broker, or advisor in the leasing of such property (including leasing transactions that would allow CIT to rely for its compensation on an estimated residual value of the leased property at the expiration of the initial lease term up to 100 percent of the acquisition cost of the property).

At the time it received approval for this expansion of service powers inside the United States, Dai-Ichi was by far the largest banking organization in the world, with $435 billion in consolidated assets. Dai-Ichi then operated branches in Chicago, Los Angeles, and New York, agency offices in Atlanta and San Francisco, and a full service bank in Los Angeles that held just over $500 million in assets (as of June 30, 1990). CIT at the time of the application operated about 30 subsidiary firms offering commercial finance, leasing, factoring, and sales finance activities, with consolidated assets of $10.3 billion.[9] Dai-Ichi's drive to establish a leading position in the U.S. business middle market first caught financial analysts' attention when the bank purchased a $200 million commercial loan portfolio from U.S. Trust Company in 1987.

Another aggressive competitor in middle-market business financing is Sanwa Bank, headquartered in Osaka. Sanwa has grown rapidly, despite the fact that it lacks a traditional relationship to a zaibatsu (conglomerate corporate group), because of its creative approaches to market expansion and the development of new commercial services. As financial analyst Richard Read (1988) has noted, Sanwa was the first Japanese bank to purchase a leading U.S. bank, Lloyds Bank of California (which was acquired for approximately $263 million in 1986). It was also the first Japanese banking institution to set up a management team to offer merger and acquisitions services, to launch a credit card program, and to organize both a factoring company and a leasing firm to carry out business lending. Sanwa's Business Credit Corp., formerly Continental Illinois' leasing subsidiary, has been advertising heavily on television inside the United States to attract business clients to its commercial finance and vendor leasing programs. One of the hallmarks of Sanwa's expansion inside the United States is its predominant use of U.S. citizens as officers and employees of the U.S. banks it acquires—a step that many other Japanese firms in the United States will eventually have to take due to pressure from U.S. courts and government agencies concerned with foreign firms' compliance with U.S. equal opportunity laws and regulations.

To most foreign banks, cultural and language barriers have meant that midsize U.S. firms are better served by acquiring a U.S. bank or other financial-service firm and leaving its personnel and policies intact so that it can continue to serve midsize companies as before. But there are still problems here for foreign bankers, including difficulties in entering many local markets either *de novo* or by acquisition, due to U.S. antibranching and holding company statutes, the antitrust laws, the need for fast credit decisions even though many foreign banks require permission from their home offices to grant business loan requests, the need among U.S. midsize firms for unconventional forms of financial services support and credit packages with which foreign banks often have little familiarity, and the demand for credit risk–hedging devices on the part of smaller U.S. companies in which most foreign banks are usually less experienced than are most U.S. banks. However, Japanese banks have two key points in their favor in reaching out to smaller U.S. businesses—a substantial physical presence already established inside the United States, and the valuable experience and knowledge of U.S. businesses they have gained from their ongoing presence. As economists Clifford Ball and Adrian Tschoegl (1982) discovered in an early study of multinational firms, both length of time and physical presence abroad are significant factors in shaping the size and scope of a foreign bank's penetration of domestic markets.

Standby Credit and Credit Guarantees: The Rise of Japanese Participation in the U.S. Guarantee Market

Increasingly, larger U.S. corporations are bypassing their banks and borrowing directly in the open market through the issuance of commercial notes, bonds, and stock issues. This appears to be an ominous development for most banks around the world because it means a decline in corporate loan demand and the loss of a major proportion of multinational banks' loan revenues. However, to the surprise of many bankers, there has been a silver lining to this dark cloud—a new source of fee income for multinational banks. In most cases these securities offerings must be backed up by credit guarantees—that is, an offer to pay off a customer's loan or bonds if that customer cannot pay—from financial institutions with high and stable credit ratings. International banks and insurance companies have become major players in the market for these "credit backstops," which typically pledge the guarantor's assets and borrowing capacity to repay a loan if the corporation selling securities falls short of available funds.

Standby guarantees today cover regular corporate loans, commercial paper, corporate and municipal bonds, securitized assets, and borrowings to purchase securities on margin. U.S. banks have found that standbys have a number of attractive features that cause them at times to prefer standby credits to regular commercial loans. Standbys grant bankers the opportunity to serve a corporate customer without using up scarce reserves and without having to raise new deposits and post reserve requirements behind those deposits. Moreover, because standbys are not booked either as conventional assets or liabilities, they do not reduce a bank's capital-to-asset ratio—an important measure of the adequacy of its capital position.

Foreign banks have grabbed a rapidly growing share of U.S.–based stand-

Table 4-6

Proportion of Standby Credit Letters Issued by All U.S. Banks Accounted for by the U.S. Offices of Foreign Banks

Year-End Data Expressed as a Percentage of All Standby Credits
Issued by U.S. Chartered Banks and U.S. Offices of Foreign Banks:

Name of Country	1980	1981	1982	1983	1984	1985	1986	1987	1988
Japan	2.44	2.41	4.99	1.96	1.04	0.84	0.74	47.92	64.18
Canada	1.28	1.52	1.68	1.94	3.14	3.15	4.37	5.24	5.41
United Kingdom	3.79	6.20	7.28	6.96	5.56	1.51	1.68	13.29	12.86
Hong Kong	1.36	1.30	1.47	1.45	1.91	0.01	0.01	2.25	2.50
France	3.92	4.23	4.32	3.08	4.03	0.35	0.24	7.89	9.96
West Germany	0.82	1.11	1.46	0.95	10.96	0.00	0.00	2.45	2.98
Italy	0.49	0.43	0.36	0.36	5.06	0.14	0.14	1.07	1.20
The Netherlands	0.64	0.57	0.79	0.62	6.51	0.05	0.09	3.05	4.23
Switzerland	0.88	1.56	2.05	2.23	3.77	0.04	0.07	8.32	10.92

Source: IBA Reports of Condition Tapes Supplied by the Board of Governors of the Federal Reserve System through the National Technical Information Service.

by credit customers. The Japanese appear to be way out in front in this market, as Table 4-6 reflects. In 1980 Japanese banks held only a 2 percent share of the volume of standbys held by all foreign banks with U.S. offices and U.S.–chartered banks. However, by year-end 1988 their share had catapulted to more than 60 percent of the total outstanding. British, Canadian, German, Dutch, and Swiss banks also significantly increased their shares of the U.S. standby credit market, but not at a pace that could match the Japanese gains. Economist Herbert Baer (1990) calculates that Japanese bank branch offices alone have accounted for about one-third of the increase in standbys issued to U.S. commercial customers over the decade of the 1980s.

Interestingly enough, not all of Japanese banking activity in the U.S. market for standby credits involves credit guarantees for business firms. A rising portion of such guarantees by Japanese banks are being issued to back state and local (municipal) government borrowing. Indeed, the Japanese now appear to have risen to a position of dominance in the municipal guarantee market. A number of local governments seem to have benefitted substantially from Japanese involvement in this municipal market in the form of lower guarantee fees and lower interest rates on borrowings due to the growth of these standby credit agreements.

The Japanese in the U.S. Acceptance Market

Japanese banks have also scored remarkable success in the U.S. market for acceptance financing. These bank-endorsed drafts are used primarily to fund international trade and commerce, and generally can be issued only by the largest and soundest banks. Acceptances typically arise when a corporate customer approaches a bank to request a letter of credit to buy goods and services (including foreign currency) overseas. The credit letter authorizes the foreign firm selling goods or services to draw a draft on the letter-issuing bank for a specific amount to be paid on a specific future date. Once the draft is drawn up (usually with the assistance of the foreign supplier's bank) and is accepted by the bank that issued the credit letter, that draft becomes a negotiable instrument and can be bought and sold any number of times before it reaches maturity. When the maturity date arrives, the accepting bank will pay the holder of the acceptance the full amount printed on the instrument's face. Because of the high credit ratings of banks issuing tradable acceptances and the fact that anyone who sells an acceptance is also contingently liable to pay if the issuing bank fails to do so, bankers' acceptances are considered to be one of the highest-quality financial instruments available anywhere and usually find a ready resale market among investors.

The close association between the volume of acceptances and the volume of international trade explains why the Japanese are so interested in this market. As the volume of trade between Japan and the United States has mushroomed, Japanese banking affiliates in the United States have sharply expanded their volume of acceptance financing. As Table 4-7 shows, the Japanese share of all U.S.–booked bankers' acceptances soared, expanding from just under 10 percent of the total outstanding to 120 percent over the 1980–88 period. Moreover, a substantial volume of U.S.–based acceptance financing has been diverted to support trade between Japan and other nations besides the United States and to fund currency purchases. These so-called "third country bills" have grown rapidly in recent years.

Japanese Banks in the U.S. SWAP Market

Another business-oriented financial market in the United States in which the Japanese are playing a growing role is the market for interest rate and

Table 4-7
Proportion of All Acceptances Outstanding Extended by U.S. Banks Accounted for by the U.S. Offices of Foreign Banks

Name of Country	Year-End Data Expressed as a Percentage of All Acceptances Outstanding at U.S. Chartered and Foreign Banks with U.S. Offices:								
	1980	1981	1982	1983	1984	1985	1986	1987	1988
Japan	9.99	11.06	13.45	14.69	37.77	2.39	2.44	100.05	120.81
Canada	1.18	1.52	1.52	1.25	1.75	0.66	0.80	3.20	3.88
Hong Kong	1.75	2.33	2.57	4.09	2.93	1.85	0.86	1.75	2.07
United Kingdom	5.41	5.97	6.75	5.53	3.70	2.81	3.08	6.41	7.33
France	1.92	2.04	1.72	1.27	2.66	0.03	0.05	3.69	6.40
Italy	0.21	0.26	0.24	0.28	0.86	0.01	0.01	0.62	0.51
The Netherlands	1.65	1.55	1.14	1.55	3.48	5.72	7.83	10.57	12.46
Switzerland	1.10	1.61	1.27	1.09	1.65	0.00	0.00	5.99	5.30

Source: IBA Reports of Condition Tapes Supplied by the Board of Governors of the Federal Reserve System through the National Technical Information Service.

currency swaps. An interest-rate swap involves an agreement by two firms to exchange interest payments, so that there is a better balance in volume and timing between the cash inflows and cash outflows of each firm and substantial savings in borrowing costs. In the most common type of interest rate swap a borrower with a high credit rating will usually issue long-term securities at a low fixed interest rate, while a borrowing company with a lower credit rating takes out a short-term loan. The two firms then periodically exchange interest payments (usually once each quarter) and each saves money because savings on interest costs due to differences in credit ratings (known as the "quality spread") typically are much greater in long-term credit markets than in short-term credit markets.

Currency swaps, on the other hand, involve the exchange of two different national currencies among two or more parties who need those currencies to make purchases of inventories or to cover other operating costs. Currency swaps also allow businesses to reduce their exposure to loss from fluctuating currency prices. Both kinds of swaps generate fee income for banks that arrange swaps for their customers. Additional fees may be earned if a bank agrees to guarantee the performance of either or both parties to a swap.

Swap transactions are also attractive to banking companies because swaps generally do not require the booking of assets which, other things equal, reduce a bank's capital-to-asset ratio. Today Japanese bankers are mindful of the need to avoid pushing their ratios of permanent capital to total assets too low relative to new international capital standards specified in the Basle Agreement, which both Japan and the United states (along with nine other nations) signed in 1988.[10] When fully in force, these new international standards will require all banks, regardless of their country of origin, to meet the same minimum ratios of long-term capital to total assets.

THE IMPLICATIONS OF JAPANESE PURSUIT OF U.S. BUSINESS CUSTOMERS

The Japanese thrust into the U.S. business sector is little cause for surprise among most economists and financial analysts. As we have seen, Japanese banks and securities firms first came to the United States to make Japanese trade with U.S. businesses and consumers flow more efficiently. They soon found a strong secondary market in the thousands of Japanese expatriates and in the personal accounts of the managers and employees of Japanese companies. The final step—reaching out to U.S. businesses of all sizes as well as to U.S. individuals, families, and governments at all levels—took longer, but it too was fully expected by those who have studied the history of international banking.

However, as we have seen in this chapter, the success of Japanese expansion inside the United States has been due not only to economic factors—the strength of the Japanese economy and the huge size of the common market formed by the 50 states—but also to the special characteristics of banking and securities regulation in Japan and the United States. U.S. restrictions on interstate banking, which prohibit full service branching across state lines, have severely limited the ability of most U.S. banks to reach all of their potential customers and to grow to a size that can successfully challenge the industry's leaders. At the same time the National Bank Act of 1933 (known as Glass-Steagall) has drawn a rigid wall between U.S. commercial banking and investment banking, limiting the ways in which U.S. commercial banks can service their largest and best corporate and institutional customers. These barriers to full service U.S. banking have opened the door to Japanese penetration of the U.S. financial system.

At the same time, banking regulations inside Japan have encouraged Japanese bank expansion abroad even as they have discouraged expansion at home. At home, Japan's banking firms have recently lost ground to nonbank financial service providers, due to government-imposed interest rate ceilings on deposits, branching restrictions, and Japan's own version of the Glass-Steagall Act. The United States has come to represent a haven to Japanese banks from the foregoing restrictions. Low-cost deposits raised inside Japan are routed to the United States, supplemented with funds raised in the interbank market centered in London and New York, and used to offer a range of financial services the quantity and quality of which U.S. banks have increasing difficulty in meeting.

The success of Japanese banks and securities firms in their penetration of the United States' financial service markets and their rapid acquisition of U.S. assets need not continue into the future, however. Some slowing had already begun by 1990 and the latter part of 1989 for a variety of reasons. U.S. economic growth slowed significantly as the 1990s began, subduing further increases in Americans' appetite for Japanese goods. At the same time, the sharp decline in the Japanese stock market during 1990 forced Japanese institutions to sell off a substantial portion of their holdings of U.S. stocks, bonds, and real estate. Moreover, the rapid run-up in world oil prices associated with the Middle East crisis appears likely to keep the pressure on corporate earnings and government revenues inside Japan as more of that nation's resources must be committed to supporting the Japanese economy. Finally, with significant deregulation underway in Japan, Japanese banks will be free to compete aggressively for domestic deposits and, therefore, less dependent on the U.S. and Eurodollar money markets for funding to help support their vast undertakings worldwide. Both Japan and the United States will find themselves moving inexorably toward a new relationship with new and equally complex problems.

NOTES

1. See especially Gary C. Zimmerman, "The Growing Presence of Japanese Banks in California," *Economic Review*, Federal Reserve Bank of San Francisco, Summer 1989, pp. 3–17.

2. Interestingly enough, as Federal Reserve Board economists Terrell, Dohner, and Lowrey (1990) illustrate, the Japanese have become net long-term lenders and, at the same time, net short-term borrowers in global capital markets. Long-term capital outflows increased dramatically during the 1980s as leading Japanese insurance companies and pension funds were freed substantially from regulations that limited their investments abroad (particularly those denominated in foreign currencies). On the short-term end, as we noted previously, deposit regulation at home has encouraged Japanese banks to borrow heavily through their branches overseas. The result has been to make the Japanese financial system a global financial intermediary—borrowing short in some markets and lending long in others—while also playing a key role as a net supplier of global savings.

3. As Federal Reserve economist Herbert Baer (1990) observes, the expansion of commercial and industrial loans to U.S. businesses by Japanese banks has accounted for virtually all the rise in the total foreign bank share of U.S. commercial and

industrial loans since 1980. In total, by the end of the decade of the 1980s, foreign banks represented almost 15 percent of all commercial and industrial loans booked in the United States, and the Japanese accounted about one-fifth of all foreign bank loans to businesses with U.S. addresses.

4. See especially Henry Sender, "Japanese Bank's Global Merger and Acquisition Assault," *Institutional Investor*, August 1988, pp. 167–72.

5. Bond rating agencies, such as Standard & Poor's and Moody's Investors Service, classify bonds and similar securities as to their degree of default risk by applying letter grades ranging from highest quality to lowest quality—from AAA to D in the case of Standard & Poor's and Aaa to C in the case of Moody's Investors Service. Bonds rated in the top four credit-quality categories are known as "investment-grade issues" and may be purchased by commercial banks in the United States and by other regulated financial institutions.

6. See Federal Deposit Insurance Corporation, *Press Release*, November 20, 1989.

7. An interesting study by Aoki (1984) suggests that Japanese bank holdings of equity shares in the corporations to which they lend money allows these institutions to charge higher loan rates to these same customers than would be the case if these banks were only creditors, due perhaps to the advantages of having at least some inside information.

8. See especially Board of Governors of the Federal Reserve System, *Press Release*, May 21, 1990, p. 6.

9. See Board of Governors of the Federal Reserve System, *Press Release*, September 17, 1990.

10. See chapters 3 and 6 for a fuller discussion of the Basle Agreement on International Capital Standards and its implications for commercial banking in both the United States and Japan.

FIVE

Japanese Expansion in U.S. Securities and Real Estate Markets

The strong foundation laid by Japanese banks in the United States during the 1960s and 1970s served to launch Japanese securities firms into the 1980s and 1990s. Once their banks were solidly grounded, Japanese securities brokers and dealers soon realized that most of the external and internal ingredients essential for successful penetration of U.S. securities markets were in place—a network for making payments for purchases of securities through Japanese or U.S. banks, a well-developed and politically stable marketplace, recent regulatory concessions that favored foreign entry, a wide array of potential business and household clients (including both domestic U.S. and foreign individuals and institutions drawn to U.S. shores), and a source of huge amounts of working capital that could be borrowed or traded through U.S. banks and dozens of foreign banks operating in U.S. money centers. Another lure drawing Japanese securities dealers to U.S. shores was the huge size of the U.S. stock market, which today accounts for about one-third of global equity trading.[1]

Moreover, as the home of the U.S. dollar—the world's most important convertible currency and principal vehicle for trading in global commodities—the United States represented a key source of international liquidity, in the form of bank dollar-denominated deposits that can serve as readily accepted borrowing collateral in international markets. An important added feature is that U.S. securities brokers and dealers have the expertise in putting together successful debt and equity securities offerings for their customers that many Japanese securities underwriters lack. U.S. financial firms lead the world in financial innovation, developing such successful recent products as securitizations, stripped securities, pass-through instruments, and zero coupon bonds.

Finally, the climate for new financial firms has been highly favorable in the United States. The number of broker-dealer firms in the U.S. nearly doubled between 1980 and 1990, giving Japanese firms in need of floating new debt and equity securities more options to choose from. And recent changes in federal regulations have made life easier for dealer firms selling new securities, due to such regulatory-inspired innovations as shelf registration and the Securities and Exchange Commission's new Rule 144a, which allows the sale of unregistered securities through private placement with "sophisticated" investors, who hold over $100 million in securities under management. Rule 144a appears to favor the largest domestic and foreign dealer firms because it gives a boost to *private placements*—securities offerings to a limited set of investors—which the largest dealers are better positioned to handle. Moreover, the recent emphasis on developing and offering many new services among leading securities firms, as well as the presence of substantial economies of size in securities offerings, have worked to concentrate the U.S. dealer market, pushing smaller regional securities firms into the background. This structural change has given the Japanese and other foreign securities firms having world-class size the opportunity to successfully penetrate the U.S. domestic market.

Moreover, smaller U.S. securities firms appear to have been hampered and their market role reduced, opening the door to the largest foreign competitors, because of a 1982 decision by the Securities and Exchange Commission known as Rule 415. This regulation allows dealers to register a new offering with the SEC *prior* to bringing the new securities to market. Rule 415 not only grants securities firms greater flexibility, but also favors the largest dealer firms that have greater capacity to time market movements and can move quickly to take advantage of favorable marketing opportunities.

To be sure, Japanese securities firms entering the United States soon discovered there were still some essential skills that they would need to either develop or compensate for, such as overcoming language and cultural barriers and understanding the terminology of U.S. securities traders and managers who have developed a language and a kit of professional tools all their own. But these problems could be overcome with education, patience, and, most importantly, sufficient capital to invest in the production and sale of quality financial services. The necessary capital was already there: huge trade surpluses with the United States presented Japanese institutions and individual investors with a surplus of dollars—claims against U.S. resources that could easily be converted into acquisitions of U.S. government and corporate securities and into the purchase of U.S. securities companies or the hiring of their most skilled staff members.

Of course, it is not just favorable conditions in the United States that have brought Japanese securities firms to America. Prevailing conditions inside Japan, particularly Japanese regulations, have been a major factor as well. As Takeo Hoshi, Anil Kashyap, and David Scharfstein (1989) point out, until recently Japanese corporations have had to raise the bulk of their domestic funds by borrowing from banks. Japanese regulations until the early 1980s made it virtually impossible to secure new capital by selling securities in Japan's capital markets. For one thing, all bonds issued inside Japan had to be fully secured by a corporation's assets. In contrast, bonds issued abroad could go unsecured, though government approval was required before a foreign sale could by launched. These restrictive rules encouraged Japanese securities firms to look overseas for greater funding opportunities. Passage of Japan's Foreign Exchange Reform Law in 1980 lifted the requirement of government approval before borrowing abroad. The Reform Law subsequently required only that the Japanese government be notified. By 1983 Japanese companies were acquiring close to half their capital funds from abroad, and both New York and London had become key points in the geography of corporate fund-raising for the Japanese. The accord reached between the United States and Japan in 1984 to internationalize the yen and stabilize its international value further accelerated Japan's investment and securities issuance abroad.

MEMBERSHIP IN THE FEDERAL RESERVE'S PRIMARY DEALER CLUB

One of the first major breakthroughs by Japanese security firms seeking power, influence, and status among professionals and investors inside the United States was the successful entry by Nomura, Daiwa, Nikko, and Yamaichi Securities into the exclusive club of U.S. *primary dealers.* In this instance, the term "primary" means dealers in U.S. government securities that are recognized by the Federal Reserve System, the United States' quasi-public, quasi-private central bank. Once a securities dealer is recognized by the Fed as having sufficient stature and financial strength in the community of investors, it is placed on the Fed's eligibility list to trade government securities with the Federal Reserve Bank of New York's open-market desk. The New York Fed enters the market almost daily, buying and selling U.S. government securities (principally Treasury bills) through the primary dealers in order to carry out its Congressional mandate of stabilizing the economy and moderating inflation (known as *monetary policy*). The Fed also enters the government securities market nearly every day to buy and sell selected securities on behalf of dozens of central banks and government agencies around the world, including the Bank of Japan, for which it acts as agent to manage their portfolios of dollar-denominated securities.

The advantages reaped by securities firms that become primary dealers are primarily prestige, which usually helps attract other clients, and the ability to obtain short-term loans from the Fed. These Federal Reserve dealer loans often arise when the Fed becomes concerned that the primary dealers are struggling to raise the funds necessary to carry their huge securities portfolios and fears that the U.S. Treasury may have trouble in placing its securities with investors. Fed loans to the primary dealers are generally accomplished through repurchase agreements in which the Federal Reserve Bank of New York agrees to temporarily purchase a portion of the dealer's securities for a few days and then sell them back at a price

Table 5-1
Leading U.S., Japanese, and Other Foreign Securities Dealer and Broker Firms Operating in North American Markets

Leading Japanese Dealer and Broker Firms	Leading U.S. Dealer and Broker Firms
Daiwa Securities	Bankers Trust
Fuji Bank	Bear, Stearns
Greenwich Capital Markets (subsidiary of the Long-Term Credit Bank of Japan)	Citicorp
	Dean Witter
	E.F. Hutton
Industrial Bank of Japan International	First Boston Corporation
	First Jersey Securities
Mitsui Bank	Goldman Sachs
Nikko Securities	J.P. Morgan
Nippon Life Insurance	Kidder, Peabody Securities
Nomura Securities	Merrill Lynch
Sumitomo Bank	Morgan Stanley
Yamaichi International Securities	Paine Webber
	Prudential-Bache
	Salomon Brothers
Leading Other Foreign Dealer and Broker Firms	Shearson Lehman Brothers
	Smith Barney
	Wasserstein, Perella (with 20 percent ownership by Nomura Securities)
Amsterdam-Rotterdam Bank	
Banque Nationale de Paris	
Barclays Merchant Bank	
Canadian Imperial Bank of Commerce	
Credit Suisse	
Deutsche Bank	
Lloyds Merchant Bank	
Swiss Bank	
Union Bank, Switzerland	

previously agreed upon. These so-called RPs are an inexpensive way for the primary dealers to raise money, because they are fully collateralized by the securities that are temporarily purchased by the Fed.

Nevertheless, being a primary dealer is not a peaceful and uneventful experience. Trading in government securities is a risky business because securities prices and yields change so rapidly. The dealer that buys government securities from the Fed at what initially looks like a bargain price may find that prices have suddenly fallen and those securities can be resold to customers only at a substantial loss. Unfortunately, no matter how securities prices behave, primary dealers cannot escape their market trading responsibilities. In order to be recognized by the Fed the dealer must agree to "make a market"—that is, stand ready at all times to buy and sell securities with the Federal Reserve. And, unlike a broker that merely matches up buyers and sellers, the dealer takes a position of risk, actually owning a large portfolio of securities out of which sales eventually can be made. Any losses in the market value of the securities held must be borne by the dealer until those securities mature or are purchased by a customer.

Securities dealing and trading is one of the most competitive and volatile occupations in the world. The dealers rely heavily on their ability to "read" trends in the market (including anticipating what the Federal Reserve's next policy move is likely to be) and to react quickly to take advantage of new market developments. Frequently the dealers guess wrong or are driven to the wall by competitors that are concerned solely with profit potential and protecting their own position. Moreover, the dealers typically invest very little of their own (equity) capital in the business, relying on massive amounts of debt (usually financing 95 percent or more of their assets with borrowed funds) to conduct their operations. In addition, the dealers buy many securities on a "when-issued" basis, which means they place orders for new issues without having to put any money down and with payment not due for several days. If prices decline after these "when-issued" commitments are issued, the dealer can be wide open to massive operating losses. Failures are not uncommon. For example, Lombard-Wall and Drysdale Government Securities failed in 1982, followed by the collapse of RID Securities and Lion Capital Group in 1984, and by Bevill, Bresher and Schulmen and E.S.M. Government Securities, which closed during 1985.

While the addition of Nomura, Daiwa, Nikko, and Yamaichi to the primary dealer club was widely heralded as good for the U.S. financial system and especially for the U.S. Treasury, which is struggling constantly to roll over its massive debt, there were several influential groups in and out of Congress that opposed the admission of Nomura and the other Japanese securities firms to the prestigious Fed-recognized dealer group. In 1989 a panel of House-Senate conferees agreed on a bill to ban non-U.S. corporations from becoming primary dealers unless parallel privileges were extended within one year to U.S. financial firms in the underwriting and distribution of securities inside the dealers' home countries. Sponsors of the bill pointed specifically to the restrictions applying to U.S. financial firms operating in Japan. While the late 1980s ushered in several significant Japanese concessions to U.S. banks and securities firms, admitting them to the Tokyo Stock Exchange, for example, and allowing them to trade and underwrite Japanese government securities, the share of these markets held by U.S. firms was both small and growing slowly. The appearance of the primary dealer bill in Congress, therefore, was designed by its sponsors to serve as an imminent warning to the Japanese that they needed to open up their financial system to entry from the outside and to do it quickly.

The threat of retaliation loomed large following the introduction of the new dealer bill. The four Japanese securities dealers seeking primary dealer status pointed to the fact that they were making substantial contributions to the growth of the U.S. government securities market, had conformed to all Federal Reserve regulations, and had entered the U.S. securities business *de novo* rather than by absorbing an existing U.S. company. Moreover, they argued, U.S. banks had already been granted the privilege of operating securities firms in the Tokyo market, while Japanese banks were not granted parallel privileges inside the United States due to the legal barriers between commercial banks and investment banks imposed by the Glass-Steagall Act of 1933. Nevertheless, the controversy surrounding foreign dealer firms operating in the United States continues to bring forth threats of international retaliation.

JAPANESE ENTRY INTO THE U.S. MERGER AND ACQUISITION BUSINESS

In 1989 and 1990 Japanese financial firms, spearheaded by such industry leaders as Fuji Bank, Mitsui Bank, Nikko Securities, Nippon Life Insurance, and Nomura Securities, made aggressive investments in leading U.S. investment banking companies in an effort to quickly become major players in the market for consulting and financing services associated with U.S. corporate mergers and acquisitions. While Japanese merger activity is limited by interlocking directorships and traditional intercorporate relationships, the merger and acquisition business inside the United States and Europe offers a tempting target for Japanese commercial banking and investment banking firms. Key U.S. investment houses, such as Goldman Sachs, Paine Webber, and Shearson Lehman, scored record profits in the mid-1980s as the number of corporate mergers and acquisitions in the United States and Western Europe, several of which involved Japanese firms, soared.

Hoping to gather in a significant share of this business, Sumitomo Bank Ltd. in 1986 purchased just over 12 percent of the equity shares of Goldman Sachs, making a $500 million contribution to that firm's capital. However, the Federal Reserve Board subsequently ruled that Goldman Sachs and Sumitomo could not engage in joint deals, due to restrictions imposed by the Glass-Steagall and Bank Holding Company Acts prohibiting commercial banks from participating in the underwriting of "ineligible" securities (mainly corporate bonds and stocks) inside the United States. The following year Nippon Life Insurance purchased 13 percent of the convertible preferred stock of Shearson Lehman for more than $530 million. Unfortunately for Nippon Life, the market value of Shearson Lehman's shares soon plunged in value, though Nippon Life appeared to gain significantly from the knowledge gained by its staff concerning U.S. financial practices and from the market contacts the company soon developed.

In 1988 Nomura Securities moved to establish a relationship with the U.S. securities firm of Wasserstein, Perella and Company, investing $100 million for a one-fifth equity share. Though their joint venture still accounts for only a relatively small share of all merger financing activity inside Japan and the United States, Wasserstein, Perella expanded rapidly in the merger and acquisition market, becoming one of the leading deal-makers as the 1980s drew to a close. Shortly thereafter Nikko Securities carried out a $100 million purchase of 20 percent of the equity shares of the Blackstone Group. Blackstone arranged the acquisition of CBS Records and Columbia Pictures by Sony Corporation and set out as one of its principal corporate objectives attracting Japanese investors into the U.S. business acquisitions market (as noted by David Lake [1990]). Not to be outdone, Mitsui Bank made a $25 million capital contribution to a fund under management by Washington D.C.'s Carlyle Group to strengthen its U.S. investment banking operations, and Yasuda Mutual Life acquired 18 percent of the voting shares of Paine Webber.

Japanese banks and securities dealers soon became major participants in financing corporate takeovers through leveraged buyouts, taking part in such important debt-financed acquisitions as RJR Nabisco, Time Warner, Inc., and United Airlines. While U.S.–owned firms still dominate securities trading and underwriting operations inside the United States and are among the leaders in global trading and underwriting, the Japanese have successfully made the transition from largely insular securities dealers to global heavyweights, fully capable of challenging leading U.S. and British securities firms on their home turf in New York and London. One important factor that many Japanese dealers benefit from is that Japan's leading industrial firms (such as Toshiba, Toyota, and Tokyo Electric Power Company) are generally cash-rich relative to Western industrial companies and, thus, have ample funds to invest abroad to open up new markets and expand their production capacity.

It is easy to forget, with all the publicity surrounding Japanese takeover activity in the United States, that until 1990 the Japanese were in *second place* to the British in both the number of U.S. merger transactions and the dollar value of U.S. mergers. (Moreover the French passed both the British and the Japanese as acquirers of U.S. companies when all the figures were in for 1990.) Of course, what helped significantly to bring about such a shift in relative importance was a decision by British firms to sharply scale back their acquisitions beginning in 1989 after their mergers had reached a record level in 1988 when the value of Britain's U.S. acquisitions totaled just over $30 billion and the number of their U.S. mergers approached 400. By comparison, in 1988 the Japanese recorded fewer than 150 U.S. business acquisitions. In 1990, when the Japanese passed the British in U.S. takeovers, Japanese companies recorded almost 180 acquisitions of U.S. industrial firms and financial institutions, while the British total of acquired U.S. firms fell just short of 170 industrial and financial mergers.

Most experts expect a continued slowing of such acquisitions, even among Japanese firms. In fact, Japanese acquisitions of U.S. firms declined in dollar terms (by about 15 percent) in 1990. Moreover, had it not been for the $6-billion acquisition of MCA Inc. in 1990 by Matsushita Electric Industrial

Company, the decrease in U.S. merger activity by Japanese companies would have been on a par with Britain's retreat from U.S. merger markets. Moreover, there is evidence of a movement among Japanese acquirers toward smaller U.S. firms, toward more cooperative arrangements with American firms rather than exclusive ownership and control, and toward an evolutionary approach to U.S. corporate expansion in which the Japanese may begin with trade agreements or licensing arrangements involving American firms and only later move toward partial equity or corporate control. In addition, the Japanese try to avoid hostile takeovers in large part due to their sensitivity to American opinion and because it clashes with many Japanese business traditions. Still, Japan's nearly $12 billion total of U.S. mergers and acquisitions in 1990 exceeded American acquisitions of Japanese firms by a ratio of about three to one.

JAPANESE SECURITIES FIRMS VENTURE INTO PROGRAM TRADING

The development of stock-index futures contracts in the early 1980s spawned a revolution in the U.S. capital market that continues to attract strong interest from foreign investors, particularly the Japanese. These index futures contracts call for delivery of the cash value of a basket of specific stocks on a specific future date for an agreed-upon price. The first of these innovative financial instruments made their appearance in February 1982 when the Kansas City Board of Trade launched formal trading in the Value Line Stock Index, which reflected the market values of some 1700 U.S. stocks. By April 1982 the Chicago Mercantile Exchange (CME) opened trading among its member firms for Standard & Poor's (S&P) 500 Stock-Index contracts. The next month the New York Futures Exchange, affiliated with the New York Stock Exchange, began offering Composite Stock Index shares based on the average value of all stocks traded on the New York Stock Exchange. All of these original contracts and similar futures contracts that have been developed subsequently share a common feature that forms the basis of their attractiveness to investors—they grant the buyer access to stock market and bond market "action" without having to purchase individual stocks, and provide a vehicle for hedging an investment position and locking in a desirable yield for the investor. As the prices of the underlying stocks rise or fall, the market value of the futures contracts usually move by an even larger amount. Generally, investors who *buy* stock-index futures expect rising stock prices, while investors who *sell* stock-index futures do so because they believe stock prices eventually will fall.

The rapid growth of stock-index trading inside the United States soon spawned a significant technical innovation in the form of *program trading*. Investors armed with sufficient computer facilities and software could profit from the discrepancies that inevitably appear between the market price of a stock-index futures contract and the current market value of the group of stocks upon which the index contract is based. The mechanism at work here is easy to follow. Suppose, for example, that the market value of the stock-index futures contract rises higher than the current market value of the stocks encompassed in that index itself. Moreover, assume the index futures contract keeps on rising in value until the surplus value of the index cones to exceed the contract's carrying cost. Alert traders will quickly detect the chance for a quick profit from buying the stocks represented in the index, while simultaneously selling index futures contracts. Because of intense competition and excellent communications on the U.S. securities and futures exchanges, such discrepancies will not last long, however. Program traders know that stock prices will soon move upward and that futures contract prices will spiral downward until the discrepancy between futures and stock values is eliminated. When this happens the program trader who bought stocks long and sold index futures contracts short will gain from both ends of this transaction, due to the higher value of the stocks held long and the lower cost of buying futures contracts to fulfill the trader's previous commitment to deliver (sell) them to another investor.[2]

Consistent use of program trading rules can earn a knowledgeable investor a higher average return than is achievable, for example, by buying and holding government bonds. Of course, such trading may result in more volatile stock and bond prices. However, there is evidence that program trading and similar forms of stock and bond index arbitrage have improved the liquidity of many stocks and bonds and also the futures contracts based on these financial instruments.

The potential benefits of program trading were not lost on Japanese securities traders. In March 1990 Nomura Securities announced the start of a program trading system intended ultimately to link financial markets nationwide and to challenge the supremacy of such leaders in the art of program trading as Goldman Sachs, Morgan Stanley, and Salomon Brothers. Aware of its need to learn more about the inner workings of program trading, Nomura chose to direct its initial program trading venture through its New York subsidiary. Nomura's announcement was especially startling to many capital market investors because program trading had been cited widely in Japan as a contributing factor in the Tokyo Exchange's rapid decline in the fall of 1987 and again early in 1990.

Nevertheless, Nomura announced it would carry on simultaneous trading in large groups of stocks, futures, and options for its preferred customers, but with the added feature of including international stocks, not just U.S.-issued equities. Among other objectives, Nomura hoped to be able to recapture a portion of program trading in the Tokyo market, which is dominated by such leading U.S. firms as Morgan Stanley, Salomon Brothers, and Goldman Sachs. Nomura's huge size—the largest securities firm in the world with equity capital of close to $12 billion and well over $500 billion in managed funds—is expected to have a major impact on both stock and futures trading in New York, Tokyo, and London in the future.

This daring move by Nomura is typical of that firm's innovative spirit and is representative as well of the aggressive acceptance of a challenge by most Japanese financial firms that have come to U.S. shores in recent years. Nomura registered a further impact on U.S. credit markets when its U.S. subsidiary announced its involvement in negotiations to purchase approximately $1 billion in troubled S&L commercial loans with the Resolution Trust Corporation (RTC), the federal agency charged by the U.S. Congress to liquidate the assets of failed savings and loan associations. If followed through, such a purchase would make this leading Japanese securities firm a major player in helping the U.S. government resolve the savings and loan crisis. Prior to Nomura's announcement, the RTC had already contracted with Greenwich Capital Markets, a corporate subsidiary of the Long-Term Credit Bank of Japan, to manage its junk bond portfolio. Only five months prior to the RTC announcement of negotiations with Nomura, the latter had functioned as a principal dealer in the repackaging and sale in Western Europe of about $1 billion of loans originally made by several U.S. banks. These transactions seem to reflect a determined effort by Japan's leading financial firm to forge closer working relationships with U.S. banks in both domestic and foreign markets.

ALLIANCES BETWEEN JAPANESE AND U.S. FINANCIAL FIRMS FOR ENTRY INTO JAPAN'S DOMESTIC MARKETS

Not all recent alliances between Japanese and U.S. securities firms represent entry by Japanese financial institutions into the United States. Some recent joint ventures have gone the other way, particularly where goods and services needed in Japan have yet to spawn aggressive and capable Japanese suppliers. A good example is the recent announcement of a joint venture between Mitsubishi Trust and Banking Corp., Japan's largest trust bank, and Chicago Research and Trading Group, Ltd. Among the principal services to arise out of this collaborative venture are currency trades on the major exchanges and the development and sale of risk-hedging instruments, particularly financial futures and options. The new agreement gives this Chicago trading firm not only increased access to financial markets inside Japan with the aid of Japanese capital, but also a link with Mitsubishi's large list of clientele.

Even more famous in this regard was the acquisition by T. Boone Pickens (of Mesa Petroleum Company) of a 20 percent interest in Kyoto Manufacturing Ltd. The estimated purchase price reportedly was close to $840 million. In the following weeks this purchase was further augmented when a small portion of Kyoto's voting shares were acquired and Mr. Pickens requested a seat on the company's board—a request that was subsequently denied, apparently out of concern about Mesa Petroleum's previous track record in buying and selling the stock of other U.S. companies.

Still, the progress of most foreign securities traders inside Japan has been quite slow compared to their counterparts in the United States. Regulatory barriers in Japan and recent fluctuations in Japanese stock and bond prices have discouraged many investors from making more aggressive moves to trade in Japanese securities. Moreover, not all Japanese purchases of U.S. securities firms reflect investment strategies designed to secure a controlling interest in U.S. companies. An apparently growing portion of recent activity has been of the portfolio investment variety—purchases of bonds and equity securities, often to secure only a minority ownership position.

For example, while the financial press was focusing during 1990 on the acquisition of a controlling interest in National Steel Corporation for $294 million by NKK Corporation and Mitsubishi's controlling acquisition of Aristech Corp. for close to $870 million, the minority investment positions taken by Nippon Life Insurance in American Express Company for about $500 million and Mitsui's fractional $150 million investment in Unisyo Corporation, also early in 1990, were overlooked. Recently an estimated two-fifths of Japanese portfolio investment in the United States has been to secure minority holdings in U.S. businesses. One reason for this trend may be recent advisories from the Ministry of Finance and the Bank of Japan to avoid high-profile U.S. takeovers. Another reason is to help cement partnerships between Japanese companies and selected U.S. firms in developing new products and in gaining access to new technologies. And finally, many of the U.S. firms attracting such minority investments have simply been well-managed companies whose track records hold the promise of solid investment returns.

JAPANESE FINANCIAL FIRMS PURCHASING SEATS ON U.S. SECURITIES EXCHANGES

Beginning in the mid-1980s, Japanese securities firms began making a strong push to gain seats on major U.S. securities exchanges. The most important targets, to the general surprise of market analysts, were the key U.S. financial futures exchanges—the Chicago Board of Trade (CBOT) and the Chicago Mercantile Exchange (CME). Japanese traders soon began to account for a rapidly growing share of trading volume on both of these exchanges.

Another surprise to many analysts has been the conservatism of most futures trading by leading Japanese securities firms. Most of the Japanese trading volume appears to be centered around interest-rate hedging strategies to protect prior purchases of U.S. Treasury and federal agency securities acquired by Japanese institutions and individuals. As they have expanded their positions in government notes and bonds, Japanese investors and their brokers have moved to protect the value of those investments by buying closely related futures contracts so that changes in interest rates will not severely damage the anticipated yields on those notes and bonds. Surprisingly little Japanese trading activity in financial futures appears to have focused on futures contracts related to purchases of corporate stocks and bonds. There is also little evidence of short-term speculative trading by the Japanese.

By and large, Japanese securities traders tend to be longer-term investors in U.S. markets, focusing on longer-range objectives and less inclined toward rapid portfolio switching. As we saw earlier, though stronger efforts are underway to promote program trading and aggressive interest rate arbitrage activity, the volume of this activity remains quite small among Japanese dealers and investors relative to the volume of more conservative trading in high-quality U.S. bonds and notes.

The relatively conservative mix of trading activity by foreign securities dealers in the United States was confirmed recently by SEC economists Robert Nachtmann and Fred Phillips-Patrick (1990), who found that the equity capital-to-asset ratios of foreign securities dealers represented in the U.S. were only about 60 percent of the average equity capital ratio for U.S. dealer firms. Because securities firms' capitalization is primarily market driven and is not determined principally by regulation, the lower capital ratios of foreign dealerships suggest that these firms are viewed as having operations and portfolios bearing lower risk than is generally true of U.S. dealer operations. One reason may be the greater average size of foreign dealers, which, Nachtmann and Phillips-Patrick found, held average assets of close to $1.2 billion (representing just over one-fifth of total U.S. dealer assets), compared to an overall industry average of less that $100 million in total assets. Moreover, these economists found that foreign securities dealers with a U.S. presence tended to underwrite larger securities issues than the average domestic dealer firms, operate with greater efficiency, and charge lower underwriting fees inside the United States. This provides an important clue as to why foreign securities firms have captured a growing share of securities trading from domestic U.S. firms (approaching one-fifth of the total U.S. market and over one-quarter of stock underwriting). On a global basis, however, U.S. securities firms (with an average worldwide share of just over 50 percent) appear to have held their market position very well and even increased it in some instances.

FORAYS BY JAPANESE BANKS INTO UNDERWRITING AND DEALING IN U.S. GOVERNMENT AND PRIVATE SECURITIES

One of the most dynamic areas of Japanese involvement in U.S. securities markets today centers around the attempt by leading Japanese banks to engage in underwriting and dealing in bonds, notes, and equity shares inside

Table 5-2

Proportion of all U.S. Loans for Purchasing or Carrying Securities Accounted for by U.S. Banks and U.S. Offices of Foreign Banks

Name of Country	Year-End Data Expressed as a Percentage of All Loans for Purchasing and Carrying Securities Extended by U.S. Chartered Banks and by Foreign Banks with U.S. Offices:								
	1980	1981	1982	1983	1984	1985	1986	1987	1988
Japan	2.07	2.70	1.88	3.95	4.38	9.58	22.30	17.37	19.85
Saudi Arabia	5.50	7.04	5.46	3.76	4.02	3.74	5.19	5.80	3.41
Canada	1.36	1.96	1.77	2.75	3.62	3.66	3.77	3.18	2.11
Hong Kong	1.68	2.36	1.88	1.64	3.18	2.62	3.35	1.38	1.15
France	2.25	1.81	1.79	1.53	1.79	1.78	1.62	1.12	NA
Italy	0.23	0.09	0.22	0.30	0.08	5.09	5.70	3.89	1.56
The Netherlands	1.14	0.95	0.37	0.50	0.63	0.72	1.32	0.49	1.61
Spain	0.03	0.03	0.11	0.13	0.05	0.04	0.35	0.55	0.32
Switzerland	0.01	0.06	0.03	0.87	2.91	7.29	4.77	6.03	0.16
United Kingdom	1.51	2.15	1.79	2.39	2.55	3.17	4.05	3.78	2.88

Source: IBA Reports of Condition Tapes Supplied by the Board of Governors of the Federal Reserve System through the National Technical Information Service.

the United States. Certainly the Japanese have proven to be highly successful bank lenders for their customers who wish to purchase U.S. securities. As Table 5-2 indicates, Japanese bank shares of all securities loans made by banks operating in the United States have grown rapidly, rising from only about 2 percent of all such loans in 1980 to nearly 20 percent in 1988. However, current U.S. law (specifically, the Bank Holding Company Act) requires foreign and domestic banking firms to seek Federal Reserve Board approval before engaging in securities *underwriting* inside the United States.

In the spring of 1990 the Long-Term Credit Bank of Japan applied to the Federal Reserve Board to underwrite and deal in municipal revenue bonds, residential mortgage–related securities, commercial paper, and consumer receivables–related securities, as well as to act as a futures commission merchant and dealer in gold and silver bullion and coins through its U.S. subsidiary, Greenwich Capital Markets, Inc. The Board approved this application on May 29, 1990, subject to the limitation that no more than 10 percent of the gross revenue of the bank's capital market subsidiary could be derived from underwriting and dealing in the securities approved.[3] The Federal Reserve Board expressed concern in this case that the Japanese bank's capital did not meet U.S. bank capital adequacy requirements, but considered the capital position of the applicant to be approximately comparable to minimum standards for U.S. banks after adjustment for Japanese banking and accounting practices. The Board expressed the belief that competition would be enhanced in the domestic market for these services if the Japanese were allowed to enter.[4]

Similar powers were requested by Sanwa Bank, the fifth largest bank in the world, and were approved by the Federal Reserve Board on May 2, 1990, subject to similar restrictions as those placed on the Long-Term Credit Bank. A few days after the Sanwa approval, Mitsui Taiyo Kobe Bank, the world's second largest banking organization, received permission to acquire up to 10 percent of the common stock of Security Pacific Financial Services System, Inc. of San Diego and of SPFs, which are both wholly owned subsidiaries of Security Pacific Corporation of Los Angeles. These firms make, acquire, and service loans, offer credit life insurance, lease personal and real property, provide collection services, and supply data processing and data transmission services.

Mitsui, too, fell below the minimum bank capital requirements of the Federal Reserve Board. However, in these instances the Board indicated that it would adhere to its longstanding policy of not second-guessing foreign governments' regulatory standards and would grant foreign banks service powers where their home countries do not deny those same powers to U.S. banks operating abroad. In this instance the Federal Reserve Board faced strong protests from the domestic insurance industry, represented by the Independent Insurance Agents of America, the National Association of Life Underwriters, and the National Association of Professional Insurance Agents, but dismissed this opposition on the ground that Security Pacific's and Mitsui's insurance activities, both those conducted in the past and those proposed for the future, did not appear to violate federal law (specifically the Garn-St. German Depository Institutions Act).

On May 21, 1990, the Fed voted approval for the acquisition by the Bank of Tokyo of certain lease servicing assets (including software and equipment) from the Bank of New England in Boston and to engage in making, acquiring, and servicing loans, providing investment and financial advice, leasing real and personal property, and supplying data processing services. Once again, the Federal Reserve Board found that the applicant's ratio of primary capital to assets was below the minimum standard required by U.S. regulations. It noted, however, that after making adjustments to reflect Japanese banking and accounting practices . . . including consideration of a portion of the unrealized appreciation in applicant's portfolio of equity securities consistent with the principles of the Basle capital framework, applicant's capital ratio meets United States' standards (Federal Reserve Board, May 2, 1990: p. 3).[5]

This application was given an important boost toward approval by the Comptroller of the Currency due to the serious financial problems then faced by the Bank of New England.

Later, on July 30, 1990, the Board approved the request of Tokyo's Fuji Bank—the world's third largest bank—to expand the activities of its wholly owned subsidiary, Fuji Capital Markets Corporation of New York, to enter *de novo* into serving as originator and principal for interest-rate and currency swap transactions and selling other risk management products such as interest-rate caps, options on swaps, and interest-rate floors and collars. The bank also requested approval to serve as a U.S. broker and agent for risk management instruments and to serve as an advisor to institutional customers regarding their risk management strategies. Fuji had to pledge to fully cover its own risk exposure from each swap transaction and monitor that exposure on a continuing basis. Once again, the Federal Reserve Board cautioned that "it expects foreign banks to meet the same general standards of strength, experience, and reputation as domestic banking organizations, and to be able to serve as a source of strength to their banking operations in the United States."[6] The Board was forced to adjust Fuji's capital figures for Japanese accounting conventions to find sufficient capital strength to approve this application and prevent strong criticism from the competing financial institutions inside the United States.

THE PROBABLE FUTURE SLOWING OF JAPANESE EXPANSION INTO U.S. SECURITIES MARKETS

Many economists and securities analysts expect a slowing in the expansion of Japanese securities trading activities in the United States in the period ahead. There are several reasons for this. One centers on the emergence of increasing inflationary pressures inside Japan. The political crisis in Iraq and Kuwait has added significantly to rising prices inside Japan due to recent dramatic increases in world oil prices, as Japan must import the bulk of its petroleum supply to fuel its factories and heat Japanese homes.

A second factor that may slow the expansion of Japanese securities operations in the United States is the recent gradual decline in Japan's huge merchandise trade surplus. Japan's trade surplus of goods and services sold abroad over imports received from abroad reached a monthly postwar record of $10 billion as 1989 opened, but by the end of that year had fallen to about $3.8 billion per month. The principal reason was the rapid growth in imports of household goods and services as Japan's consumers became more aware of the growing availability of foreign-manufactured products. Moreover, the Japanese have begun to travel more extensively, particularly in the United States and Western Europe. The net result of all of these trends has been a significant decline in Japan's current account surplus with the rest of the world. For example, according to the Bank of Japan, Japan's current account position swung from a surplus of $87 billion in 1987 to only $57 billion in 1989, with a drop to $39 billion recorded in the final quarter of 1989 alone. Almost simultaneously, the deficit in the current account of the United States declined by approximately the same amount.

For most of the 1980s, Japan's expansion into U.S. securities markets was fueled by powerful forces reshaping property values inside Japan relative to the rest of the world. Prices of real property on Japanese soil rose to heights of almost fourfold above the value of comparable U.S. real estate, spurred on by rapid internal economic growth and trade barriers that served to shelter transactions taking place inside Japan from global economic forces. The result was a massive overflow of Japanese portfolio investment into purchases of foreign securities and direct investments in foreign production and distribution facilities, as Japanese institutional and individual investors found what appeared to be real bargains abroad compared to property values inside Japan. Not surprisingly, the prices of commercial and residential space overseas, particularly in London, New York, Los Angeles, and San Francisco, soon rose as well. The result, predictably, was an eventual erosion of the huge value gap that motivated much of the earlier Japanese overseas investment. Moreover, the recent decline in Japan's total trade surplus will give Japan less capital to spend abroad, making it difficult for the Japanese to continue the record pace of their earlier overseas investment activity.

Still another factor supporting the likelihood of a future pullback or at least a slowing in Japan's securities operations in the United States is the gradual liberalization of Japanese securities laws. As we noted at the outset of this chapter, it was not until the 1980s that restrictive regulations on corporate borrowing inside Japan were gradually throttled back, substantially augmenting the financing vehicles Japanese companies could employ. Passage of the Foreign Exchange Reform Law in 1980 allowed Japanese firms to issue bonds abroad without first obtaining the government's permission. A year later warrant bonds were legalized, and the accompanying option to purchase equity shares was made detachable at the end of 1985. Two years earlier (in 1983) the Japanese government lifted its requirement that all bonds issued by Japanese companies had to be fully secured by those companies' assets and authorized the issuance of noncollateralized bonds with government approval. The result, as Hoshi, Kashyap, and Scharfstein (1989) note, has been a profound change in business sector fund-raising, with bank loans significantly declining as a source of corporate funding and the issuance of debt and equity securities inside Japan sharply on the upswing. By the middle of the 1980s, bonds and stocks issued inside Japan had pushed close to 40 percent of all capital raised, compared to less than 15 percent at the beginning of the decade.

Moreover, as the 1990s began, a controversy over public policy involving the Bank of Japan and the Ministry of Finance—the two key government agencies responsible for Japanese economic policy—was emerging. These two powerful policy-making agencies recently have aired their differences in public over the relative merits of controlling inflation through higher interest rates and other credit-tightening moves, versus continuing stimulation of the Japanese economy and stock market. Japanese financial markets prior to the 1990s faced relatively low rates of price inflation compared to other leading industrialized nations, relatively modest costs of capital, a rising value for the yen in international markets, large balance-of-trade surpluses with the United States and the rest of the world, and relatively low prices for imported energy fuels. However, most of these strong propelling factors for the Japanese economy have recently weakened. Moreover, in the second half of 1990 Japan's leading securities firms reported historic declines in liquid reserves and in net profits, as both Japanese stock values and broker commissions fell precipitously.

Ultimately, these developments should weaken Japanese securities trading activity inside the United States. One offsetting and strongly positive factor is the expected continuation of rapid growth in other leading countries that make up the Pacific Basin region, especially Australia, Hong Kong, Indonesia, Korea, Malaysia, New Zealand, the Philippines, Singapore, Taiwan, and Thailand. Regional integration within the Pacific Basin is underway, with intraregional trade now growing in unprecedented volume, supported by massive injections of capital investment and economic aid from Japan. This large-scale investment in regional economic development by the Japanese should begin to provide even larger markets for Japanese products and services in the ensuing decade.[7]

While Japanese banks, securities dealers and insurance firms are likely to play a key role in the future growth of the U.S. financial services sector, it would be a gross exaggeration to place responsibility on Japan for any adverse trends or financial problems of U.S. financial companies. Indeed, there are powerful forces at work inside the United States that suggest a future slowing in the financial services industry. One is the slowing U.S. economy, which should generate both less-rapid growth of savings and reduced demands for credit. Moreover, domestic banks, thrifts, insurance companies, mutual funds, and securities dealers are invading each other's service areas. In the mutual fund industry, for example, banks, savings and loans, insurance companies, and securities brokers and dealers are threatening intensified competition for the U.S. consumer's savings dollar through the offering of mutual fund investment products and cash management programs for both businesses and households. What growth does occur in the financial services sector is likely to center around common stock investments, due to growing public interest in retirement plans as the population ages and the cost of education that continues to rise for households with children in the family.

CHANGING JAPANESE INVESTMENTS
IN U.S. REAL ESTATE

As we saw in chapter 1, the 1980s ushered in a buying spree in U.S. real estate as Japanese banks, insurance companies, pension funds, manufacturers, and suppliers as well as individual investors bought large quantities of commercial office and warehouse space, residential properties, and farm and ranchland. Prominent examples include Rockefeller Center and the ABC headquarters, both in New York City. What is often forgotten, however, is that foreign investors currently own only about 1 percent of all U.S. farmland and less than 10 percent of the assets of U.S. manufacturing firms. They also represent less than 3 percent of all U.S. employment.

However, the plunging Japanese stock market coupled with a slowing in Japanese trade surpluses in 1990 ushered in a new trend in U.S. real property investments by the Japanese. The basic elements of this new trend appear to be:

1. Direct offerings and sales of U.S. properties previously acquired by the Japanese
2. Refinancing of previous U.S. real estate purchases in order to lower debt service costs and free up cash for other investment needs and operating expenses
3. Property syndications that bring other parties and their capital into the financing of U.S. real estate investments and, therefore, liberate capital for investments in other markets.

To date, the primary Japanese sellers appear to be investors with relatively short time horizons (such as real estate brokers) or those funded with relatively short-term loans (such as property acquisitions supported with loans from commercial banks). Where long-term investors are involved, however, especially Japanese pension funds and insurance companies, these investor groups tend to have longer planning horizons and tend to hold for long-term returns.

Indeed, the expansion of Japanese real estate investment in the United States may have already reached its peak growth rate and is likely to proceed more gradually for the foreseeable future. In 1988 U.S. real estate investment by the Japanese reached almost $17 billion and it has been less than that every year since 1988, totaling about $13 billion in 1990. U.S. regions that had drawn intensive Japanese investment interest during the 1980s— the Northeast, the South, and the West—weakened substantially in the first recession of the 1990s, especially in the commercial real estate sector. Moreover, problems plaguing Japan's domestic real estate market prompted the Ministry of Finance and the Bank of Japan to take countermeasures as the 1990s began, one of which was to restrain real estate lending by Japanese banks. In Japan, as in the United States, commercial banks are at the center of the flow of credit into real estate. With Japanese banks less willing to lend under the informal guidance of Japan's regulatory community, some cutback in both domestic and foreign real-estate purchases by the Japanese was almost inevitable.

Another interesting development that was hidden in the general trend of Japan's real estate acquisitions inside U.S. shares has centered upon *property* and *geographic diversification.* The Japanese have moved toward a significant broadening out of their real estate purchases. Today they hold commercial or residential properties or both in a majority of states (now approaching 40 different states and all U.S. geographic regions). Initial Japanese property purchases were heavily concentrated along the East and West Coasts, especially California, New York, New Jersey, Oregon, Washington, and Hawaii. However, recently, Japanese real-estate buyers have shown a surge of interest in the Rocky Mountain States (most notably, Montana with its abundant agricultural and mineral resources), in the South (especially Georgia, Florida, and North Carolina), and in the Midwest and Southwest (where attractive real estate prices have been very much in evidence). Moreover, they have moved toward smaller properties, larger in number but lower in price. This compositional change reflects more emphasis upon ranch and resort properties and property development projects and less eagerness to acquire highly visible commercial properties in U.S. financial centers (particularly in the New York metropolitan area). Consistent with this last objective, the Japanese in the latest period appear to have shifted more of their real-property acquisitions back toward the West Coast of the United States.

The causes of this fundamental change in the magnitude and direction of Japanese real estate investment inside the United States are many. Among the most important are falling stock values in Japan, which have made it more difficult to acquire and retain investments overseas as well as to make domestic acquisitions. In addition, recent increases in market interest rates inside Japan have substantially closed the gap with U.S. interest rates, negating much of the previously favorable situation when Japanese real restate investors could borrow short-term funds inside Japan at short-term rates well below U.S. interest rates and invest in U.S. properties with substantially elevated expected yields. Moreover, as we noted earlier, decreasing Japanese trade surpluses have resulted in Japanese individuals and institutions recently accumulating fewer U.S. dollar claims to invest in U.S. properties. At the same time, the decreasing value of Japanese securities and property pledged as collateral to buy U.S. property has forced some Japanese lenders to call in their loans. In turn, this has forced the sale of some U.S. property previously purchased on credit.

Moreover, new international bank capital standards have encouraged both Japanese and U.S. banks making real estate loans to either reduce the size of their commitment to the real estate sector or to demand more collateral behind those real estate loans remaining in force. Finally, and by no means least important, is the recent appearance of attractive real estate investment opportunities in other regions of the world, especially Hong Kong, Singapore, China, and Southeast Asia, and in portions of Western and Eastern Europe.

Nevertheless, we must keep in mind that Japan's real estate market is unlike any other real estate market in the world. Japanese real estate purchases give their owners little or no liquidity; there are few subsequent sales. The reason is that Japanese real property buyers face an extraordinarily high capital gains tax that usually causes them to use their real estate acquisitions as collateral for borrowings to meet other cash needs rather than selling out. Thus, we are more likely to see a slowing in Japanese real estate investment in the future if global interest rates rise or if Japan's trade surplus weakens further, rather than a massive sell-off of foreign and domestic real estate holdings by Japanese investors.

THE LIKELY RESULTS IF JAPANESE INVESTORS CUT BACK OR WITHDRAW THEIR INVESTMENTS IN U.S. SECURITIES AND REAL PROPERTY

The Tokyo stock market debacle in 1990, when share prices on the Tokyo exchange declined by close to 40 percent, and the scattered signs of a developing U.S. recession raised a key issue among U.S. policymakers and investors: will Japanese investors cut back or withdraw their funds from U.S. domestic markets due to economic problems at home, recession in the United States, or simply because of more attractive investment options elsewhere? Implicit in such a question was a not-well-concealed fear that any significant slowing in Japanese investments inside the U.S. could lead to highly damaging effects on the U.S. economy because of sharply rising U.S. interest rates and falling securities prices and property values. A counterargument has emerged that economic pressures inside Japan may, in fact, lead to an acceleration of Japanese investments in U.S. markets as Japan's investment community seeks a safer haven for its funds. Moreover, there is evidence that Japanese firms with U.S. investments tend to adopt substantially longer time horizons for their investment planning than most U.S. investors, particularly among major institutional investors.

Most frequently Japanese investments are recorded at cost—an accounting practice followed widely by U.S. firms as well—and short-term losses due to fluctuations in market price usually are not recorded. Instead, securities trading losses generally will only be recognized when those securities mature or are sold. Moreover, market declines are often looked upon positively by Japanese investors as opportunities to lock in relatively cheap prices and, therefore, to preserve higher total returns over long holding periods. Of special concern, however, is the behavior of the largest Japanese financial institutions that make relatively short-term investments, particularly the city and regional banks and securities brokers and dealers. This concern usually surfaces with special intensity at the beginning of the second quarter of each year, when many of Japan's leading institutional investors plan their investment strategies for the new fiscal year, which typically begins for them on or about April of each calendar year.

Historically, the United States has attracted the largest share of Japan's foreign securities purchases, due to the tremendous size of the common market formed by the 50 states, the superior stability of the U.S. economy and political system, and the enormous volume of trading in most U.S. stocks, bonds, and notes, which gives them superior liquidity (in case emergency cash is needed) than possessed by most securities traded abroad. Added to this is the international recognizability and financial strength of major U.S. corporations, and the continuing need for U.S. dollars to fund international purchases of commodities and services. However, a number of changes along these various dimensions of U.S. investment may be anticipated. For one thing, the need for a more diversified portfolio may dictate increased investments in Western and Eastern Europe (especially following German unification) and in other areas around the Pacific Rim. Some Japanese investment companies, banks, and securities companies appear to have become top-heavy with investments in U.S. securities and real estate. Their need for rebalancing their investment portfolios, especially if the U.S. economy enters a recession, with a substantial representation in other global markets should become more evident in the 1990s and beyond.

An added factor contributing to the probable future need for some Japanese repositioning of U.S. investments is the strength of selected other foreign currencies, particularly the deutsche mark. Financial managers at leading Japanese banks, insurance companies, and pension and trust firms have expressed growing interest in investments in West Germany to take advantage of expected economic gains following German unification. Moreover, the corporate mergers and acquisitions market, which grew rapidly in the United States during most of the 1970s and 1980s, has been rapidly declining in the 1990s. In Japan, however, mergers and acquisitions appear to be on the rise. During the first nine months of 1990, for example, more than 500 Japanese businesses launched acquisition programs. Moreover, almost three-fifths of these acquisitions involved Japanese firms reaching abroad for new assets. With more merger and acquisition activity originating from Japan, U.S. investment banking firms and securities traders may experience slackening demand.

However, not all the market signals point toward reduced Japanese investments in the United States and expanded Japanese investment spending in

European and Pacific markets. One problem with such an investment strategy is the limited size of many foreign markets, particularly the French and German capital markets in which large-scale Japanese investment purchases and sell-offs could have substantial effects on market prices, locking in Japanese investors to some European securities that they could not readily dispose of without absorbing substantial losses. Moreover, the Japanese response to rapid share price erosion in the Tokyo stock market during the spring of 1990 indicated that European financial markets may be one of the first areas to experience a pullback in Japanese investment if significant problems are encountered in other market areas, such as in the United States.

One example of such a pullback may already be surfacing among Japanese securities dealers operating in the Eurocurrency markets. Taking over from U.S. firms that led in Euromarket trading in the early 1980s, Japanese securities firms, led by Nomura, Yamaichi, Daiwa, and Nikko, recently came to dominate Euromarket trading. Nomura, for example, climbed to the leading position among Euromarket underwriters, followed distantly by Daiwa and Nikko Securities. The nearest non-Japanese underwriter was Credit Suisse-First Boston Corp. However, by early 1990 Nomura's share had slumped noticeably and was being closely pressed by Deutsche Bank of West Germany, followed by the Union Bank of Switzerland. Nomura's Euromarket underwriting volume dropped by almost half in the first quarter of 1990, while Nikko and Daiwa experienced even steeper declines. A principal reason centered around falling market demand for the warrants issued by Japanese companies after a moratorium was declared by Japanese dealers on further warrant agreements.[8]

Indeed, the pullback of Japanese foreign investments, if it occurs in large volume in the 1990s, is likely to affect all markets around the world, including the United States and Western Europe. As we have discussed in other parts of this book, there is growing evidence of a recent retrenchment by Japanese investors in their holdings of U.S.–issued securities. For example, in April and May of 1990, foreign investors as a whole were net sellers of common stock traded in the United States. U.S. stock sales by foreign investors exceeded U.S. stock purchases by more than $3 billion in those two months. Of course, not all categories of U.S. securities registered net sell-offs among foreign investors. Foreign buyers purchased nearly $600 million in U.S. government obligations and just over $2 billion in U.S.–issued corporate bonds during those same months. The figure for net purchases of U.S. government securities is particularly surprising, however, because it is so anemic. During the comparable period in 1989, purchases of U.S. government securities, net of sales, exceeded $7 billion, while net purchases of U.S. corporate bonds tallied a little less than $3 billion and net stock purchases, just under $1 billion.

This abrupt change in the pattern of foreign purchases of U.S. securities has raised immediate concern over the future course of U.S. stock and bond prices and U.S. interest rates. With the likely upward pressure on market interest rates in these circumstances, it would be both more difficult and more costly for the U.S. government to market its debt and put downward pressure on an already weak U.S. economy that, in the second half of 1990, had already begun to experience slowing consumer and business investment spending as well as rising unemployment.

JAPANESE SECURITY AND REAL ESTATE ACTIVITIES IN THE UNITED STATES—A CONTINUING CENTER OF CONTROVERSY

Regardless of the evidence that Japanese investment in the United States is slowing, Japanese purchases of U.S.–issued securities and acquisitions of highly visible firms, office buildings, shopping centers, and ranch and farm-land continue to arouse a storm of controversy in virtually every region of the United States. Some U.S. observers see it as an unwanted confirmation that the United States is now a debtor nation and that, ultimately, those debts must be paid, draining resources from the United States. Japanese purchases of U.S. government securities are frequently viewed as an undesirable "mortgage on our future" that must be paid for by taxing future generations. Perhaps such investments might also result in handing over control of some of the vital decisions Americans and their government must make to foreign investors.

Foreign purchases of U.S. assets have also been seen by some Americans as painful reminders of the huge trade deficits incurred by the United States in recent years and the apparent lack of competitiveness of U.S.–made goods in foreign markets. Well-publicized acquisitions of U.S. property by foreigners are often catalysts for painful questions about the quality of the U.S. educational system, about whether Americans have lost their sense of direction and vitality, and about the willingness of Americans to take on challenges and work toward better products and a higher standard of living.

But are these truly serious problems that should demand attention on the United States' agenda? Are they legitimate worries that Americans can ill afford to ignore? In the last two chapters of this book we turn to these issues of public policy—first in the banking field and then, in the final chapter, in the broader securities and real estate fields. We explore what recent trends in U.S. and Japanese banking, securities trading, and real estate purchases may mean for the distant future that beckons us forward.

NOTES

1. Interestingly enough, the U.S. stock market ranked first in trading volume among the world's 20 principal equity markets until October 1987, when U.S. stock

prices dropped at a record pace. In contrast, when the Tokyo market plunged sharply in the spring of 1990, the U.S. stock market climbed back to about 34 percent of all equity values outstanding, versus less than 33 percent for Japan.

2. Conversely, suppose stock-index futures contracts have recently declined in value further than the current market value of the stocks making up the index. This situation has great profit potential for those program traders who are willing to buy the recently devalued stock-index futures contracts and simultaneously sell stocks. As stock prices fall due to an increase in sell orders and futures contracts rise in value as demand for them picks up, program trading results in a gain.

3. These restrictions were certainly not unique. Similar restrictions were imposed on Citicorp, J.P. Morgan and Company, Chemical New York Corp., Bankers Trust New York Corporation, Manufacturers Hanover, and Security Pacific Corporation.

4. See Federal Reserve Board, Press Release, Washington, D.C., May 29, 1990, 4.

5. See Federal Reserve Board, Press Release, Washington, D.C., May 2, 1990, 3.

6. See Federal Reserve Board, Press Release, Washington, D.C., July 30, 1990, 7.

7. There is also evidence that the United States has benefitted from the acceleration of trade with the remaining Pacific Rim nations, particularly exports of consumer goods and services and automotive products, though in sales of capital goods the United States appears to have lost market share in Asia, principally to the Japanese. See especially Susan Hickok and James Orr (1989-90).

8. Stock index warrants, linked to the performance of Japan's stock market (particularly the Nikkei 225 stock index), became very popular in Japan as the decade of the 1980s began. In the spring of 1990 interest began to grow among U.S. investors in the seven warrants offered through underwriters, and trading volume in Japanese-linked instruments on the American Stock Exchange, in particular, soured. These warrants promise holders cash payments if stock market performance moves favorably for the investor.

SIX

An Assessment of the Benefits and Costs of Japanese Banking Activities Inside the United States

Japanese banks represent the greatest financial force from abroad operating in U.S. financial service markets today. Yet, we must develop a proper sense of perspective in assessing how important they really are. As we observed in chapter 1, Japan's city banks rank among the world's largest in terms of total assets, whereas by this measure the largest U.S. bank barely makes it into the top 20. However, other measures may be far more relevant than total assets in capturing the real importance of Japanese financial firms within the U.S. and global financial systems. For example, measured by strength of capital (ownership funds), National Westminster and Barclays Bank, both of Great Britain, rank first and second in total equity capitalization, followed by Citicorp in third place. The most capital-rich Japanese bank, Fuji, ranks fourth on this list, though Japanese banks do capture half the list of the 20 banks worldwide holding the most shareholder capital. Moreover, measured by size of bank staff, several leading British and U.S. banks outstrip the largest Japanese banks by a substantial margin.

The principal reason for these differences in ranking between various measures of bank size appears to be the rapid growth of "off-balance-sheet" activities among leading banks. Particularly prominent among these activities are credit guarantees to back customer loans and securities issues and the provision of services that generate fee income, such as securities underwriting and agency functions, but do not result in additional asset bookings. Moreover, leading banks like Morgan Guaranty, Chase Manhattan, and Citicorp are worldwide players in arranging securities issues for their customers, which enhances their stature in worldwide markets but is missed by the most widely used measures of bank size.

Nevertheless, as we have seen in the foregoing chapters, the recorded growth in assets and capital of Japanese banks over the past two decades is truly phenomenal. During the 1984–88 period alone these banks accounted for close to one-half of the increase in all banking assets worldwide, approximately half of all foreign banking activity in the United States, and nearly 40 percent of all foreign banking activity centered in Great Britain. In total, Japanese banking institutions hold about two-fifths of global bank assets and currently have a market value about five times that of all U.S.–owned multinational banks.

AN EMPHASIS ON COMPARATIVE ECONOMIC ADVANTAGE

The rapid expansion of Japanese banks in the United States should not obscure the fact that these financially powerful institutions have primarily focused on those activities in which they have a significant comparative economic advantage. These primary areas of Japanese banking activity in the United States center on the financing of trade with Japan and Southeast Asia and the provision of banking services to Japanese citizens and firms who have moved to the United States and to U.S. citizens of Japanese heritage. Superior knowledge of Japan's culture, business practices, and markets gives Japanese bankers a significant advantage with customers having Japanese backgrounds and with Americans transacting business with Japanese firms and governmental bureaus and agencies. Moreover, much of the expansion of Japan's banks inside the United States has been by acquisition of other foreign banks—most notably, British-owned banks in California.

In a broader context, the increasingly globalized economy in which international trade is growing faster than the U.S. GNP (and, in fact, is growing faster than the world's total output of goods and services) has made it virtually inevitable that more banks will cross national boundaries. Their objective will be to finance an even larger share of global trade and to protect their institutions against the risk of loss from declining domestic economic activity and falling currency prices by employing greater geographic diversification. Nowhere is this foreign bank expansion likely to be greater than in the United States for the foreseeable future. As Alan Greenspan, Chairman of the Federal Reserve Board notes:

Since the U.S. dollar is still the key international currency . . . diversification has been, and may continue to be, disproportionately into assets denominated in the dollar. For the same reason, many foreign financial institutions find it beneficial to be represented by banking offices in this country so that they can play an intermediary role based on dollars. (May 1990:4)

THE IMPACT ON U.S. BANKS

Without question, the rapid growth of Japanese banks inside the United States has resulted in substantial savings for both U.S. and Japanese customers of these banks in the form of lower interest rates on loans and reduced charges for noncredit services, such as cash management and trust services. Moreover, the growing Japanese presence in U.S. markets appears to have resulted in a substantial expansion of the number and range of financial services available to U.S. consumers and, especially, to U.S. businesses.

Unfortunately, we are much less sure about the impact of Japanese bank expansion on U.S. banks. This impact is not easy to assess, for some very sound reasons. In the first place, the great majority of U.S. banks do not compete head-to-head with Japanese banks. Those U.S. banks principally affected by Japanese banking competition are usually labeled *international banks* and *regional money-center banks*—roughly, the 400 U.S. billion-dollar banks that are headquartered in the largest U.S. cities and money centers. These internationally competitive institutions represent scarcely more than 3 percent of the 13,000 commercial banks chartered by U.S. authorities and little more than 2 percent of the 10,000 independent U.S. banking organizations, counting all bank holding companies. Most of these smaller banking firms serve local businesses and households in the thousands of cities, counties, and rural towns that dot the U.S. landscape.

Over the last two decades a cadre of several dozen regional banks has emerged—institutions like NCNB of Charlotte, North Carolina, BancOne of Columbus, Ohio, and First Interstate Banks of Los Angeles—that have expanded within selected groups of states, most of these concentrating their operations mainly on households and businesses within their chosen states and regions. These regional banks have displayed a growing appetite for funding U.S. and foreign corporations that has brought them on a collision course with foreign banks, especially the Japanese. But these regional institutions—despite the fact that they have been among the fastest growing of all U.S. banks in recent years—still hold relatively few foreign assets in their portfolios. Federal Reserve Board Chairman Alan Greenspan (May 1990:6) has estimated that fewer than 5 percent of all the assets held by regional banks in the United States are from foreign sources.

The bulk of international banking activity is, in fact, centered in a handful of the largest U.S. banks. Just ten U.S. bank holding companies account for more than four-fifths of all the overseas assets held by the domestic banking industry, and four of these banking companies hold about 50 percent of all international assets under the control of U.S. banks. Thus, any assessment of the thrust of Japanese banking's impact on the U.S. domestic banking environment must take into account the limited number and range of institutions that are directly confronted by the Japanese.

Another factor that must be carefully weighted is the changing nature of banking services and activities among the largest international banks. As Alan Greenspan (May 1990:7) has observed:

The international role of banks has changed from one of simply extending credit to one of facilitating transactions. Partly for this reason, and partly also to economize on costly equity capital, U.S. banks have tended to cut back on those activities that result in assets that must be booked on a balance sheet. For example, they have chosen to reduce drastically their interbank lending business, which is essentially a high-volume, low-spread business. U.S. banks have devoted their resources instead to banking services that often do not result in assets held by the bank.

It is in this field of assisting customers in securing credit by acting as agent to market their securities in international markets, by the issuance of credit guarantees, and by acting as efficient channels for moving funds and information that U.S. banks today rank at or near the top in global financial markets. Yet, because such activities usually do not result in the booking of assets on the balance sheet, the traditional measures of bank size—total assets or total deposits—can, in today's market, be highly misleading and result in exactly the wrong prescriptions for public policy.

Moreover, the United States has become a world leader in the development of innovative financial instruments, many of which do not show up on traditional bank financial statements. Among the most notable of these in recent years have been risk-hedging instruments, such as interest rate and currency swaps, standby credit letters, options on stocks and debt securities, and financial futures contracts. Citicorp, Morgan Guaranty, Security Pacific, and other leading U.S. banks are major players worldwide in selling or arranging for the acquisition of all of these instruments. However, because these instruments in most cases do not give rise to the booking of bank assets or the posting of deposits, conventional bank financial statements convey a blurred, if not false, image of the relative importance of U.S. and Japanese banks within the global financial system. Moreover, international banks often book loans and deposits in locations other than where they were made or received. For example, the largest U.S. and foreign corporations that borrow from foreign banks in the United States themselves operate around the world and can and do borrow from the same lenders at many different locations all over the world.

A corollary to this reasoning is that mere shifts in the relative sizes of international banks, even substantial changes in their world rankings in terms of total assets or total deposits, do not necessarily imply that U.S. banks are losing ground to foreign banks or are losing their competitive edge. This could be true only if there is a significant size-to-operating-cost relationship in banking—a fact not firmly in evidence from recent research—and if total assets or similar indicators are an accurate barometer of how efficient an individual bank is. The impact of bank size on bank operating efficiency is simply too controversial and too much an unresolved issue today for us to draw any confident conclusions about how efficient the Japanese banks are relative to their competitors.

THE MINIMAL EFFECT OF JAPANESE BANK EXPANSION ON SMALLER U.S. BANKS

Discussions of the impact of Japanese banking operations in the United States usually turn very quickly toward concern over the fate of the smallest banks in the system. The smallest U.S. banks over the past decade have been buffeted by deregulation, which had a particularly significant negative influence on their funding costs as federal deposit interest rate ceilings were lifted, and by regional economic problems, which in some cases were severe enough to undermine the quality of their loan portfolios, bring instability to their earnings flows, and erode their capital. The sudden prominence of Japanese banks and their rapidly broadening beachhead inside key U.S. markets seemed to represent a severe jolt to these institutions at one of the worst times in their history. Dozens of the smallest U.S. banks and hundreds of savings and loan associations failed during the financial debacle of the 1980s and early 1990s. Economists and financial analysts quickly searched around for the basic causes—excessively rapid deregulation of the financial sector, overbuilt real estate markets, government mismanagement of the regulatory process, and even outright fraud among owners and managers.

But were foreign bankers, including the Japanese, to blame in any way? What does existing research evidence suggest about the fate of smaller U.S. banks in the wake of the rapid expansion of foreign banking in the United States, especially by Japanese banks? Is there any evidence of specific damage to the small bank sector of the economy?

Direct evidence on the foregoing questions is severely limited, as we saw in earlier chapters. One of the few formal studies was prepared recently by economist Gary Zimmerman of the Federal Reserve Bank of San Francisco (1990), who examined the performance of "small" (under $100 million in total assets) banks in California.

Certainly if there is damage to the profitability and long-run viability of smaller banks, California is likely to be one of the very best places to look for it. Not only must the smallest California banks compete with some of the most successful U.S. money-center banks for both business and household accounts, but the Japanese have become major players in that state, gaining control of the ten largest California banks and several medium-size state banks as well. Moreover, the Japanese have made their strongest pitch for a share of U.S. retail banking markets—the principal market segment served by the majority of small banks—in California. In this sense the California banking environment, accounting for approximately 10 percent of all bank deposits in the United States, comes close to being an ideal banking market in which to assess the impact of the Japanese on U.S. banking.

Zimmerman's study of 290 small California banks, which represented two-thirds of that state's aggregate banking population, revealed that these banking firms as a whole did *not* suffer a decline in their market shares over the period when the Japanese and other foreign bankers entered. In fact, adjusted for banks moving across asset-size boundaries into larger-size groups, there appeared to be a *gain* in the small bank share of statewide banking assets, even as the ten largest California banks lost some of their former percentage share. Moreover, while small bank profitability, measured by return on assets, weakened in the United States in the middle of the 1980s, profits of small West Coast banks generally moved upward late in the decade to compare favorably with the profit ratios of larger California banks. The smallest California banking institutions as a group apparently were successful at increasing spreads between interest revenues and interest costs, suggesting they were having some success at differentiating their services from those of competitors in the minds of customers. Among the more successful service offerings of smaller U.S. banks have been agricultural credit programs, small business loan and cash management services, lending for small business and residential construction, automobile loans, and consumer credit card and installment lending.

This does not necessarily mean that smaller banks face no serious challenge from Japanese and other foreign banks. For one thing, California may represent a special case because of its relative economic prosperity and rapid population growth that permit most banks to succeed without severe financial stress. Of course, the heavy dependence of most small banks on the economies of smaller local market areas makes them especially vulnerable to economic downturns, but they also benefit significantly when a local economic boom is underway. Some small banks have at least partially offset this form of economic risk by shifting a greater proportion of their earning assets into securitized loans and government-backed securities from other cities and regions, thus providing greater geographic diversification for their loan portfolios. This diversification strategy has helped buoy up the profitability of smaller commercial banks even when their local economies weaken and new competitors enter their localized markets.

OMINOUS FACTORS FOR THE FUTURE OF JAPANESE BANKS IN THE UNITED STATES

Despite the rapid growth of Japanese bank operations in the United States over the past decade, particularly in California, there are signs that these banks will face a number of potentially serious problems in U.S. financial service markets in the future. For one thing, the number of potential acquisition targets—among both foreign and domestic banks—is declining, because there are fewer banks not already affiliated with U.S. bank holding companies. Moreover, as interstate banking becomes more widespread, Japanese banks will likely face greater challenges from domestic banks that strive to enter the same local markets in thousands of communities across the United States.

Still another problem centers around Japanese banking's most recent strategic thrust into retail banking services offered to U.S. individuals and families. By and large, this newest customer group has few identifiable relationships with Japanese firms or individuals and little, if any, background in Japanese culture. It is not at all clear from the research evidence to date that Japanese banking firms possess a comparative economic advantage in dealing with U.S. households. There is no research evidence currently available that demonstrates that Japanese banks operating in the United States can raise funds at lower cost, hire management and staff more cheaply, or construct or lease physical facilities at lower cost than U.S. banks serving the same domestic markets. Moreover, if the Japanese choose to focus their marketing efforts even more intently on domestic individuals and small firms as customers, such a strategy will subject them to the same economic forces within states and regions (including the persistent problems faced by the real estate, agricultural, and energy sectors) that U.S.–owned banks must now grapple with in their respective credit and deposit markets.

Much of the growth in the U.S. assets of Japanese banks and securities firms arises from the rapid expansion of Japanese trade within the United States. In 1987 Japan passed Great Britain as the leading receiver of payments from U.S. firms and individuals. As Japan's trade surpluses with the United States have continued to mount, their claims on U.S. reserves (including dollar deposits) have increased enormously. Fortunately for the United States' position in global markets, Japanese businesses and governmental agencies have been willing to convert the majority of those dollar claims into holdings of U.S. securities and real estate rather than demanding to withdraw capital resources and foreign exchange reserves from U.S. shores. If those trade surpluses weaken significantly in the future, however, the growth of Japanese claims against U.S. assets could slow and, in fact, even begin to contract.

Indeed, there is already limited evidence supporting such a trend. For example, in trade figures released by the Japanese Ministry of Finance for August 1990, Japanese trade surpluses narrowed sharply against both the United States and Western Europe, even before the full effects of rising global oil prices from the conflict in the Middle East had been registered. Japan's trade surpluses with the United States may well shrink further should the Iraqi conflict not come to an early resolution, because higher world oil prices will tend to raise the market value of Japan's imports relative to its exports. Overall, Japan's trade surplus with the United States and Western Europe in the summer of 1990 declined 6 percentage points from the levels of a year earlier, as total exports declined relatively faster than imports.

The slowing of economic growth in the United States is another potentially ominous factor for Japan and its foreign investment activity. Japan's key exports to the U.S.—particularly automobiles and electronic equipment— are known to be sensitive to business cycle fluctuations. Thus, both the mix and the volume of Japanese trade with the United States make Japanese banking and investment unusually sensitive to variations in the growth of the U.S. economy. Nevertheless, we must not overemphasize this factor. Japan and the United States have one of the lowest ratios of imports to gross domestic product in the world (about 10 and 11 percent, respectively, compared to about 27 percent for Great Britain and almost 30 percent in West Germany).

The Japanese themselves appear to be shifting emphasis in their sales abroad away from their current heavy reliance on U.S. domestic markets toward greater marketing opportunities in Southeast Asia and Europe. Recent economic growth in South Korea, China, Singapore, and other portions of Asia has been accompanied by growing demand for automobiles, computers and robotics, electronic communications equipment, and machinery— all areas in which the Japanese have demonstrated a strong comparative advantage in production and performance. A combination of weakening demand in the U.S. economy plus growing demands for Japanese goods in Asia and Europe would exacerbate the declining trade surplus with the United States and, more than likely, slow the recent buildup of Japanese banking assets and acquisitions inside U.S. territory.

Finally, looming on the horizon is a new path for banking regulation worldwide—an effort to place all banks on the same regulatory footing to help ensure the safety and soundness of the global financial system and to promote greater competition for the benefit of consumers, regardless of their location or situation. The most dramatic example of the past decade is the Basle Agreement, reached in 1988 among leading industrialized nations, that focuses on common international capital standards for commercial banks. The motivations for these new risk-based global bank capital standards are technical ones. Among the most important is the rapid growth of off-balance-sheet bank risk exposure occasioned by the rise of such banking services as standby credit letters, interest rate and currency swaps, and other financial instruments that add to banking's risks but usually are not recorded on bank balance sheets. Far more important, however, is the intensification of competition among leading banks and securities firms worldwide that has eroded bank profit margins—pressures so intense that they have brought into sharp relief the differences in banking regulation from nation to nation. Bankers feeling the pressure of what they regard as excessively burdensome regulations in their home countries, while their competitors appear to enjoy the advantages of less constraining rules, have pushed strongly for greater regulatory equity.

The Basle Agreement is only the beginning in a growing international trend toward more equal regulation for banks and securities firms. Other examples include a recent recommendation of the international trade organization represented by the Group of 30 nations which, in 1990, called for the creation of new international standards for the clearing and payment of corporate securities transactions, and recent discussions by the International Organization of Securities Supervisors (IOSCO) on the possibilities for coordination in securities firm supervision.[1] Moreover, in November 1990 officials from leading industrialized nations met in Tokyo to discuss levying minimum capital standards on securities firms and insurance companies, with an ultimate goal of implementing common capital standards by 1993 if preliminary plans hold.

One important motivation for these discussions was the perception that, following more complete integration within the European Economic Community scheduled for 1992, financial systems all over the world would, perforce, become more closely intertwined so that some form of common regulatory standards would become a virtual necessity. Otherwise, financial institutions located in countries with stricter rules will simply book their assets and funds sources in less stringently regulated regions of the world. One special problem that must be faced here is that in some countries—for example, the United States and Japan—securities firms, insurance companies, and banks tend to be separate businesses, independent of one another, whereas in other areas, such as Western Europe, they may be closely linked, creating real problems in trying to estimate common capital requirements. (The 1991 banking reform proposals of the Bush Administration, if adopted, could change this unique feature of U.S. banking, but it will not happen overnight.) If this trend toward greater equity in financial services regulation persists, there will be fewer comparative advantages to lure Japanese banks and other financial service banking firms into U.S. markets.

The new international capital agreement may also create some serious problems for Japanese banks working to meet the new Basle standards, especially the agreed-upon goal of an 8 percent bank capital-to-asset ratio by 1993, which Japanese banks must adhere to by the start of their fiscal year in April 1993. Financial analyst Vivian Lewis (1989) estimates that Japan's 33 largest banks will have to raise nearly $80 billion in new equity funds by 1993, even under the assumption that their total assets will remain unchanged. Recent stock market declines in Tokyo have made both domestic and international markets less receptive to Japanese bank paper. Indeed, Japanese insurance firms have purchased most of the capital securities issued by the largest Japanese banks, and these firms appear now to be facing fund-raising and capital adequacy problems of their own. Moreover, a gradual lifting of government controls on domestic bank deposits has meant that, by the beginning of the 1990s, 60–70 percent of domestic yen-denominated deposits carried market-driven or market-influenced interest rates, raising significantly the average cost of domestic fund-raising for Japanese banks.

Confronted with higher deposit and permanent capital costs as they strive to meet the new international capital standards, Japanese banks may be forced to slow the growth rate of their assets, making their current capital-to-asset ratios look better, or to increase returns on their invested assets. The latter route is now a much less promising option than it was in the rapid growth era of the 1980s. Not only has economic growth and the expansion of global trade slowed, but also two of the markets that fueled a substantial portion of Japanese bank growth in the 1980s—commodities lending and the issuance of standby credit guarantees—are today more crowded with competing suppliers and growing at a substantially slower pace. Moreover, the retail and small business markets most recently targeted by these banks have become intensely competitive in the United States and Western Europe as well as inside Japan itself.

We must not lose sight of the fact, however, that Japanese bankers have a history of developing creative solutions to their most pressing problems. In this case, with spreading domestic deregulation and the date for imposition of international capital standards looming closer, mergers and acquisitions among the key Japanese players in international banking markets are a potential solution that some of Japan's banks will pursue readily. Indeed, signs of the development of such a problem-solving strategy are already unfolding. For example, in November 1990 two of Japan's city banks—Kyowa Bank and Saitama Bank—announced a merger to be consummated in April 1991. These two institutions have a primary focus on retail banking and small business markets inside Japan and, therefore, could put heavy pressure on Japan's regional banks to pursue mergers of their own and, perhaps, clear away any remaining regulatory barriers to further mergers among the Japanese city banks.

Of course, there are those who argue that the Basle Agreement on bank capital standards is, in fact, *not* a real step toward fairer and more equitable international banking rules. Financial economist Edward Kane (May/June 1990) contends that the new capital standards will not increase the funding costs of Japanese banks relative to U.S. banks. Rather, he argues that global capital requirements will merely prolong the existence of government subsidies to banks in many countries, including such protectionist measures as low-cost government deposit insurance and legal entry barriers into certain credit and deposit markets that give protected banks unfair advantages over their competitors. Professor Kane points out that the Basle Agreement covers only book-value bank capital, not market-value capital, and ignores the interrelated effects of other regulations (such as those surrounding legal reserves and deposit insurance) that may countermand the impact of the new capital regulations. Thus, the revised capital rules may confront only one problem out of a whole set of serious regulatory discrepancies between trading nations. Kane sees the new global capital standards as, first, an attempt at retribution against the Japanese in order to slow their growth relative to Western banks and second, a vain effort to halt the erosion of prestige among Western versus Japanese regulatory authorities.

Professor Kane contends that the Basle Agreement was based on a serious misunderstanding of the reasons for Japanese banks having relatively low capital-to-asset ratios and comparatively low overall funding costs. These lower funding costs appear, at least in part, to arise from Japan's relatively high savings rates compared to other industrialized nations with lower savings rates and correspondingly weaker currencies. Capital fund-raising in Japan has benefitted greatly from the relatively high market values attached to Japanese bank stock (where bank stock prices often exceed their book values by a factor of seven or eight times). Moreover, financial system regulations inside Japan limit domestic competition for funding among Japanese banks and restrict the efforts of foreign banks to attract Japanese deposits. Kane concludes that, if bank regulators in the West were really interested in restoring a measure of regulatory equity with Japan, they should have targeted Japanese restrictions against foreign entry and their control over deposit interest rates and the types of domestic deposits that may be offered. Instead, bank regulators in the United States and Western Europe were apparently willing to exchange banking deregulation for securities deregulation, which tends only to prolong any remaining regulatory advantages of Japan's banks. Moreover, the Basle Agreement could be viewed as an attempt at postponing troublesome regulatory reforms at home and deflecting attention from weaknesses in the current U.S. bank regulatory structure.[2]

RECOMMENDATIONS FOR BANK REGULATORY POLICY IN THE UNITED STATES

The history of bank regulatory policy in the United States is one of concern for safety and for the avoidance of monopolistic power. The latter objective has often been expressed as a wish to maintain local control over banks, their services, and their power to expand geographically. Local control could be enforced by prohibiting or restricting the ability of each bank to establish branch offices and by prohibiting banks from one state entering another state without the express approval of the latter. The proponents of these restrictions have argued for decades that they were designed ultimately to protect the public welfare. If the largest money-center banks were permitted to enter, they might drive smaller, locally owned banks out of business. The fear arose in all parts of the nation in the late nineteenth and early twentieth centuries that such banking giants would divert scarce capital from local areas and route those funds into distant markets, thus stifling the economic development of states and local communities.

In the case of foreign bank expansion, additional fears surfaced repeatedly in the years that followed World War II. For example, a foreign-owned banking facility might follow the policies of its home nation and thereby work against state and federal government objectives. Moreover, such banks allegedly would be more difficult to control, supervise, and regulate because the bulk of their business sales as well as their ownership were positioned outside U.S. territory. During the 1960s and 1970s there was even fear that a foreign bank headquartered in a country taken over by communism might come to possess a substantial measure of influence over U.S. banking regulation (as noted, for example, by Neil Osborn [1979]).

Few of these fears have materialized in concrete form. Moreover, recent history suggests that many of the territorial restrictions on banks have subsequently not resulted in more competition, but instead have protected some inefficient institutions from the cleansing force of competition. Federal and state restrictions against the territorial expansion of U.S. and foreign banks simply (and, for some banks, fatally) ignored the question of operating efficiency. How large should banks be allowed to become so that they can supply the public with the services it demands at the lowest possible cost in terms of scarce resources? If U.S. banks are prevented from reaching efficient operating size due to regulatory restrictions, it is the public that will suffer in terms of fewer services at higher cost.

As a group, U.S. banks have not been able to grow as fast as the U.S. economy. And the regulatory restrictions against branching and holding company activity within individual states and across state borders may have stifled U.S. banking's growth and fostered inefficiency. But what about the foreign competitors of U.S. banks? Is there evidence of a developing "efficiency gap" between banks inside the United States and Japan?

Evidence is accumulating that Japanese banks are among the most efficient banking operations in the world. Recent estimates (in particular, Grant Reuber [1990]) suggest that the average cost of capital for Japan's multinational banks is only about 3 percent. In contrast, U.S. bank equity capital costs, on average, may be three to four times as high. Among major industrialized countries, U.S. capital costs in banking are among the highest; only banks in the United Kingdom appear to have higher average equity costs.

Such a discrepancy in the price of owners' capital is of more than passing interest, because it places U.S. banks at a decided economic disadvantage in the most competitive financial service markets in the world—the markets for large corporate and institutional loans where bank profit margins are extremely narrow. (For example, the spread between bank borrowing costs and lending rates in the global Eurodollar market frequently hovers around one-eighth of a percentage point or less.) Other things being equal, high-cost banks will be driven from the market by institutions able to operate with lower required rates of return to owners' capital. It is still true that U.S. financial institutions display a high level of expertise in such specialized and profitable fields as interest rate hedging, syndicating loans, arranging mergers and acquisitions, and asset securitization, but these advantages are unlikely to prevail in the long run. Indeed, they are already eroding, as the knowledge of foreign bankers continues to grow through observation and joint ventures with U.S. financial service firms.

An added problem that burdens U.S. banks vis-à-vis their Japanese competitors is largely a legacy from the U.S. savings and loan crisis. Domestic depositors, particularly those not fully covered by deposit insurance, have demanded greater risk premiums on their accounts due to the failure of hundreds of S&Ls and commercial banks. This problem has been exacerbated by the forbearance policies of the federal government, which have allowed many insolvent S&Ls to continue to operate and compete with healthy banks and thrift institutions for insured deposits by paying higher and higher interest rates.

An additional burden that also swells U.S. banks' capital costs is domestic reserve requirements on deposits and selected nondeposit borrowings that are, generally speaking, much larger than reserve requirements overseas.

Placing cash in a reserve account in an amount that exceeds a bank's actual liquidity needs acts as a form of taxation and requires U.S. banks to earn a higher rate of return on invested capital simply to offset the effects of the reserve tax.

U.S. banks can combat higher capital costs to some extent by moving into other service lines where profit margins are significantly higher or by improving the efficiency of their operations. As we have seen in this book, to a large extent this is what U.S. banks have done by moving more aggressively into household financial services markets and into the markets for financial services offered to small and midsize business firms. Ultimately, however, there are limits to how economically effective such switches into higher-margin service markets can be. As more U.S. banks emphasize retail and small business financial services, profit margins in these product markets will be eroded, *ceteris paribus*. Moreover, as we saw in chapter 3, Japanese banks are themselves making a strong effort to capture a larger share of U.S. retail banking markets.

We must hasten to add that, because of regulation, not all high-margin markets are open to U.S. banks inside the United States. Federal and state restrictions prevent the offering of a complete menu of financial services that would allow U.S. banking firms to fully utilize all of their expertise in serving customers. Nowhere is this more evident than in the restrictions against offering securities underwriting services to corporate customers, originally legislated in the National Bank Act of 1933 (Glass-Steagall). Under its provisions, a U.S.–chartered bank can lend funds directly to a corporation, but it cannot purchase that corporation's stocks and bonds for resale to investors in the open market. As we saw in earlier chapters, this restriction has hit U.S. bank earnings particularly hard over the past decade, because so many major domestic and foreign corporations have turned away from bank loans in preference to selling their own securities in the open market to raise capital.

While the Federal Reserve seems to be moving toward greater U.S. commercial bank involvement in securities underwriting, it remains well behind Western Europe in this service area. As economist Chester Feldberg (1990) of the Federal Reserve Bank of New York notes, European banks generally have broad authority to carry on banking and securities underwriting simultaneously. In Germany, for example, underwriting activities typically are carried on within the banks themselves, while in Great Britain banks normally offer underwriting services through separate subsidiary firms. To be sure, Japanese banks face similar restrictions at home. Article 65 of their banking code places barriers comparable to those in the United States between commercial banking and investment banking. In fact, Japanese banks have entered the United States and the United Kingdom, in part, to avoid these domestic restrictions inside Japan.

As we noted in chapter 4, significant strides have been made by the Federal Reserve Board in granting broader securities underwriting powers to leading U.S. banks. For example, in September 1990 the Board granted J.P. Morgan the right to underwrite corporate stock for its customers, and in January 1989, the Board granted several leading banking companies permission to underwrite corporate notes and bonds. But the Federal Reserve Board's stock underwriting decision was a controversial one. Many members of the U.S. Congress are groping for ways to support the beleaguered government deposit insurance fund and to make sure that U.S. banks adequately strengthen their capital positions before granting them broad new service powers. However, factors that may mitigate Congress' objections include the fact that J.P. Morgan possesses a strong capital position and that tight restrictions were placed on Morgan's stock underwriting activities similar to those placed earlier on the underwriting of corporate debt—namely, all such activities must be conducted through a special subsidiary effectively sealed off with "fire walls" from banking units within the same company.

Clearly, there is risk for U.S. banks in the conservative, highly measured approach of the Federal Reserve Board. The burden of restrictive regulation is further extended, prolonging the disadvantage of U.S. banks by the Fed's "fire walls" approach to securities underwriting activities. Moreover, potential gains in bank operating efficiency from offering combined banking and underwriting services are wasted and the potential risk-reducing benefits from service diversification are artificially limited.

The Glass-Steagall Act's prohibitions against securities underwriting are not the only barriers to U.S. banking firms striving to achieve full competitive equality with Japanese banks. Perhaps equally damaging have been the prescriptions laid down by the McFadden Act of 1927, the Banking Act of 1933, and the Bank Holding Company Act of 1956 (and its numerous amendments) against wider authority to establish branch offices and acquire bank and nonbank businesses. The McFadden Act allowed U.S. national banks to establish branch offices only in the city where they were headquartered, provided state law granted similar powers to state-chartered banks. The Banking Act of 1933 (Glass-Steagall, Section 23) permitted national banks and state-chartered Federal Reserve member banks to branch anywhere within their home states if state law allowed state-chartered banks the same privilege, but not otherwise. While the United States seems to be moving toward nationwide banking in the 1990s, skirting around the McFadden and Glass-Steagall Acts, this movement may not be fast enough to avoid further significant erosion in U.S.–chartered bank market shares at home. Worse, as we noted earlier, legislation permitting interstate banking to date (passed at the state level and not at all at the federal level) has usually permitted expansion only via holding company acquisitions—an expensive way to diversify geographically—and not by creating new branch offices or by chartering new banks. Facing significant capital and earnings constraints, few U.S. banks have been able to take advantage of the new laws allowing cross-border, full-service expansion. And few are likely to do so until new legislation appears at either the state or federal level to make full service interstate banking an economically viable reality.[3]

U.S. banks have a history of creativity in developing new services that meet pressing customer service needs. Prominent examples in recent years include interest rate and currency swaps and money market–linked deposits, but U.S. regulations tend to stifle that creativity and limit U.S. bankers' capacity to develop new skills and services so that they remain competitive both at home and abroad. There is no apparent plan or long-range strategy in the United States to systematically improve the competitiveness of U.S. banks. Rather, we have had only piecemeal reform, usually occurring state-by-state or through small changes in regulations occurring principally at the federal level through such agencies as the Federal Reserve Board and the Comptroller of the Currency, at least until the appearance of the Bush Administration's banking reform proposals in February 1991. Moreover, as we saw earlier, recent attempts at common international regulation may convey the impression that something is being done to streamline U.S. regulations themselves, particularly the faulty deposit insurance system, when, in fact, very little is being done to make the United States' banking regulations consistent with a freer market for financial services.

In the final analysis, the United States appears to face a grim but critical decision about how it regulates its banks. By using regulation as a subsidy to protect weak and inefficient banks and small depositors, we thereby raise the cost of doing business for our banks and, potentially at least, weaken their competitive position in global markets. The global market share held by U.S. banking firms inevitably must decline if their cost of capital exceeds that of foreign banks. Perhaps the optimal role that government can play here is, as Federal Reserve Board Chairman Alan Greenspan (May 1990:10) suggests, to reduce the cost of capital U.S. banks must bear—that is, the minimum rate of return they must be able to earn in order to attract and hold capital contributed by stockholders, depositors, and other creditors. This is an especially significant challenge vis-à-vis Japanese banks, because the price-earnings ratios posted on the stock of Japanese banking firms are remarkably high, which has sharply lowered their equity capital costs relative to most other foreign banks. Moreover, Japanese financial accounting practices tend to reinforce the impression of relatively low capital costs.

As we have seen in earlier portions of this book, the critical advantage of lower capital costs is partly the result of strong economic performance in the Japanese homeland and an exceptionally high national savings rate that lowers real interest rates in Japan relative to the United States and stimulates investment. The U.S. government can make a significant difference here by working to keep the U.S. economy as stable an operating environment as possible for U.S. banks and other firms and by reducing the federal government's budget deficit. In addition, the federal government must soon begin to reduce the restrictions U.S. banks face at home that prevent them from achieving greater geographic and produce line diversification to reduce risk, including lowering or eliminating current limitations on branching across state lines and on offering investment banking and insurance services along the lines of the U.S. Treasury's banking reform proposals of February 1991, as well as reducing deposit reserve requirements, liberalizing antitrust rulers, and simplifying credit regulations.

Indeed, one of the key reasons Japanese banks have established substantial office facilities in the United States and the United Kingdom is to escape the burden of regulation at home (particularly in the area of raising funds), which only in the last decade has become appreciably lighter. In this sense the prominence of Japanese banks within the U.S. financial system appears to be overstated, as we saw earlier, because much of the volume of lending and fund-raising activity that might otherwise have flowed through offices in Japan gets booked in the United States, even when the funds involved ultimately flow back to Japan. It seems eminently reasonable to expect that, as deregulation proceeds in Japan toward more freedom for domestic firms, the rate of expansion of Japanese banking abroad is likely to slow significantly in the years to come.

Whatever the rate of Japanese expansion abroad, however, the United States must not hesitate to push for those sound principles of banking regulation and supervision it has tried to promote in other parts of the world. U.S. legislators and regulators must press for equal treatment of foreign and domestic banks inside Japan as well as in the United States. Indeed, this appeared to be the intent of the U.S. Treasury in negotiations with Japan during the spring and summer of 1990, when U.S. officials asked that bank deposit interest rates be deregulated in 1991 under the threat of retaliation against approving new services for Japanese banks operating in the United States. Such a near-term deadline is probably unreasonable, however. As business journalist Anthony Rowley (1990) reports, Japan's city banks quickly responded to the U.S. Treasury's suggestion with calculations to show that the profits of these leading multinational institutions would be reduced by almost 20 percent if such an event were to occur suddenly.

More reasonable, perhaps, is the proposal from the Japanese Ministry of Finance that calls for complete deregulation of time deposits by the end of March 1992. Other deregulatory moves affecting the terms of Japanese bank deposits have been gradually phased in in a manner similar to U.S. deposit deregulation, which took almost five full years between 1981 and March 1986 to complete (and, indeed, is still not complete as regular checking accounts sold by U.S. banks in the domestic market are still subject to a regulatory ceiling). Research evidence from the United States (e.g., Paulus [1976] and Dunham [1983]) suggests that gradual deregulation of bank deposits, particularly after decades of close control, is the preferable route, because of the danger to banks operating at the margin with low earnings and thin capital margins and the need to give all financial firms affected adequate opportunity to restructure their pricing schedules and operations to conform to a deregulated market environment. Evidence from the spread of interest-bearing checkable deposits (NOWs) in New England in the 1970s indicates that bank earnings are likely to fall initially. However, over the long run, as Peter Rose (1987) has observed, New England banks learned to price their deposits more conservatively, to stabilize their market shares, and, in most cases, to experience a recovery in their net earnings.

In brief, insisting that Japanese banks deregulate their services, particularly deposits, on a schedule that is substantially faster than the United States followed would probably be unreasonable. However, the United States must press for steady progress toward financial deregulation inside Japan. Available research evidence from the United States strongly suggests that deregulation causes no lasting harm to individual banks, especially those that are as heavily capitalized as Japan's multinational banks and the more numerous Japanese regional commercial banks and savings depositories. Recent research suggests that the benefits to the public in terms of improved returns on savings outweigh what is essentially a transitory loss to most individual banking firms.

As economist David Hale (1990) has suggested, we need to have a worldwide commitment to national treatment in which both domestic and foreign firms are allowed to play by the same rules, and nowhere is this more essential today than between the United States and Japan. Careful monitoring of the performance and market shares of U.S. financial firms inside Japan as well as in Western Europe and elsewhere around the Pacific Rim is a necessity. That monitoring serves as an ever-present reminder to us and to the Japanese of how far all of us must travel together toward a global financial system free and open to all with unfair advantage to no one. When financial markets are not free, they invite calls for protectionism and government interference in private decisions to allocate resources that, so often in the past, have led to disastrous consequences. We are, indeed, a long way from an ideal global banking and financial system, but that journey has begun and we must support it with an equal measure of concern and reason every step of the way.

NOTES

1. See especially Feldberg (1990), p. 32.

2. It is not clear how burdensome the new international capital standards will be for Japanese banks. Recent stock price declines on the Tokyo stock exchange have lowered the value of bank stock issues substantially, but prices still appear high enough to give Japanese banks an above-average net worth cushion compared to most other international banks in the West. However, the new standards are stated in book-value terms and require Japanese banks to have a capital-to-asset ratio of 8 percent by March 1993. International and Japanese capital markets appear to be much less receptive to new bank-issued paper than earlier, which means that Japanese bankers could have a difficult time meeting the full tier-one (permanent equity) capital and tier-two (supplemental) capital requirements. Recently the Ministry of

Finance approved the issuance of capital debentures subordinated to deposits, but this is a more costly form of capital with a less well-developed market. For example, in July 1990 Sumitomo Bank sold subordinated debt through London and New York amounting to close to $1.2 billion—a step not likely to be encouraged by Japanese regulatory agencies and likely to be available only to a few of Japan's multinational institutions. It appears likely that the Japanese will have to slow bank asset growth somewhat in the ensuing decade.

3. It is interesting that the United States has always tended to treat foreign banks somewhat more leniently than domestic banks with regard to territorial expansion, especially branching activity. Prior to 1978 there were no federal restrictions on foreign banks branching across state lines, while domestically chartered banking institutions were subject to such restrictions. At that time, the principal barriers foreign banks faced in reaching across state lines were in the form of state laws, though the most important states for foreign banks—New York and California— allowed them considerable latitude. Even when the International Banking Act (IBA) of 1978 was passed it contained a proviso known as the Stevenson Compromise. Section 5 of the IBA permitted foreign banks to branch across state lines if state law allowed them to do so—a parallel privilege possessed by domestic banks as well. However, foreign banks could also seek federal and state approval to establish *limited* branch offices that would serve as channels for most services, except that only deposits arising from international transactions could be accepted. Moreover, foreign banks with existing U.S. branches were allowed to keep all of those facilities. (See especially Van Patten [1979].)

SEVEN

Japanese Investment Activities Inside the United States: Implications of Their Rise and Fall

Nations, markets, and institutions are becoming increasingly interdependent—economically, politically, and socially. This generation is characterized more than in any preceding era by the globalization of economics and of society, and by growing interdependence across the whole fabric of societal relationships. Global trade over the past decade has grown faster than global output, and cross-border financial transactions have increased faster than global trade. Foreign-owned financial institutions and foreign investors today perform indispensable roles within the U.S. financial system. In one market alone—the buying and selling of U.S. government securities—foreign purchases and sales of U.S. securities rose from about $100 billion at the beginning of the 1980s and to more than $4 trillion by the close of that decade.

These massive cross-border movements of goods and services, especially of financial capital, have been facilitated by a revolution in technology, particularly in the processing and transfer of financial information. Satellite communications, automated teller machines and clearinghouses, fiber-optic cable transmissions, and artificial intelligence systems are prominent examples—but only examples—of an unprecedented wave of technological innovation that has led to greater operating efficiency, even for relatively small businesses and financial institutions. These and other new technologies have made possible the rise of smaller firms and more compact production methods—the global downsizing of economic output.

In the financial sector of this increasingly global economy, the new technologies have led to a proliferation of new financial services and instruments designed to reduce capital market costs, speed payments and credit transactions, and provide protection against risk exposure. Improved methods of controlling risk through such devices as futures and option contracts and currency and interest rate swaps, coupled with faster and more efficient means of long-range communication, have facilitated and accelerated the flow of financial services and financial transactions across national boundaries, creating more chances to profit from the arbitraging of goods and financial capital, stimulating even more international investment and still greater interdependence among societies and the markets that allocate their resources and create or destroy jobs for their citizens. In addition, capital market investors have sought the greater portfolio diversification that purchases of securities and real property in a variety of different countries can offer, helping to shield investors from the greater economic risks that any one nation's economy and currency can present.

Not surprisingly, most of the foreign investments of the past decade have been denominated in U.S. dollars—the principal currency in which international reserves are held and in which globally traded commodities, such as crude oil, are valued. In addition, the majority of new risk-hedging instruments and other financial service innovations have arisen in markets where the U.S. dollar is the principal medium of exchange. Without question, today the United States remains a world leader in financial innovation. Foreign institutions and investors have found that access to U.S. dollar deposits and to U.S. institutions is absolutely essential in today's international financial marketplace, if not because of the attractive investment returns offered by dollar-denominated assets, then because of their superior liquidity that opens the door to tradable assets worldwide. This is one of the chief causes of the rapid expansion of Japanese banks in the United States and of the rapid accumulation of U.S. stocks, bonds, and real estate by the Japanese and other foreign investors.

Massive capital flows into and out of U.S. dollars coupled with growing economic interdependence have, in turn, pressured governments in Europe, Asia, and the Americas to take a fresh look at the rules and regulations that bind foreign trade and international financial transactions. Technological change, particularly in the financial services sector, has made many narrowly focused local regulations bearing upon banks and other financial firms obsolete and damaging to both the regulated institutions themselves and to their regulators. There are strong economic incentives today among businessmen and women to find ways around constraining regulatory barriers if they are to survive in an intensely competitive international marketplace that does not forgive either poor products or counterproductive regulations. The result is a worldwide trend toward financial services deregulation and toward international cooperation to remove or modify the remaining regulations in order to make the rules of commerce and trade fair for all. We find ourselves, regardless of differences in culture or background, caught in the midst of a global resurgence of competition, of technological and financial innovation, and of a compelling drive toward greater efficiency in the use of scarce resources. It is an environment that demands flexible thinking, openness to new ideas and approaches, and a receptivity to change that readily adapts to, rather than resists, social and technological innovations.

To be sure, the growing entry by foreign firms into the U.S. domestic marketplace has aroused both fear and anxiety—emotions that have, at times, shown forth in open hostility. As Manuel Johnson (1989:2), former Vice-Chairman of the Federal Reserve Board, noted in a recent speech:

Certain analysts argue that such increased foreign investment and ownership will mortgage our future since the obligation of interest payments abroad will generate an impossible burden. Also, there seems to be a growing fear that increased indebtedness to foreigners will cause Americans to lose control of their own destiny. . . . Because such capital inflows bring about dollar appreciation, they "crowd out" exports and encourage imports, thereby increasing existing [U.S.] trade deficits.

It is difficult for most of us (and impossible for some) to view the burgeoning influx of foreign firms and institutions into U.S. markets and into the fabric of American life with a long eye and from an intellectually balanced perspective. It is not necessarily reassuring to learn that foreign holdings of U.S. assets remain well below the relative amounts of foreign investment in other industrialized nations, such as Canada or Great Britain, or that foreign investors hold no greater proportion of U.S. government debt than was true two decades ago. As a society and as individuals with significant influence over our own economic destiny, we must resist the temptation to look backward. For example, it does not help in any positive sense to note that foreign holdings of the United States' net wealth more than doubled during the 1980s (or from about 5 percent to 12 percent of net U.S. assets). Instead, we must focus on the economic realities of today's marketplace and how we can promote and encourage capital inflows, whatever their source, so that employment will be a reality for all those who seek jobs and production and prices will be stabilized to encourage saving and investment that will maximize living standards in every corner of the nation.

THE IMPACT OF JAPANESE INVESTMENT ACTIVITY ON U.S. PROPERTY VALUES, SECURITIES PRICES, AND FINANCIAL SERVICES

There is a growing awareness that, on balance, we have benefited as a society and as a global community from the presence of foreign players in the U.S. financial system. The competition they have brought to the markets for financial services sold to U.S. businesses, federal and local units of government, and, to a lesser extent, households undoubtedly have resulted in substantial savings in borrowing costs and a wider availability of credit to all qualified borrowers. Japanese banking and investment firms have played a significant role in stimulating real estate development, including the building of new shopping centers, office buildings, and production facilities, by lowering the cost of capital to both U.S. and foreign investors. Moreover, much of the foreign inflow of capital has come at a time of crisis in the real estate and savings and loan markets, where a glut of commercial and residential space has led to thousands of bankruptcies, a lowering of public confidence in the U.S. banking and financial system, and a shortfall in domestic capital due to unprecedented government deficits.

The consequences for U.S. businesses, consumers, and institutions if foreign investors withdraw, even partially, from U.S. securities markets was hinted at in February and March of 1990, when elections in Japan combined with political uncertainty over Germany's future led to sharply falling bond prices and rising interest rates over a broad spectrum of U.S. government and privately issued bonds. The same pattern of falling U.S. securities prices and rising market rates of interest appeared again in the late summer and fall of 1990 as the conflict in the Middle East surrounding Iraq's invasion of Kuwait intensified, leading to increased inflationary pressures inside Japan and a significant slowing in the U.S. economy. Japanese and other foreign investors cut their purchases of U.S. securities and began to sell off previously accumulated holdings of U.S. bonds and stocks, driving interest rates higher and U.S. debt and equity securities prices sharply downward. These adverse movements were moderated somewhat as Japanese institutional investors borrowed against U.S. properties they had acquired earlier in order to protect their investments and position themselves for new investment opportunities.

Of special concern as the 1990s began to unfold was the appearance of a *negative investment gap* in U.S. financial markets. The so-called "investment gap" is measured from the simple formula:

Net Inflow (+) or Outflow (−) of Capital into or from the United States

= Total Capital Inflows − Total Capital Outflows

= Purchases of U.S. Securities and Acquisitions of Businesses and Real Property by Foreign Investors − Purchases of Foreign Securities and Acquisitions of Businesses and and Real Property by U.S. Investors

For most of the decade of the 1980s, the United States experienced a positive net inflow of foreign capital as foreign purchases of U.S. securities, businesses, and real estate substantially outpaced similar foreign purchases by U.S. investors. While the growing presence of foreign investment inside the United States aroused many concerns, it had the beneficial effect of supplying sufficient capital to absorb huge U.S. government deficits and to support the expansion of U.S. businesses and jobs.

As the 1990s began, however, quite the opposite trend was ushered in as U.S. investors accelerated their overseas investments, particularly in Europe where, for example, General Motors recently announced an expansion of its Opel car subsidiary through a joint venture in East Germany, and both IBM and Digital Equipment Corporation recently reinvested record European profits in further European ventures. Capital outlays abroad by U.S. companies rose to more than $50 billion in 1990 alone, according to Department of Commerce estimates, up from just over $30 billion in 1986, with U.S. acquisitions of European companies approaching close to 200 per year. At the same time, foreign investors, led by the Japanese and the Germans, began to sharply scale back their purchases of U.S. assets, resulting in substantial net outflows of U.S. capital that are reminiscent of the fateful experience in October 1987 when foreign investors fled the crash of stock and futures prices on U.S. exchanges in New York and Chicago. Such trends directly impact both U.S. interest rates and the exchange value of the dollar in international markets, pushing market rates higher inside the United States and slowing the growth of the U.S. economy, while lowering the U.S. dollar's exchange value abroad and adding to domestic inflationary pressures.

Another consequence of the recently emerging U.S. negative investment gap falls upon the nation's balance of payments. The huge deficit in the United States' current account, which measures the net volume of U.S. exports less imports of goods and services, has been balanced in the past by massive net capital inflows from abroad. The United States has paid for this excess of imported goods and services over exports by attracting foreign investor purchases of U.S. securities, businesses, and real estate, but that source of international financing has begun to erode rapidly in the 1990s. If this trend persists, the U.S. government will have to surrender a substantial portion of its foreign exchange reserves and attempt to sell substantial quantities of federal government securities.

At the same time, the U.S. dollar is likely to fall against other trading currencies, particularly the yen and the deutsche mark, until sufficient U.S. assets are purchased at depressed market prices to cover the nation's balance-of-payments deficit. Moreover, real interest rates in Japan and West Germany have remained sufficiently high to attract a growing volume of investment and to divert funds previously slated for U.S. markets into internal projects in those countries. If there is an easing of U.S. credit conditions by the Federal Reserve System due to signs of an impending U.S. recession, then the negative investment gap could widen because the Fed would likely nudge U.S. interest rates toward lower levels, making U.S. securities less attractive relative to investment opportunities around the Pacific Rim and in Western and Eastern Europe.

Nevertheless, the United States must prepare itself for a more volatile future in which Japanese support of our financial markets will fluctuate over wider ranges, building and then unwinding investments as market signals change. The possibilities for significant cutbacks in the presence of Japan (and other foreign investors as well) in our economic and financial system are numerous. A retrenchment in Japan's substantial role with the U.S. economy may arise from:

1. A cessation or significant reduction in the flow of oil from the Middle East, which would erode Japan's trade surpluses, generating fewer U.S. dollars for them to invest abroad, sharply increase production and costs inside Japan, and drive Japan's domestic interest rates upward, stimulating greater investment at home and less capital investment in the United States

2. A slower rate of economic growth in the United States (especially if annualized growth in the real U.S. GNP drops below 2 percent) which would leave Americans' standard of living stuck at current levels, lead to near-term increases in unemployment, and risk rekindling serious inflation—all of which would reduce the attractiveness of the United States as a target for foreign investment

3. The growth of attractive investments in other parts of the world, particularly in Korea, Southeast Asia, and Eastern and Western Europe, as legal and regulatory barriers fall all over the world

4. A slowing in world trade that would affect the international markets Japan relies heavily upon to market its growing production of electronic equipment, automobiles, and other goods and services

5. Changing consumer demands and life-styles inside Japan that point toward more leisure time, less emphasis on achieving production quotas, and a developing appetite for imported goods from Asia, Europe, and the United States (illustrated most recently, for example, by a surge in Japanese imports of alcoholic beverages, automobiles, art works, and sports equipment)

6. The continued expansion of U.S. investments inside Japan which, in the short run at least, will result in capital outflows from the United States and slower growth in domestic employment and capital investment.

It can be argued that slower economic growth in Japan could have as many significant consequences for Japan's involvement in U.S. domestic markets as did the rapid expansion of Japanese businesses abroad that characterized much of the 1970s and 1980s. Indeed, such a scenario began to develop as 1990 drew to a close and the Japanese economy began to display signs of softening demand. Real GNP in the domestic Japanese economy rose in the fourth quarter at less than its rate of advance in the third quarter of 1990, led by a significant drop in long-term consumption spending and an unexpectedly high rate of inflation in consumer prices. This slide in domestic spending has encouraged Japanese authorities to begin emphasizing the role of exports in order to strengthen the Japanese economy and to avoid following the U.S.

into the latest recession. While, on the surface, this would seem to run the risk of expanding Japan's politically unpopular trade surpluses with the United States, it seems likely that most of the added Japanese trade activity in the near-term will move toward China, Korea, India, and the Asian continent as a whole and toward Eastern and Western Europe.

The foregoing possibilities are not mutually exclusive. The United States could easily be confronted with a taste of all or most of these scenarios. Moreover, there are elements within each that lie well beyond the United States' control or sphere of influence. The best the United States can do is to set its own "economic house" in order, ensuring an economic growth path sufficiently rapid to absorb new entrants into the labor force and to increase living standards, but not so rapid as to invite a rekindling of price inflation and economic instability.

One of the most important steps the nation can take is to curtail growing federal, state, and local government deficits so that more domestic savings flow into increased private investment in plant and equipment, which would expand production, improve productive efficiency, and accelerate U.S. exports. Economic growth, buttressed with stability in the markets for goods and services, will attract, rather than repel, foreign investment.

The U.S. economy needs to be rebalanced by encouraging increased domestic savings. Controlling inflation is one of the most important ways to accomplish this goal, because rapid inflation stimulates consumption spending, rather than saving, as consumers and businesses rush to purchase goods and services before their prices rise even higher. To further stimulate savings, favorable tax treatment should be given for accumulated savings dollars, as in tax-free annuity programs where savers are not taxed on interest earnings, but only on drawings from the annuity fund that normally occur several years later when the annuitant is in a lower tax bracket (usually in retirement). Actually, there are forces at work in the U.S. economy that may bring a resurgence in total savings in the 1990s and beyond. In fact, the U.S. personal savings rate, measured by the volume of household savings relative to total personal income, has generally risen since 1987, when it reached an historic low near 3 percent.

The reasons for the growing belief that the U.S. savings rate will rise in the future center on a concept developed during the 1950s and 1960s by economists A. Ando and Franco Modigliani (1963) and others, known as the *life-cycle hypothesis*. The basic notion behind the life-cycle theory is that individuals and families do not save at a constant rate (that is, at a constant percentage of their income) throughout their lives. For much of their early adult years (especially in their twenties and thirties) individuals typically become net borrowers of funds, with annual borrowings substantially exceeding their savings. Somewhere in their forties, families and individuals usually change that pattern, however, scaling back their borrowings and accelerating their savings. By their late forties and early fifties, most individuals become net savers, particularly as retirement approaches. Recent research by Alan J. Auerbach and Lawrence J. Kotlikoff (1989), among others, suggests that the driving force in this familiar pattern of individuals' economic behavior is income expectations. Individuals and families formulate a long-run view of their income and borrow based on that forecast of probable future cash flows. In the early years, most working people anticipate rising income in the future, so they are quite willing to borrow more than their current savings in the expectation that higher income in the future will be sufficient to pay off those borrowings and allow additional saving to take place. Typically, however, family incomes peak in the age bracket that encompasses the late forties and fifties, so that borrowing in excess of saving becomes more risky, with limited or even negative growth in expected future income. Older individuals and families, then, typically save more than they borrow, and much of that saving flows to younger individuals and families who are in the net borrowing stage of their life cycle.

As the U.S. population continues to age rapidly, the life-cycle hypothesis suggests that saving will become a more and more critical priority, because a greater proportion of adults will have reached or surpassed their maximum level of personal income. The supply of savings flooding into banks, insurance companies, and other financial institutions will rise significantly if the life-cycle hypothesis holds, providing amply loanable funds to support domestic investment and cover government budget deficits. Other factors held constant, interest rates—the price of credit—will fall, stimulating domestic investment spending on plant and equipment to fuel the nation's economic growth and absorb a substantial proportion of the upward surge in personal savings. The United States will, then, need less foreign capital because internal sources of capital will more fully meet domestic borrowing needs. A paramount objective of U.S. economic policy in the 1990s and beyond must be to foster and encourage that projected growth in personal savings.

THE POLICY EFFECTS: SUPPORT OF U.S. GOVERNMENT POLICY INITIATIVES AND STATE AND LOCAL GOVERNMENT BORROWING AND GOVERNMENT PROGRAMS

Federal, state, and local governments in the United States in recent years have saved billions of dollars in interest costs because of the significant role played by Japanese banks in supplying credit to U.S. government programs and projects. By purchasing government securities and thereby creating additional demand for federal and local government securities, these borrowing instruments were able to be sold at higher prices (and, therefore, lower interest costs), saving U.S. taxpayers billions of dollars in potential tax levies. State and local governments in recent years have become more aggressive in soliciting Japanese firms to set up operations in their local communities. Today Japanese banks are market leaders in supplying letters of credit guaranteeing the notes and bonds issued by state and local governments inside the United States.

What can U.S. governments and agencies do to encourage this kind of beneficial involvement by foreign investors in U.S. markets? One vital step is to use the nation's most potent economic policy tools, especially monetary and fiscal policy, to promote greater economic stability and more rapid economic growth at home. We must provide a favorable investment climate where inflation is subdued and economic growth is steady and measured, rather than volatile and uncertain. We must also reduce remaining barriers to trade in goods and services that the U.S. government still maintains and encourage other nations, particularly Japan, that are still maintaining restrictions on the foreign entry of banks and other U.S. businesses to open their borders more fully. We must simplify and consolidate regulations and regulatory bodies that have jurisdiction over financial institutions and the trading of capital market securities and derivative financial instruments, such as corporate and government bonds, futures, and options.

However, we must also proceed cautiously, with considered restraint, on measures that threaten economic or financial retaliation against Japan and other U.S. trading partners. We must avoid, except as a possible last resort when negotiation has failed completely, enacting legislation that creates new barriers in a marketplace that increasingly erodes such barriers and economically punishes those that hope to hide behind them. One pertinent and recent example was the Omnibus Trade Act, passed by the U.S. Congress in 1988, which required the Federal Reserve Board to decide if U.S. securities dealers operating in Japan were receiving the same treatment and freedom of operation as was extended to Japanese primary dealers marketing their services in the United States.

The 1988 Trade Act also required the U.S. Treasury Department to carry out a market access study of global markets to determine if retaliatory measures needed to be taken against other groups of foreign firms. A second example of potentially dangerous legislation from the standpoint of capital investment in the United States is the so-called Fair Trade in Financial Services Act, which proposes a mechanism for rejecting applications by foreign companies—principally commercial banks and securities firms—that wish to open or expand operations inside the United States if the nations involved do not extend similar privileges to comparable U.S. firms. On its surface, such legislation appears to seek only fairness and equity, but it sends a threatening signal to the international investment community as a whole, not just to the Japanese.

The greatest danger is that it makes existing and potential targets for investment in the United States vulnerable to raiding by firms from other nations that offer less threatening environments for economic development. For example, there is the prospect of dramatic reductions in barriers to entry by foreign financial institutions into the European Economic Community and into Eastern Europe in 1992 and beyond. In 1986 the EEC unanimously approved the Single European Act, calling for an economy "without frontiers, in which the free movement of goods, persons, services, and capital is assured." The language of the Single European Act envisages the eventual emergence of a consolidated and integrated European Common Market. Moreover, the EEC's subsequent issuance of a Second Banking Directive calls for the development of a single license that will grant permission for lending institutions to operate throughout the common market's geographic area.

Japan appears to be moving toward a globally free system in order to take maximum advantage of the unfolding opportunities in Western and Eastern Europe, including developing securities powers and facilities for their banks in Europe. The United States, however, still enforces the barriers to commercial and investment banking defined by the Glass-Steagall and McFadden Acts which, as we have seen, place U.S. banking firms at a significant competitive disadvantage. As Gary Welsh (1990:9–10) observes:

Against this backdrop of change, the United States' continuing failure to restructure its financial services industry for competition into the twenty-first century poses long-term competitive problems for the U.S. and its banks. Banks' larger corporate customers are increasingly demanding a sophisticated menu of financial products and services that allows them access to funds worldwide at the least cost. If U.S. banks cannot provide this mix of products or services here or abroad, their customers will go to financial institutions that can. The EC, Japan, Canada, and others are building markets that will serve these customers. The United States is not.

But we need to do more than merely avoid ill-advised new legislation; a positive and proactive response is also needed. Existing barriers to the growth of both domestic and foreign firms need to be reduced or eliminated. Moreover, there is a pressing need to promote U.S. exporting ventures, particularly among smaller companies. Thus far, federal government programs to provide information on marketing opportunities abroad and to encourage the growth of trade financing by domestic lenders have been largely ineffective. Much of the problem arises from gross underfunding of U.S. Department of Commerce trade promotion efforts compared to other leading exporting countries.

As Ron Chernow (1990) notes, we appear to be on the eve of the twentieth century's third crest of financial reform legislation, in the wake of a glut of commercial and residential real estate properties and resulting bank and savings and loan failures rivaling the collapse of U.S. depository institutions during the Great Depression of the 1930s. At the beginning of this century, a series of financial panics and institutional failures resulted in the Aldrich-Vreeland Commission and, ultimately, creation of the Federal Reserve System in 1913. In 1933, the Pecora hearings in Congress and President Franklin Roosevelt's Bank Holiday led to passage of the Glass-Steagall Act, creating the Federal Deposit Insurance Corporation and an elaborate system of constraining regulations surrounding U.S. banks. Now, we face not only large numbers of failed and deeply troubled financial institutions, but also a substantial slowing in the U.S. economy, threatening still more financial system problems.

The danger in this cauldron of reform and financial failures is that it will not lead to greater freedom in the financial sector, but possibly to new and more punishing restrictions against domestic and foreign firms alike, to the long-run detriment of the U.S. economy and U.S. business firms. As Federal Reserve Board Chairman Alan Greenspan (May 1990:15–16) has said:

It would clearly be counterproductive to close our own markets to foreign competition merely because foreign markets are less open than we would like. Such an action would invite retaliation and would not be very effective in any case. The globalization of financial markets means that most of the business that foreign banks do with U.S. customers could alternatively be done offshore. In the long run, this would clearly be harmful to the best interests of both U.S. consumers and U.S. producers.

The growing role of Japanese banks, securities firms, and other investors in U.S. markets, if nothing else, has served as a powerful reminder that U.S. isolationism, if it ever really existed, is now passing into history. The U.S. economy and financial system, more than ever, is not the sole master of its own fate. The two leading economies today in terms of the size and stability of their economic growth and international competitiveness are Japan and Germany, and their investors and institutions are heavily involved in U.S. securities and real estate markets. As long as the U.S. government and scores of state and local governments post record budget deficits that drain massive funds from the capital markets, the Japanese, Germans, and other foreign investors will be indispensable in funding a substantial portion of the capital needs of U.S. borrowers. Otherwise, U.S. business investment in new plant and equipment, housing, and other job-creating projects will be choked off. The United States will face a deep recession with rising unemployment and a declining standard of living. Ultimately, the key role of the U.S. dollar as the world's chief reserve currency will erode away.

Appendixes

Table A-1

Japanese Banking Organizations Having U.S. Offices as of Year-End 1989

Name of Banking Organization	Principal Cities Where Offices Are Located	Total Assets in Thousands of Each Foreign Banking Firm in the U.S.
Ashikaga Bank	New York	$418,286
Bank Kyoto	New York	600,979
Bank of Fukuoka	New York	671,827
Bank of Tokyo	Coral Gables, Honolulu, Houston, Los Angeles, New York, Portland, San Francisco, Seattle	47,161,185
Bank of Yokohama	Los Angeles, New York	2,142,361
Chiba Bank	New York	3,301,884
Chuo Trust and Banking	Los Angeles, New York	2,693,437
Dai-Ichi Kangyo Bank	Atlanta, Chicago, Los Angeles, New York, San Francisco	37,295,946
Daiwa Bank	Chicago, Los Angeles, New York	12,229,740
Fuji Bank	Atlanta, Chicago, Houston, Los Angeles, New York, San Francisco	35,168,770
Gunma Bank	New York	539,489
Hachijuni Bank	New York	886,485
Hiroshima Bank	New York	1,436,656
Hokkaido Bank	New York	551,986
Hokkaido Takushoku	Los Angeles, New York, Seattle	4,104,831
Hokuriku Bank Ltd.	New York	1,481,142
Hyakujushi Bank	New York	1,077,485
Industrial Bank of Japan	Chicago, Los Angeles, Miami, New York	28,770,741
Iyo Bank, Ltd.	New York	137,416
Joyo Bank, Ltd.	New York	2,735,378
Kyowa Bank	Chicago, Los Angeles, New York	5,239,969
Long-Term Credit Bank	Chicago, Los Angeles, New York	12,917,908
Mitsubishi Bank	Chicago, Houston, Los Angeles, New York, San Francisco	39,463,891
Mitsubishi Trust and Banking	Chicago, Los Angeles, New York	13,341,478
Mitsui Bank	Chicago, Los Angeles, New York	18,712,166
Mitsui Trust and Banking	Chicago, Los Angeles, New York	13,873,789

Table A-1 (continued)

Name of Banking Organization	Principal Cities Where Offices Are Located	Total Assets in Thousands of Each Foreign Banking Firm in the U.S.
Nippon Credit Bank	Los Angeles, New York	7,357,038
Norinchukin Bank	New York	3,944,157
Saitama Bank	Chicago, Los Angeles, New York	4,948,320
Sanwa Bank	Atlanta, Boston, Chicago, Dallas, Los Angeles, New York, San Francisco	31,806,402
Shizuoka Bank Ltd.	Los Angeles, New York	1,606,065
Shoko Chukin Bank	New York	1,349,139
Sumitomo Bank	Atlanta, Chicago, Houston, Los Angeles, New York, San Francisco	26,719,470
Sumitomo Trust and Banking Co.	Los Angeles, New York	11,372,161
Suruga Bank Ltd.	New York	223,110
Taiyo Kobe Bank	Chicago, Los Angeles, New York, Seattle	9,664,805
Tokai Bank	Atlanta, Chicago, Los Angeles, New York	18,793,697
Tokyo Tomin Bank Ltd.	New York	15,100
Toyo Trust and Banking Co.	Los Angeles, New York	5,072,869
Yasuda Trust and Banking Co.	Los Angeles, New York	9,691,159
Zenshinren Bank	New York	<u>1,225,880</u>
Total Assets for All U.S. Offices of Japanese Banking Firms		$420,745,567

Source: Board of Governors of the Federal Reserve System, Structure Data for U.S. Offices of Foreign Banks by Type of Institution, Washington, D.C., April 20, 1990.

Table A-2

Foreign Bank Shares of Deposits and Loans Inside Japan (Figures as of September 30 of Each Year)

Percentage of Deposits and Loans Held by Foreign Banks Relative to Japanese Banks:

Year	Deposit Percentage	Loan Percentage
1980	0.95%	3.27%
1981	1.09	3.49
1982	1.13	3.50
1983	0.99	3.43
1984	0.98	3.40
1985	1.05	2.72
1986	0.72	2.12
1987	0.57	2.15
1988 (June)	0.58	2.08

Source: Federation of Bankers Associations of Japan (Zenginkyo), Japan Financial Statistics 1989, Tokyo, 1989, Table II-14, 30.

Table A-3

Market Shares of Banks in Japan

Institution	Proportion of Total Funds Raised as of:	
	Year-End 1988	Year-End 1989
City Banks	19.5%	20.7%
Regional Banks	12.7	13.5
Sogo Banks (the majority changed to ordinary banks in March 1989)	10.0	5.4
Financial Institutions Servicing Small and Medium-Size Corporations	9.7	10.4
Trust Banks	9.4	10.1
Long-Term Credit Banks	4.9	5.1
Foreign Banks	0.2	0.2
Government Financial Sector	26.0	26.8
Other Institutions	7.8	7.8
TOTALS	100.0%	100.0%
City Banks	24.2%	27.0%
Regional Banks	12.9	14.7
Financial Institutions for Small and Medium-Sized Corporations	9.3	10.6
Trust Banks	6.7	7.3
Long-Term Credit Banks	5.2	5.8
Sogo Banks (the majority changed to ordinary banks in March 1989)	5.2	5.9
Foreign Banks	0.9	1.0
Government Financial Sector	32.4	24.1
Other Institutions	3.4	3.6
TOTALS	100.0%	100.0%

Notes: Funds raised include deposits, debentures, and trusts.

Source: Federation of Bankers Associations of Japan (Zenginkyo), Japanese Banks' 90, Tokyo, 1990, p.1 and Japanese Banks' 89, Tokyo, 1989, p. 1.

Table A-4
Types of Banks Serving the Japanese Financial System (Data as of July 1990)

Bank Category	Number of Banks in Category	Deposits in Billions of Yen as of:		Total Branch Offices	Foreign Branch Offices
		June 1989	July 1990		
City Banks	12	294,698	335,273	3,072	173
Regional Banks	64	123,607	144,044	6,532	15
Member Banks of the Second Association of Regional Banks	62	43,472	52,438	4,215	0
Trust Banks	7	108,672	125,278	404	33
Long-Term Credit Banks	3	60,008	64,666	91	22
Totals	148	630,457¥	721,699¥	14,378	257

Notes: Deposit totals include CDs that were first recorded in September 1988. The branch total includes head offices. In the case of city banks and long-term credit banks some deposit totals include debentures. Deposit totals for trust banks include money in trust, loan trusts, pension trusts, and employees' property formation benefit trusts.

Source: Federation of Bankers Associations of Japan (Zenginkyo), List of Member Banks, June 1989, 1-5; and List of 152 Member Banks, July 1990, 1-6.

Table A-5

Key Steps in the Deregulation of the Japanese Banking and Financial System

Time Began	Description of Steps Taken
April 1983	Public bonds were made available to small domestic investors.
June 1983	Short-term Euroyen loans were made more readily available to foreign individuals and firms.
April 1984	Commercial paper and CDs issued abroad were opened to Japanese investors.
June 1984	The regulations limiting the conversion of foreign currencies into yen were eliminated; banks were permitted to deal in public bonds and the Japanese were granted greater access to short-term Euroyen loans from abroad.
December 1984	Foreign and Japanese banks were permitted to issue Euroyen CDs through their overseas branch offices.
April 1985	Money-market certificates were made available for sale, while middle and long-term Euroyen loans were made available to foreign investors under more liberal conditions.
June 1985	A bankers' acceptance market was launched with these bank drafts denominated in yen.
July 1985	Japanese banks were authorized to issue foreign currency denominated convertible bonds overseas.
October 1985	A market for futures contracts for the delivery of government bonds was begun while the restrictions on the posted yields on large-denomination time deposits were loosened.
November 1985	Foreign banks were permitted to own new domestic trust banks.
December 1985	Foreign banks were authorized to establish 50% subsidiaries to carry on securities operations through their branch offices in Tokyo.

Table A-5 (continued)

February 1986	Six foreign-owned securities firms were admitted to the Tokyo Stock Exchange and the Japanese government began issuing six-month government bonds.
June 1986	Foreign banks were allowed to issue Euroyen bonds. Twenty-year government bonds were first issued publicly.
February 1987	Japanese banks were permitted to underwrite foreign commercial paper issues through their overseas branches.
April 1987	Japanese banks were permitted to issue domestic convertible bonds.
May 1987	Japanese banks, securities houses, and insurance companies were permitted to participate in overseas financial futures markets.
June 1987	Trading in stock futures contracts was allowed to begin on the Osaka Exchange.
September 1987	A public auction was established for trading in long-term government bonds.
November 1987	A domestic market for commercial paper was begun and foreign firms were allowed to issue Euroyen commercial paper.
January 1988	Domestic commercial paper was allowed to be issued by foreign businesses.
March 1988	Spot option contracts were allowed to be issued and traded overseas.
September 1988	Two new stock-index futures contracts were developed.
October 1988	Banks were allowed to securitize home loans.
December 1988	Regulations on the issuance of commercial paper at home and abroad were liberalized.
April 1989	An option market for bonds was begun.
May 1989	Medium and long-term Euroyen loans were opened to residents of Japan.

Table A-5 (continued)

June 1989	Restrictions on the issuance of Euroyen bonds by nonresidents of Japan were liberalized and banks and other traders were allowed to act as brokerage firms in foreign financial futures markets and permitted to launch brokerage operations in bond futures contracts. The Tokyo International Financial Futures Exchange was begun with trading in Euroyen and Eurodollar deposit and currency futures.
July 1989	The rules restricting the holding of offshore deposits by Japanese residents were eased as were the restrictions on residents issuing foreign-denominated bonds; at the same time bonds were permitted to be issued by foreigners in Tokyo. Japanese banks were granted the power to securitize loans extended to local units of government.
October 1989	New stock index option contracts were allowed to trade on the Nagoya and Tokyo exchanges.
December 1989	A market in financial futures for U.S. Treasury bonds was begun.
March 1990	Corporate loans made by Japanese banks were permitted to be securitized.
May 1990	The Tokyo Stock Exchange began trading in option contracts for government bond futures; the following month subordinated loans were approved.

Source: Federation of Bankers Associations of Japan (Zenginkyo), _Japanese Banks' 90_, Tokyo, 1990, pp. 4-6; _Japanese Banks '89_, Tokyo, 1989, pp. 4-10.

Table A-6
**Changes in the Share of Japan's Domestic Savings and Capital Market Flows
Accounted for by Japanese Banking Institutions**

Calendar Years	Proportion of Yen-Denominated Capital Market Flows (%) Accounted for by:				
	Japanese Banks	Other Privately Owned Financial Institutions	Government Financial Institutions	Securities Markets	Foreign Markets
1965	39.6%	39.0%	15.5%	5.6%	0.3%
1970	36.8	34.2	16.7	8.4	3.9
1975	36.5	33.3	23.3	7.1	-0.2
1980	23.5	31.4	31.2	8.6	5.3
1985	35.6	23.3	27.8	6.6	6.7
1987	35.5	45.4	16.6	-0.1	2.6

Type of Institution	Percentage Share of Personal and Postal Savings in Japan in:					
	1978	1980	1982	1984	1986	1988
Banks*	33.9%	33.1%	32.1%	31.4%	31.7%	32.9%
Other Financial Institutions	39.7	38.9	37.8	36.9	35.9	35.0
Postal Savings System	26.4	28.0	30.1	31.7	32.4	32.1

Note: *includes 87 member banks of the Federation of Bankers Associations of Japan.
Source: Bank of Japan, Economic Statistics Annual and Economic Statistics Monthly, selected annual and monthly issues; and Federation of Bankers Associations of Japan (Zenginkyo), Japan Financial Statistics 1989, Tokyo, 1989, Table I-6, 10, and Table I-9, 13.

Table A-7

Principal Components of the Balance Sheet of Japanese Banks (Percentage of Total Assets as of March 31, 1988)

Type of Bank	Proportion of Total Assets (%) in:				Proportion of Total Liabilities and Capital (%) in:		
	Cash and Deposits Due from Other Banks	Loans Out-standing	Security Holdings	Other Assets	Deposits*	Money Market Borrow-ings	Other Liabili-ties
City Banks	20.0%	52.9%	10.5%	16.6%	72.7%	10.4%	14.7%
Regional Banks	6.9	62.3	17.8	13.0	83.8	3.5	9.3
Trust Banks		18.2	43.0	23.6	15.2	51.0	12.4
Long-Term Credit Banks	13.8	57.5	16.8	11.9	79.4	6.1	12.1

<u>Notes</u>: *Excludes trust accounts but includes overseas accounts.

<u>Source</u>: Federation of Bankers Associations of Japan (Zenginkyo), <u>Japan Financial Statistics 1989</u>, Tokyo, 1989, Table II-3, p. 18.

Table A-8

Types of Deposits Customers Served by Japanese Banks (Data for Yen-Denominated Deposits as of March 31, 1988)

Percentage Shares of Total Deposits at Each Type of Japanese Bank Represented by:

Type of Bank	Corporations	Individuals and Families	Government Sector
City Banks	48.6%	37.9%	5.1%
Regional Banks	35.4	49.7	5.8
Trust Banks	75.0	14.1	1.7
Long-Term Credit Banks	77.7	1.7	5.5

Percentage Shares of Demand Deposits at Each Type of Japanese Bank Represented by:

Type of Bank	Corporations	Individuals and Families	Government Sector
City Banks	60.7%	26.9%	----
Regional Banks	48.6	32.9	----
Trust Banks	71.5	21.1	----
Long-Term Credit Banks	92.7	2.7	----

Percentage Shares of Time Deposits at Each Type of Japanese Bank Represented by:

Type of Bank	Corporations	Individuals and Families	Government Sector
City Banks	46.9%	47.9%	----
Regional Banks	29.8	63.5	----
Trust Banks	88.9	8.5	----
Long-Term Credit Banks	94.3	1.6	----

Source: Federation of Bankers Associations of Japan (Zenginko), _Japan Financial Statistics 1989_, Tokyo, 1989, Table II-2, 16-17.

Table A-9

Shares of Yen-Denominated Deposits and Loans Accounted for by the Different Kinds of Banks and Other Financial Institutions Operating in Japan (Figures as of July 31, 1988)

Type of Bank or Outstanding: Financial Institution	Percentage Share of Deposits and Loans	
	Deposits	Loans
City Banks	21.0*	24.2*
Regional Banks	12.7	12.5
Trust Banks	10.0	6.8
Long-Term Credit Banks	8.3	5.3
Foreign Banks	0.2	0.9
Sogo Banks	5.2	5.2
Shinkin Bank	7.1	6.1
Credit Cooperatives	1.7	1.6
Agricultural Cooperatives	5.0	1.8
Government Financial Institutions	NA	10.6
Trust Fund Bureau	23.2	20.1
Other Institutions	8.6	4.9
Totals	100.0*	100.0*

Note: * Deposit percentages also include debentures and trust accounts.

Source: Federation of Bankers Associations of Japan (Zenginkyo), _Japan Financial Statistics 1989_, Tokyo, 1989, Table II-1, 15.

Bibliography

Alexander, James. "Muscle or Mirage?" *The Banker*, March 1990, pp. 33–34.

Anderson, Gerald H. "Three Common Misconceptions About Foreign Direct Investment." *Economic Commentary*, Federal Reserve Bank of Cleveland, July 15, 1988.

Ando, A., and Frances Modigliani. "The Life Cycle Hypothesis of Savings." *American Economic Review*, March 1963, pp. 55–84.

Andrews, Suzanna. "Foreign Banks Take Aim at the Middle Market." *Institutional Investor*, 18 (March 1984), pp. 277, 278, 280, 282, 284.

Aoki, Masakiko. "Shareholders' Non-unanimity on Investment Financing: Banks vs. Individual Investors." In *An Economic Analysis of the Japanese Firm*, ed. M. Aoki. Amsterdam: Elsevier Science Publishers B.V. (North-Holland), 1984.

————, ed. *An Economic Analysis of the Japanese Firm*. Amsterdam: Elsevier Science Publishers B.V. (North-Holland), 1984.

Arvan, Alice. "Japanese Banks Consider Trust a Must." *Bankers' Monthly*, 57, 2 (February 1990), pp. 62–63.

Auerbach, Alan J., and Lawrence J. Kotlikoff. "Demographics, Fiscal Policy, and U.S. Saving in the 1980s and Beyond." National Bureau of Economic Research, Working Paper No. 3150, October 1989.

Baer, Donald. "Anxiety in America's Heartland." *U.S. News & World Report*, April 25, 1988, p. 24.

Baer, Herbert L. "Foreign Competition in U.S. Banking Markets." *Economic Perspectives*, Federal Reserve Bank of Chicago, May–June 1990, pp. 22–29.

Ball, Clifford A., and Adrian E. Tschoegl. "The Decision to Establish a Foreign Bank Branch or Subsidiary: An Application of Binary Classification Procedures." *Journal of Financial and Quantitive Analysis*, 17, 3 (September 1982), pp. 411–23.

Bank of England. "Developments in International Banking and Capital Markets in 1988." *Bank of England Quarterly Bulletin*, 29, 2 (May 1989), pp. 252–63.

Bank of Japan. *International Cooperative Statistics*. 1988.

————. "Balance of Payments Adjustment in Japan: Recent Developments and Prospects." Bank of Japan Special Paper No. 178, May 1989, pp. 1–59.

Board of Governors of the Federal Reserve System. *Press Release*, May 21, 1990.

————. *Press Release*, September 17, 1990.

Bourantas, Dimitris, and Yiorgos Mendes. "Does Market Share Lead to Profitability?" *Long-Range Planning*, 20, 5 (1987), pp. 102–108.

Bownes, Geoffrey. "Nikko's Spreading Global Network." *Director*, 42, 5 (December 1988), pp. 121–122.

Brady, Simon. "The Sun Rises Again in the West," *Euromoney*, December 1988, pp. 41, 43–44, and 47–48.

Brauchli, Marcus W. "Big Japan Investors Try to Quell Rumor They'll Sell U.S. Holdings." *The Wall Street Journal*, February 2, 1990, pp. C1 and C12.

Brecher, Charles, and Vladimir Pucik. "Foreign Banks in the U.S. Economy: The Japanese Example." *Columbia Journal of World Business*, Spring 1980, pp. 5–13.

Buell, Barbara, William Glasgall, Richard A. Melcher, and Jonathan B. Levine. "The Tidal Wave That's Sweeping International Finance." *The Economist*, July 1988, pp. 15–21.

Butler, Alison. *International Economic Conditions*, Federal Reserve Bank of St. Louis, January, 1990.

Cargill, Thomas F., and Shoichi Royama. *The Transition of Finance in Japan and the United States: A Comparative Perspective*. Stanford, California: Hoover Institution Press, 1988.

———. "The Evolution of Japanese Banking: Isolation to Globalization." Bank Structure and Competition Conference, Federal Reserve Bank of Chicago, May 1990.

Caves, Richard. "International Trade, International Investment, and Imperfect Markets." Special Papers in International Economics, No. 10, Princeton University, November 1974.

Chernow, Ron. "Don't Punish the Banks, Liberate Them." *The Wall Street Journal*, September 24, 1990, p. A14.

Cho, Yang Roe, Suresh Krishnan, and Douglas Nigh. "The State of Foreign Banking Presence in the United States." *International Journal of Bank Marketing*, 5, 2 (1987), pp. 59–75.

Christiano, Lawrence J. "Understanding Japan's Saving Rate: The Reconstruction Hypothesis." *Quarterly Review*, Federal Reserve Bank of Minneapolis, Spring 1989, pp. 10–25.

Clyde, P. *The Institutional Investor and the Theory of the Firm*, The University of California at Los Angeles, Unpublished Manuscript, 1989.

Cooper, Wendy. "Banking: The Financial Services Trade War." *Institutional Investor*, 21, 11 (November 1987), pp. 203–06.

Corrigan, Gerald E. "Trends in International Banking in the United States and Japan." *Quarterly Review*, Federal Reserve Bank of New York, Autumn 1989, pp. 1–6.

Crabbe, Matthew. "Japan Turns to Cheap Financing." *Euromoney*, March 1989, pp. 79, 82–90.

Damanpour, Faramanz. "The State of East Asian Banking Structure and Activities in the United States." *Asia Pacific Journal of Management*, 1, 2 (January 1988), pp. 139–51.

———. *The Evolution of Foreign Banking Institutions in the United States*. Westport, Conn.: Quorum Books, 1990.

Diamond, Douglas. "Financial Intermediation and Delegated Monitoring." *Review of Economic Studies*, 51 (1984), pp. 393–414.

Dohner, Robert S., and Henry S. Terrell. "The Determinants of the Growth of Multinational Banking Organizations: 1972–86." *International Finance Discussion Paper 326*, Board of Governors of the Federal Reserve System, June 1988.

Dunham, Constance. "Unraveling the Complexity of NOW Account Pricing." *New England Economic Review*, Federal Reserve Bank of Boston, May–June 1983, pp. 30–43.

Evans, Garry. "Why IBJ Could Oust Nomura." *Euromoney*, May 1989, pp. 46–55.

Fagerberg, Jan. "International Competitiveness." *The Economic Journal*, 98 (June 1988), pp. 355–74.

Fairlamb, David. "Foreign Banks Take an Increasing Share of the Cake." *The Banker*, June 1989, pp. 34–41.

Federal Deposit Insurance Corporation, RIL-18-89, Press Release, November 20, 1989.

Federal Reserve Board. Press Release. Washington D.C.: May 2, 1990

———. Press Release. Washington, D.C.: May 29, 1990.

———. Press Release. Washington, D.C.: July 30, 1990.

Federation of Bankers Associations of Japan (Zehginkyo). *Financial Liberalization and Internationalization in Japan*. International Affairs Department, May 1987.

———. *The Banking System in Japan*. Tokyo, 1989.

———. *Japanese Banks' 89*. International Affairs Department, Tokyo, 1989.

———. *Japanese Banks' 90*. International Affairs Department, Tokyo, 1990.

———. *Japan Financial Statistics 1989*. Tokyo, 1989.

———. *List of Member Banks*. June 1989.

———. *List of 152 Member Banks*. July 1990.

Feldberg, Chester B. "The Supervisory Implications of Financial Globalization—Competitive Equality and Supervisory Competence." *Economic Perspectives*, Federal Reserve Bank of Chicago, May–June 1990, pp. 30–32.

"Finance: Another Piece of the Puzzle," *Economist*, 312, 7623 (October 7, 1989), pp. 95–96.

"Financial Deregulation Has Accelerated in Japan Since 1984 Notes BIS Paper." *IMF Survey*, 19, 5 (March 5, 1990), pp. 70–71.

"Financial Globalization and Reformation of Japan's Financial System." *Sanwa Bank Economic Letter* (Japan), April 1989, pp. 3–7.

Fingleton, Eamonn. "Tokyo Watch: Night and Day." *Euromoney*, June 1989, pp. 17–21.

France, Boyd, Carla Ann Robbins, and Ronald Grover. "Collision Course: Can the U.S. Avert a Trade War With Japan?" *Business Week*, April 8, 1985, pp. 50–55.

French, Kenneth R., and James M. Poterba. "Are Japanese Stock Prices Too High?" Center for Research in Security Prices, Working Paper No. 280, February 1990.

Gilbert, Nathaniel. "Foreign Banks in the U.S.: A Tide of New Capital." *Management Review*, 77, November 1988, pp. 44–47.

Goldberg, Ellen S. "Comparative Cost of Foreign-Owned U.S. Banks." *Journal of Bank Research*, Autumn 1982, pp. 144–59.

Goldberg, Lawrence G. "The Competitive Impact of Foreign Commercial Banks in the United States." Paper Presented at the Fifteenth Annual Economic Policy Conference, Federal Reserve Bank of St. Louis, October 1990.

Goldberg, L.G., and Anthony Saunders. "The Determinants of Foreign Banking Activity in the U.S." *Journal of Banking and Finance*, March 1981, pp. 17–32.

———. "The Growth of Organizational Forms of Foreign Banks in the U.S.," *Journal of Money, Credit, and Banking*, 13, 3 (August 1981), pp. 365–74.

Greenspan, Alan. Chairman of the Federal Reserve Board. Testimony Before the

Committee on Ways and Means, U.S. House of Representatives, January 25, 1990.

———. Testimony Before the Financial Institutions Supervision, Regulatory, and Insurance Subcommittee, U.S. House of Representatives, Chicago, Illinois, May 14, 1990.

———. Testimony Before the Subcommittee on Telecommunications and Finance of the House Committee on Energy and Commerce, U.S. House of Representatives, October 5, 1987.

Griffith, T.F., and Frank Tuzzolino. "International Banking in the 1980s: A Global and Regional Perspective." *Arizona Business*, 28 (August–September 1981), pp. 15–21.

Grosse, Robert, and Lawrence G. Goldberg. "Distribution by State of Foreign Bank Activity in the United States." Unpublished Manuscript, University of Miami, March 1990.

Grubel, Herbert G. "A Theory of Multinational Banking." *Banca Nationale De Lavoro Quarterly Review*, December 1977, pp. 349–64.

Gurwin, Larry. "Foreign Banking in America: A Gallery of Foreign Bankers." *Institutional Investor*, 13 (September 1979), pp. 170–88.

Hale, David D. "Global Finance and the Retreat to Managed Trade." *Harvard Business Review*, 68 (January–February 1990), pp. 150–62.

Hamilton, Adrian D. "Financial Decontrol in Japan: A Case of When, Not Whether." *Banker*, 134, 702 (August 1984), pp. 29–33.

Hanley, Thomas H. *The Japanese Banks: Positioning for Competitive Advantage.* New York: Salomon Brothers, 1986.

Hanley, Thomas H., John D. Leonard, Diane B. Glossman, Ron Napier, and Steven I. David. *Japanese Banks: Emerging Into Global Markets.* New York: Salomon Brothers, September 1989.

Hardouvelis, Gikas, and Steve Peristiani. "Do Margin Requirements Matter?: Evidence from U.S. and Japanese Stock Markets." *Quarterly Review*, Federal Reserve Bank of New York, 14, 4 (Winter 1989–90), pp. 16–35.

Hatanaka, Sugio. "The Deregulated Japanese Banking System." *Business Japan*, 32, 5 (May 1987), pp. 30–33.

Hayashi, Fumio. "Is Japan's Savings Rate High?" *Quarterly Review*, Federal Reserve Bank of Minneapolis, Spring 1989, pp. 3–9.

Heller, H. Robert. *International Banking and Bank Regulation.* Speech by a Member of the Board of Governors of the Federal Reserve System to the Bankers' Association for Foreign Trade, Annual Conference, Phoenix, Arizona, May 1, 1989.

Helm, Leslie, and Sarah Bartlett. "How Japan Wants to Conquer Global Finance." *Business Week*, April 8, 1985, pp. 58–59.

Hervey, Jack L. "Changing U.S. Trade Patterns." *Economic Perspectives*, Federal Reserve Bank of Chicago, March–April 1990, pp. 2–12.

Hickok, Susan. "Japanese Trade Balance Adjustment to Yen Appreciation." *Quarterly Review*, Federal Reserve Bank of New York, Autumn 1989, pp. 33–47.

Hickok, Susan, and James Orr. "Shifting Patterns of U.S. Trade with Selected Developing Asian Economies." *Quarterly Review*, Federal Reserve Bank of New York, 14, 4 (Winter 1989–90), pp. 36–47.

Hirasawa, Sodaaki. "The Role of Japanese Banks in the Financial World." *Business Japan,* 34, 1 (January 1989), pp. 45–47.

Holden, Dennis. "Japanese Bank Strategy in U.S." *The Oriental Economist,* 51 (October 1983), pp. 22–25.

Hoshi, Takeo, Anil Kashyap, and David Scharfstein. "Bank Monitoring and Investment: Evidence from the Changing Structure of Japanese Corporate Banking Relations." *Finance and Economics Discussion Series,* 86, Washington, D.C.: Division of Research and Statistics, Federal Reserve Board, August 1989.

Houpt, J.V. *International Trends for U.S. Banks and Banking Markets.* Staff Economic Study No. 156, Board of Governors of the Federal Reserve System, May 1988.

———. "Foreign Ownership of U.S. Banks: Trends and Effects." *Journal of Bank Research,* 14, 2 (Summer 1988).

Hultman, Charles W., and Randolph McGee. "Factors Affecting the Foreign Banking Presence in the U.S." *Journal of Banking and Finance,* 13, 3 (July 1989), pp. 383–96.

Inouya, Minora. "Japan's New Role in Global Finance." *Sloan Management Review,* 30, 1 (Fall 1988), pp. 73–77.

Ioannou, Lori. "Global Custody: What Is a Custodian?" *Euromoney,* March 1989, pp. 6–8.

Irvine, Laura, and Stephen Vaught. "The Asian One Hundred." *Euromoney,* December 1988, pp. 89, 91, 93, 95, 97–98.

Japan Economic Institute. *Japanese Banks in the United States.* Washington, D.C.: Japan Economic Institute, January 12, 1988.

"Japanese Bank Buys Stake in Manufacturers Hanover." *Bank Notes,* Federal Reserve Bank of Boston, 17, 39 (September 22, 1989), p. 1.

"Japanese Banking Industry Faces Adjustment to Changes in Domestic, Global Environment." *International Monetary Fund Survey,* 18, 5 (March 1989), pp. 66–69.

"Japanese Banks in the U.S.: On the Same Team." Special Supplement to *Euromoney,* July 1988, pp. 1–48.

"Japanese Financial Deregulation: Surely but Oh So Slowly." *Economist,* 315, 7657 (June 2, 1990), p. 89.

"Japan: Reciprocity Vital to Market Reform." *Asian Finance,* 16, 8 (August 15, 1990), pp. 44–45.

Johnson, Christopher. "A Tale of Three Cities." *Lloyds Bank Economic Bulletin* (UK), 125 (May 1989), pp. 1–4.

Johnson, Manuel H., *Foreign Investment and the Economy.* Speech by a Member of the Board of Governors of the Federal Reserve System to the Conference Sponsored by Citizens for a Sound Economy Foundation, Washington, D.C., June 6, 1989.

Jones, Randall S. "Japan's Expanding Role in World Financial Markets." *Columbia Journal of World Business.* 24, 3 (Fall 1989), pp. 3–9.

Kane, Edward J., Haluk Unal, and Ashi Demirguc-Kunt. "Analyzing Hidden Capital at Japanese Banks." Conference on Bank Structure and Competition, Federal Reserve Bank of Chicago, May 1990.

———. "The Supervisory Implications of Financial Globalization—Incentive Conflict in the International Risk-Based Capital Agreement." *Economic Perspectives*, Federal Reserve Bank of Chicago, May–June 1990, pp. 33–36.

Kasman, Bruce. "Japan's Growth Performance Over the Last Decade." *Quarterly Review*, Federal Reserve Bank of New York, Summer 1987, pp. 45–55.

Key, Sydney J. "International Banking Facilities," *Federal Reserve Bulletin*, LXVIII (October 1982), pp. 565–77.

Key, Sydney J. "Is National Treatment Still Viable? U.S. Policy in Theory and Practice." *International Finance Discussion Papers*, No. 385, Board of Governors of the Federal Reserve System, September 1990.

Key, Sydney and Henry S. Terrell. "International Banking Facilities," *International Finance Discussion Papers*, No. 333, Board of Governors of the Federal Reserve System, September 1988.

Khoury, Sarkis J. "International Banking: A Special Look at Foreign Banks in the U.S." *Journal of International Business Studies*, 10, 3 (1979), pp. 36–52.

Lake, David. "Country Watch: Japan—A Prized Link to Takeover Market." *Asian Finance*, 16, 2 (February 15, 1990), pp. 42–44, 79.

———. "M&A Fever Begins to Sweep Japan." *Asian Finance*, 16, 2 (February 15, 1990), pp. 38–40.

Landis, Ken. "Wall Street Bows to Japan." *Banking Technology* (UK), 6, 3 (March 1989), pp. 18–21.

Lawrence, Edward C. "Performance of Foreign-Owned U.S. Banks Since the International Banking Act of 1978." *The Review of Research in Banking and Finance*, 5, 1 (Spring, 1989), pp. 57–77.

LeBlanc, Maureen, and Andrew C. Suarre. *The Japanese Financial System*. Federal Reserve Bank of New York, April 22, 1988.

Lewis, Vivian. "Enter the U.S. Bank Raider?" *Banker*, 139 (November 1989), pp. 20–22.

Lyon, Simon. "Ever Upwards." *The Banker*, January 1989, pp. 67–68, 71, 73–75.

McCauley, Robert N., and Steven A. Zimmer. "Expanding International Differences in the Cost of Capital." *Quarterly Review*, Federal Reserve Bank of New York, Summer 1989, pp. 7–28.

McDougall, Rosamund. "Empire II: The West." *Banker*, 139, 755 (January 1989), pp. 54–60.

McNamee, Michael, Blanca Riemer, Christopher Farrell, and Robert Neff. "It's a Global Game." *Business Week*, March 15, 1990, pp. 24–25.

Maidment, Paul. "International Banking: All In It Together." *Economist*, 316, 7649 (April 7, 1990), pp. 934–40.

Mann, Catherine L. *Determinants of Japanese Direct Investment in U.S. Manufacturing Industries*. International Finance Discussion Papers, No, 362, Board of Governors of the Federal Reserve System, September 1989.

Matsuoka, Takeo. "Banks Hatch Plans for Expansion, Specialization Amid Sweeping Change." *Business Japan*, 35, 6 (June 1990), pp. 37, 39.

Mikuni, Akio. "Evaluating Japanese Banks," Speech to the International Banking Conference, Washington, D.C., February 17, 1988.

Miller, Alex, William B. Gartner, and Robert Wilson. "Entry Order, Market Share, and Competitive Advantage: A Study of Their Relationship in New Corporate Ventures." *Journal of Business Venturing*, 4 (1989), pp. 197–209.

Nachtmann, Robert, and Fred Phillips-Patrick, "The Competitive Impact of Foreign Securities Firms in the United States." Paper presented to the Fifteenth Annual Economic Policy Conference, Federal Reserve Bank of St. Louis, October 19, 1990.

Nadler, Paul S. "The Slow Death of the Glass-Steagall Act." *Journal of Cash Management,* 9, 5 (September–October), pp. 58, 60.

Nathans, Leah. "U.S. Innovators Still Ahead." *Banker,* 137, 733 (March 1987), pp. 47–49.

Osborn, Neil. "Foreign Banking in America I: Will Foreign Takeovers of U.S. Banks Be Stopped?" *Institutional Investor,* 3 (September 1979), pp. 155–68.

———. "Japanese Tackle Frankfurt Determined to Win." *Euromoney,* November 1988, pp. 140, 142.

Osterberg, William. "LBOs and Conflicts of Interest," *Economic Commentary,* Federal Reserve Bank of Cleveland, August 15, 1989, pp. 1–4.

Ostrom, Douglas. "Japanese Banks in the United States." *JEI Report,* No. 22A, Japan Economic Institute, June 8, 1990, pp. 1–17.

Osugi, K. *Japan's Experience of Financial Deregulation Since 1984 in an International Perspective.* Pamphlet No. 6, Basle, Switzerland: Bank for International Settlements, 1990.

Ott, Mack. "Is America Being Sold Out?" *Review,* Federal Reserve Bank of Chicago, May–June 1990, pp. 33–36.

Palmer, George. "California Here We Come." *The Banker,* 137, 746 (April 1988), pp. 49–51, 53.

Parry, Robert T. "Hawaii and the Pacific Basin." *Weekly Letter,* Federal Reserve Bank of San Francisco, November 2, 1990, pp. 1–3.

Paulus, John D. *Effects of NOW Accounts on Costs and Earnings of Commercial Banks in 1974–75.* Staff Study No. 88, Board of Governors of the Federal Reserve System, 1976.

Pettway, Richard H., T. Craig Tapley, and Takeshi Yamada. "The Impacts of Financial Deregulation Upon Trading Efficiency and the Levels and Risk of Return of Japanese Banks." *Financial Review,* 23, 3 (August 1988), pp. 243–68.

Popper, Helen. "The Term Structure of Interest Rates in the Onshore Markets of the United States, Germany, and Japan." *International Finance Discussion Papers,* 382, Board of Governors of the Federal Reserve System, June 1990.

Poulsen, Annette B. "Japanese Bank Regulation and the Activities of U.S. Offices of Japanese Banks." *Journal of Money, Credit, and Banking,* 18 (August 1986), pp. 366–73.

Prindle, Andreas. "Change and Continuity in Japanese Finance." *Banking World,* 7, 3 (March 1989), pp. 21–24.

Prowse, Stephen D. *Institutional Investment Patterns and Corporate Financial Behavior in the U.S. and Japan.* Finance and Economics Discussion Series No. 108, Washington, D.C.: Board of Governors of the Federal Reserve System, January 1990.

Rabino, Samuel. "The Growth Strategies of New York-Based Foreign Banks." *Columbia Journal of World Business,* Winter 1981, pp. 29–35.

Read, Richard. "Crossing the Tracks to Success." *Euromoney,* June 1988, pp. 177–80.

Reuber, Grant. "The Supervisory Implications of Financial Globalization—Implications of Globalization for Regulation and Safety." *Economic Perspectives*, Federal Reserve Bank of Chicago, May–June 1990, pp. 36–38.

Rhoades, Stephen A. "Market Share as a Source of Market Power: Implications and Some Evidence," *Journal of Economics and Business*, 37 (1985), pp. 343–63.

Robbins, Brian. "Japan Warms to Financial Reform." *Triple A* (Australia), 4, 5 (March 1989), pp. 28–29.

Rose, Peter S. *The Changing Structure of American Banking*. New York: Columbia University Press, 1987.

———. "Japanese Banks Inside the U.S.: Dynamic Changes in Their Sources and Uses of Funds." *Columbia Journal of World Business*, 4 (Winter 1989), pp. 45–59.

———. "Affiliates of Japanese Banks in the United States: Responsiveness to Economic and Financial Conditions in the U.S. and Japan," *Journal of Business and Economic Perspectives*, XVI, No. 2 (Fall 1990), pp. 84–92.

Rowley, Anthony. "Japanese Banks Recoil From U.S. Interest-Rate Demands: Survival of the Fattest." *Far Eastern Economic Review*, June 21, 1990, pp. 86–88.

Salomon Brothers. *Japanese Banks—At a Crossroads?* New York: Salomon Brothers, 1988.

Saltzman, Michael I. "Government Access to Foreign Branch Records." *The Bankers Magazine*, 167, November–December 1984, pp. 77–82.

Sender, Henry. "Japanese Bank's Global Merger and Acquisition Assault." *Institutional Investor*, August 1988, pp. 167–72.

———. "Will the Gaijin Ever Get a Grip on Tokyo?" *Institutional Investor*, January 1989, pp. 51–56.

Smith, Charles. "A Taste for Takeovers: Japanese Securities Firms Join the U.S. Acquisitions Business." *Far Eastern Economic Review*, 141, 33 (August 18, 1988), pp. 72–73.

Smith, Lee. "Fear and Loathing of Japan." *Fortune*, February 26, 1990, pp. 50–60.

Suzuki, Yoshio. *The Japanese Financial System*. New York: Salomon Brothers, 1988.

Tatewaki, Kazuo. *Banking and Finance in Japan: An Introduction to the Tokyo Market*. London: Routledge, 1990.

Terrell, Henry. Statement to the Task Force on the International Competitiveness of U.S. Financial Institutions, Committee on Banking, Finance, and Urban Affairs, U.S. House of Representatives, August 2, 1990.

Terrell, Henry S., and S.J. Key. "The Growth of Foreign Banking in the United States: An Analytical Survey." In *Key Issues in International Banking*, Federal Reserve Bank of Boston, Conference Series No. 18, 1977.

———. "U.S. Banks in Japan and Japanese Banks in the United States: An Empirical Comparison." *Economic Review*, Federal Reserve Bank of San Francisco, Summer 1979, pp. 18–30.

Terrell, Henry S., Robert S. Dohner, and Barbara R. Lowrey. "The U.S. and U.K. Activities of Japanese Banks, 1980–1988." *International Finance Discussion Paper* 361, Board of Governors of the Federal Reserve System, September 1989.

———. "The Activities of Japanese Banks in the United Kingdom and in the United States, 1980–88." *Federal Reserve Bulletin*, February 1990, pp. 39–50.

U.S. House Committee on Banking, Finance, and Urban Affairs, Subcommittee on

Financial Institutions, Supervision, Regulation, and Insurance. Oversight Hearing on Foreign Competition in the Banking Industry, May 14, 1990.

Van Patten, Robert F., Jr. "The Regulation of Interstate Bank Branching Under the International Banking Act of 1978." *Northwestern Journal of International Law and Business*, 1 (Spring 1979), pp. 281–98.

Walters, Dennis, "Stunned U.S. Banks Fear Deeper Market Inroads by Foreign Firms." *American Banker,* January 26, 1982, p. 22.

Walton, R.J., and Desmot Trimble. "Japanese Banks in London." *Bank of England Quarterly Bulletin*, 27 (November 1987), pp. 518–24.

Waterhouse, Brian. "Banking: Artful Japanese Turn the Tables on Cooke." *Asian Business*, 24, 10 (October 1988), pp. 76–78.

"Weakening Position Irritates Foreign Banks in Japan." *The Oriental Economist,* July 1978, pp. 6–10.

Wellons, Philip A. "Competitiveness in the World Economy: The Role of the U.S. Financial System." In B.K. Scott and G.C. Lodge, eds., *U.S. Competitiveness in the World Economy.* Cambridge, Mass.: Harvard University Press, 1985.

Welsh, Gary M. Esq., "Europe 1992: Implications for U.S. Commercial Bankers," *Journal of Commercial Bank Lending*, 72 (January 1990), pp. 4–10.

White, Betsy B. "Foreign Banking in the United States: A Regulatory and Supervisory Perspective." *Quarterly Review,* Federal Reserve Bank of New York, Summer 1982, pp. 48–58.

Wilson, Dick. "Japan: The Other Side of the Trade War." *Banker,* 132, 681 (November 1982), pp. 31–32, 37–38.

Zimmerman, Gary C. "The Growing Presence of Japanese Banks in California." *Economic Review,* Federal Reserve Bank of San Francisco, Summer 1989, pp. 3–17.

————. "Small California Banks Hold Their Own." *FRSF Weekly Letter,* Federal Reserve Bank of San Francisco, January 26, 1990, pp. 1–2.

Index

About the Author

PETER S. ROSE holds the Jeanne and John Blocker Chair of Business Administration at Texas A & M University and is Professor of Finance. He previously served as a Financial Economist with the Federal Reserve System and has written several books, including *The Interstate Banking Revolution: Benefits, Risks, and Tradeoffs for Bankers and Consumers* (Quorum, 1990).

DATE DUE

JAN 0 5 1995			
			Printed in USA